Grow something
to eat every day

Jo Whittingham

DK

LONDON, NEW YORK, MUNICH, MELBOURNE, DELHI

Project Editor Chauney Dunford
Editor Ann Baggaley
Senior Art Editor Alison Shackleton
Designers Vanessa Hamilton, Lucy Parissi
Jacket Designer Mark Cavanagh
Production Editor Joanna Byrne
Picture Researcher Sarah Hopper
DK Picture Library Jenny Baskaya, Lucy Claxton

Managing Editor Esther Ripley
Managing Art Editor Alison Donovan
Associate Publisher Liz Wheeler
Art Director Peter Luff
Publisher Jonathan Metcalf

First published in Great Britain in 2011 by
Dorling Kindersley Limited. 80 Strand, London WC2R ORL

Penguin Group (UK)
Copyright © 2010 Dorling Kindersley Limited
2 4 6 8 10 9 7 5 3 1 – 001 – 177864 – Feb/2011

A CIP catalogue record for this book is available from the British Library

ISBN 978-1-4053-6227-6

Colour reproduction by Colourscan, Singapore
Printed and bound by Star Standard, Singapore

Discover more at
www.dk.com

Jo Whittingham is a gardener and writer with a postgraduate degree in horticulture from the University of Reading and a passion for growing fruit and vegetables. Awarded the Garden Writers' Guild News Journalist of the Year 2004, she writes a monthly column for *The Scotsman* newspaper, as well as features for many leading gardening magazines. She authored DK's bestselling *RHS Simple Steps to Success: Vegetables in a Small Garden*, and was consultant on *Grow Vegetables*, *Allotment Month by Month*, and *Grow Fruit*.

Contents

Introduction

More and more people are discovering that the advantages of growing your own fruit and vegetables go far beyond being able to pop outside and pick something to eat.

Home-grown produce tastes better than anything in the shops because it's freshly picked and perfectly ripe, which shines through even when cooked or preserved.

Grow fresh

For those who look for local, seasonal produce, what could be better than a perfect summer strawberry or handsome winter cabbage, picked at their prime, footsteps from the kitchen? Fruit and vegetables from your garden can also be produced organically if you choose, and it's amazing how trivial the odd chewed leaf and misshapen apple becomes when they've been raised under your own watchful gaze.

Whether you are starting out or a seasoned gardener, growing your own fruit and vegetables is enormously satisfying, even if the yields are small at first. It doesn't matter if you have just a few patio pots, some spare space in a border, or a large allotment, anyone can grow their own, and it's a lot easier than you might think.

Something every day

Eating something every day of the year that you have grown yourself might sound like an impossible dream, achievable only for those with a country estate and a team of gardeners. But with careful planning, and the most basic food preservation and storage methods, anyone with growing space can enjoy home-grown produce, fresh or stored, throughout the year.

(right) **Preserve** surplus summer crops to enjoy during the colder, leaner months.

(far right) **Allotments** are ideal if you don't have a big garden. Share one with a friend.

(below) **Small beds** are all you need for many crops. Make use of every inch of space.

The aim here is not full self-sufficiency, rather the pleasure in knowing that you and your family will be able to enjoy something tasty and nutritious, every day, grown on your own plot. Come summer, that could well be a feast of fresh crisp salad leaves, juicy fruit, and wholesome beans, while autumn brings a glut of tree fruits and hearty root crops. You won't go hungry winter to spring either if you take advantage of stored produce, not just dried beans or bagged potatoes, which are good anyway, but also rich chutneys, sweet jam, and indulgent homemade wines.

Even if you only grow a few radish in a pot, they're yours, and you'll never taste fresher.

How to use this book

This month-by-month guide takes you through all the stages of growing, picking, storing, and preserving your own fruit and vegetables. Each chapter opens with a summary of what you might be eating, and tells you what to do each month. Features suggest good varieties to try, or explain the best growing practices and techniques.

Ready to eat calendars
These guides highlight crops to enjoy now, picked fresh or taken from your stores. There's something every day.

What to sow/plant
These pages offer clear advice on what to sow and plant, taking into account weather and climate. The central bar shows the final produce.

What to do
Use these pages as a calendar of tasks that will keep your crops growing and healthy. The central bar illustrates the developing crops.

What to harvest
Pick your crops when they are at their best, especially if you plan to store them. These pages help you identify when they are ripe and explain the best techniques.

Your growing space

You might imagine that you would need ample space to make growing your own fruit and vegetables worthwhile, when in fact even the tiniest sunny corner or windowsill is enough to make a good start. With a little imagination, time, and effort, you can transform almost any space into a productive plot.

Where to grow

The happy truth is that you can grow fruit and vegetables anywhere with reasonable soil, as long as it's not in deep shade all day long. If you're lucky enough to have a large garden, you might consider setting out a dedicated vegetable plot, several fruit trees, and even a cage to protect soft fruit bushes from marauding birds.

Having a smaller garden need not restrict the range of crops you grow, you just need to be more creative in how you use space to fit them in. For instance, you might try filling the vertical space on walls and fences with trained fruit trees and bushes, or plant climbing crops, like peas, beans, and cucumbers. Productive plants can also make attractive additions to your flower borders – don't be afraid to plug summer gaps with fast-growing lettuces, add height to your planting with tall, leafy, sweet corn, or give a neatly pruned redcurrant pride of place.

Containers are another way of turning almost any outside space into a burgeoning edible garden.

It is possible to grow almost any fruit and vegetables in pots on sunny patios, roof terraces and balconies, as long as they are protected from strong winds; and you can keep them well watered and fed. Even small windowboxes and hanging baskets can provide good crops of salads, herbs, and cherry tomatoes, if well cared for.

Try experimenting with crops in pots, from pears to potatoes, French beans to figs, and look out for special dwarf varieties that have been specifically bred to suit cultivation in containers.

(above) **Vertical spaces** allow you to grow more crops in a smaller space. Fruit trees, such as apples, pears and figs can be trained against walls.

(left) **Crops in containers** are the ideal solution if you have limited growing space. Any good-size container with adequate drainage is suitable.

(above) **Sunny windowsills** are warm and bright, and provide a convenient spot to raise young plants for extra early crops.

(right) **Community gardens** offer welcome growing spaces; and are a great way to meet like-minded people to share advice and produce. Ask your council about local schemes in your area.

Alternative spaces

If your own garden doesn't have enough space to fulfil your ambitions, consider taking on an allotment, or investigate local shared community gardens and land-share schemes. These can be great places to learn the ropes, with more experienced gardeners who are usually generous with their advice. They may even organize practical workshops for novice growers.

With the increased popularity of growing your own, there is often considerable demand for a patch to cultivate, so be patient, and be prepared to join a waiting list if necessary.

Where outdoor garden space is limited, don't overlook growing indoors on windowsills, and in glazed porches and conservatories. The light and warmth found here is ideal for raising seedlings and for growing heat-loving plants, such as tomatoes, sweet peppers, chillies, and aubergines, which may struggle outside in a cooler regions. Choose smaller varieties though, so the mature plants don't block too much daylight when fully grown.

Many herbs thrive growing on windowsills, where they are convenient for picking. Seeds can also be sprouted on the kitchen work top at any time of year.

Plan your plot

Whether you have a generous plot or a tiny postage stamp in which to grow, it is important to plan how you use the space, both to maximize productivity, and to make maintenance easier.

First consider the location of permanent structures – work out if the greenhouse will get enough sunlight, the paths are wide enough, and the compost bins sited in a convenient place.

Once you have decided a layout, think about where you will plant trees, fruit bushes, and perennial vegetables like rhubarb. It's important to put these in the right place first time because they take a few years to establish and start cropping, and will be set back if you have to move them. The great thing about the rest of your vegetable crops is that you grow them afresh each year. Be bold, because any mistakes won't be with you for long.

Well planned spaces make growing fruit and vegetables easier and more productive. Take time to work out where permanent features, such as paths and greenhouses, should go.

Using space

Constructing raised beds (see page 33) is one of the best ways of creating growing space where there was none before. As long as the beds themselves are well drained, they can be built on very poor or badly drained soil, or on a patio, then filled with plenty of good topsoil and compost to give good results.

If you have, or are planning, a dedicated kitchen garden, you can make the most of your space by using a bed system, setting up a series of narrow beds separated by access paths (see page 16). With this system you don't need to allow room for walking on the soil between rows, so you can pack your plants more closely in the growing area for a higher yield.

(right) **Raised beds create instant** growing space on any surface; filled with good-quality soil and compost they can be very productive. Keep them small for easy access and maintenance.

Flowers, fruit, and veg

Using flower beds to grow crops is a more attractive idea than it might sound. Many vegetables have appealing foliage and flowers, while fruit bushes and trees bear blossom and bright berries that merit a place in any garden. Just be aware that crop plants are more demanding than flowering plants; dig in plenty of manure or compost before planting, and give them ample light and space. Perennial herbs and edible flowers are particularly suitable as border plants, but colourful salads, kales, and Swiss chard can be highly effective, too, especially if you use every scrap of space by intercropping them between ornamentals (see pages 124–125). Train climbing beans or squashes up decorative supports with spectacular results.

(above left) **An old tin bath** makes an interesting container for this crop of garlic. Ensure that recycled containers have adequate drainage.

(left) **Make the most of your growing** area, whether it is large or small, by planting your crops as closely as practicable in evenly spaced rows.

Crops in pots

Containers are an obvious way to make the best use of space; and can instantly imbue your plot with its own style. Sleek metal, rustic terracotta, or quirky reclaimed containers, such as old sinks, and tin buckets and baths, can all look great. However, plants will be just as happy in functional plastic pots or growing bags, as long as they have good drainage.

Fill your containers with good-quality compost, mixed with water-retaining granules to help prevent them drying out. Since containers make plants mobile, you can move smaller planters into the sun, away from the wind, and under cover during winter, when necessary.

(above) **Even a tiny patio** has room for a few container-grown crops. They look attractive and can be moved around as required.

(above left) **Make a vegetable plot** on a windowsill. Small plants such as herbs will love the sun.

(left) **Hanging baskets** don't encroach on your growing space and look wonderful crammed with trailing tomatoes or edible flowers.

Be realistic

Hopes are invariably high when sowing gets under way in spring but, sadly, disappointment sometimes follows. To keep your enthusiasm going for years to come, it is vital to be realistic about what you are likely to achieve in the space and time you have available. Don't make the mistake of initially clearing a huge plot if you have only limited time to spend on it. Nothing is more disheartening than watching the weeds regain the upper hand after you have recently spent hours digging them out. It is better to start out small and expand as knowledge and experience increase. Success will soon build confidence.

There is no escaping the fact that whichever methods you use to grow fruit and vegetables, time and effort invested at every stage of the process are what bring good returns. Think carefully about how much you can plant without giving yourself an impossible amount of work later on.

Crop care

Planting directly into the soil involves early preparation, but once young plants are well established they usually grow happily without much input, except periodic weeding, watering during dry spells, and routine checks for pests and diseases.

Getting plants started in containers is initially less effort than planting in beds, but then you will have to spend time watering them, possibly twice daily in a hot summer, for as long as you want them to crop.

Keep it simple

If you have never grown your own before, keep it simple. Start with crops that are easy to cultivate and almost guaranteed to harvest. Buy in plants, so not everything has to be raised from seed.

Radishes, salads, potatoes, and beans are all reliable crops, while courgettes and tomatoes fruit all summer, paying back your investment if you choose to buy in plants. Leave challenging melons, cauliflowers, and grapes until you're confident with other crops.

(top) **Cut-and-come-again** salad leaves will produce several crops from just one sowing. They can be grown all year round.

(above) **If you want freshly picked greens** in midwinter, then try growing kale, one of the most resilient of all brassicas.

(left) **Asparagus** needs time and plenty of room to grow. It has a short season, but an established bed will crop for many years.

What to grow

It seems obvious, but use your space to grow what you like to eat. Although it's tempting to try weird and wonderful crops seen in catalogues, or to plant a glut of the latest superfood, what you really want is everyday produce that tastes fabulous. Even in a large garden there won't be time or space for everything, and to grow something to eat every day, you need to consider a few points.

The most important thing to weigh up is the return that each crop will give for the amount of space it takes. Asparagus, for example, needs a large dedicated bed to produce a decent crop over a couple of months. On the other hand, a few rows of cut-and-come-again leaves can keep a family in salad all year round. Many winter crops, such as parsnips and sprouting broccoli, need to be in the ground for months before they are ready for harvesting; so you either need to be clever and squeeze fast-growing crops between them or limit their numbers in small spaces.

Locally grown

You should also take into account which crops grow well locally. If you are not sure, find out by visiting nearby gardens, talking to your neighbours, or asking the growers at your local farmers' market. Use your common sense, too, when it comes to selecting crops that will do well on your plot. If you live in an area where the summers are cool and wet, then heat-loving crops such as aubergines and tomatoes will crop well only in a greenhouse or indoors. Gardeners in hot, dry climates may struggle to keep leafy salads and brassicas going during the height of summer.

It makes sense to put your effort into growing things that are either expensive or impossible to buy in the shops. What these crops might be depends on your local suppliers, but soft fruits, such as currants and berries are often pricey, as are herbs, runner beans, and good salad varieties. Globe artichokes, borlotti beans, and the full range of winter squashes are often simply unavailable, so if they take your fancy, why not grow your own?

If you have never harvested food fresh from the garden before then you might not know how incredibly different it can taste, even compared to produce bought straight from the farmers' market. When there are just minutes between picking and eating, none of the precious sugars have been turned to starch and the cells are still plumped with water, so you get sweetness and crispness that simply cannot be bought. Some crops, including peas, beans, sweetcorn, tomatoes, and new potatoes, lose this freshness faster than others, making them worth growing just because their flavour can't be matched in the shops.

Smaller plots

Where space is at a premium, grow high-yielding fruit and vegetables that get the most out of every scrap of soil by cropping quickly or consistently over a long period. Look out for dwarf and bush varieties, bred to take up less room and often to grow well in containers. Use pots and grow bags and fill them with attractive varieties for a colourful display.

- **Bush tomatoes** – Great in hanging baskets, these can produce sweet cherry fruit for most of the summer.

- **Dwarf beans** – French and runner beans are available as dwarf varieties that crop heavily in a tiny space.

- **Herbs** – Both perennials and annuals deserve space for their long picking seasons and good looks.

- **Salad leaves** – Cut-and-come-again salads, like rocket and mizuna, will regrow three times in summer.

- **Blueberries** – These compact bushes thrive in pots; their berries ripen gradually for picking right through late summer.

- **Strawberries** – They look pretty in pots or at the edge of a border. Plant early, mid- and late varieties to extend the cropping period.

- **Summer radishes** – Ready to eat 6 weeks after sowing, peppery radish is perfect for filling a gap in your crops.

- **Beetroot** – The striking red-veined leaves look beautiful and are as good to eat as the earthy baby roots.

- **Swiss chard** – Neon-coloured stems make this leafy crop a must.

- **Courgettes** – A single bush can provide more than 20 fruits, along with glorious yellow flowers.

(right) **Raspberries** often produce heavy crops that give you enough fruit to freeze or make into preserves, as well as to enjoy straight from the bush.

(below) **Freshly lifted new potatoes** have an incomparable flavour. You could grow a small crop in containers if you don't have room for a vegetable plot.

Growing under cover

This isn't some kind of covert gardening, but the practice of protecting plants from the worst weather, to extend the growing season. It is particularly useful if you live in a cold area where spring comes late and autumn early, but almost all gardeners looking to produce crops year-round will need to grow under cover at some stage.

(above) **Greenhouses** come in a range of materials and styles to suit all plots. They can be expensive, so consider buying a second-hand one locally.

(left) **Ideal growing conditions** are the main advantage of greenhouses and polytunnels, and they also provide somewhere to work in bad weather.

Grow indoors

Greenhouses and polytunnels take the lottery out of growing tender summer crops, providing the ideal environment to grow tomatoes, peppers, and aubergines, but you needn't stop there. Even unheated, these structures provide enough protection to grow extra early strawberries in spring, to raise winter crops such as radish and cut-and-come-again salads, and give many crops a head start.

Greenhouses are expensive to buy new, so make sure the shape and size you choose suits your garden and growing ambitions. Also ensure that there is adequate ventilation to keep air flowing around your plants; aim for one roof- and one side-vent for every 2m (6ft) of length.

Polytunnels are cheaper, but their functional appearance best suits allotments rather than gardens. The plastic that covers them has a limited lifespan, as does the plastic used in some greenhouses, and they are more difficult to ventilate, but they still provide a great growing space.

Whichever structure you choose, position it on a bright, level site, away from the shade of buildings and trees, and sheltered from strong winds. Be sure to provide good access, and try to find space outside for a rain barrel and also a tool shed.

Simple cover

Small-scale covers, such as cloches and cold frames, are invaluable for warming the soil to allow seeds to be sown early. They can also be used to harden off plants raised indoors, keep out damaging winds and hungry pests, and to protect overwintering crops.

Cloches, whether made of glass, plastic or fleece, are relatively cheap and have the advantage that they can be moved where needed, although they must be securely pinned to the soil. Use cut-off plastic bottles to cover individual plants, or low, wire-framed tunnels to protect whole rows.

Cold frames usually have a soil base and a sloping, glazed lid. Although lighter frames can be moved where required, most are permanently positioned against south-facing walls, to give maximum light and heat, and extra frost protection. They are ideal for raising early-sown seeds, hardening off young plants, or growing heat-loving crops like cucumbers and melons.

Plastic mini-greenhouses perform many of the same functions as a cold frame. Taller models are ideal for protecting growing bags planted with tomatoes, although they must be anchored securely, and have a sheltered, sunny site.

Even sunny windowsills are perfect for raising tender plants from seed. To stop seedlings bending towards the light, grow them in a simple light box made by cutting the front away from a small cardboard box, and lining the back with reflective silver foil.

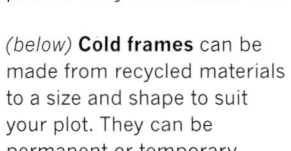

(far left) **Cloches** provide enough warmth and protection to give crops a useful head start.

(left) **Mini-greenhouses** are ideal for tender crops, like tomatoes, if you have limited space. They can be easily packed away when not in use.

(below) **Cold frames** can be made from recycled materials to a size and shape to suit your plot. They can be permanent or temporary.

A perfect spot for crops

You will want your vegetable and fruit plants to deliver large, healthy crops over the longest period possible. To help them achieve this, offer them the best possible conditions for growth. Provide your plants with light, water, good airflow, and well-drained, fertile soil – in other words, give them a perfect spot for crops.

Ideal conditions

A long-neglected corner where nothing much ever seems to grow is not the right place to start a vegetable patch. Provide an open site for your crops, with plenty of sunshine during the day to warm the soil and give the plants energy for rapid growth. A position away from the shade and competing roots of hedges or large trees is essential. If your site isn't ideal, try to improve it as best you can. This will not only ensure better harvests, but also make growing them simpler.

Let in as much light as possible by cutting back overhanging growth, and create raised beds to lift crops above competing roots.

Good exposure

Open ground gets the full benefit of any rainfall, meaning you are less likely to have to water plants yourself. However, an open site can leave your crops at the mercy of the weather, particularly damage from strong winds.

In exposed gardens, put up windbreaks to reduce the force of gusts as much far as possible. Don't build a solid wall, because air pressure creates turbulence on the leeward side of the barrier that can be worse than the unimpeded wind. Choose a permeable barrier,

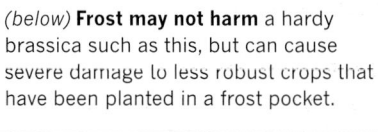

(left) **For healthy plants** and maximum productivity, choose the site of your vegetable plot with care, taking account of light, temperature, and soil quality.

(below) **Frost may not harm** a hardy brassica such as this, but can cause severe damage to less robust crops that have been planted in a frost pocket.

Trellis makes an effective and attractive windbreak for the vegetable plot, and can be used to support crop plants or ornamental climbers.

such as a fence or a hedge, that will break the force of the wind without creating unpredictable eddies. Also watch out for gaps between buildings and walls that could funnel wind.

Frost pockets

Temperature is another important consideration when it comes to choosing a site for your crops. Some gardens have frost pockets, which are low-lying areas, where cold air gets trapped on still winter nights, increasing the likelihood of frosts. Check your garden after a hard frost to see if there's a patch that is still white when everywhere else has thawed. Planting in such a cold spot will lead to frost damage and slow growth, so should be avoided.

Know your soil

Soil is a vital source of nutrients and water for plants. Knowing what type of soil you have and how it can be improved is key to growing success. To establish the soil type of your garden or allotment, take a small handful, wet it slightly and squeeze it lightly in your palm. If it sticks together into a smooth, shiny ball you have a heavy, clay soil. If it feels gritty and doesn't clump together, your soil is light and sandy. Often soils are a combination of these two types, and contain fine silt particles as well, which gives good garden soil known as a loam.

Soil types have different characteristics that influence the way plants grow, as well as how you should treat them.

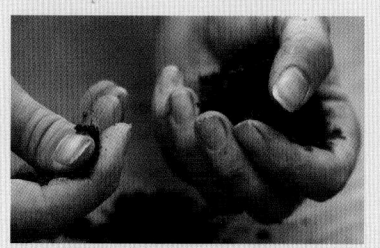

Sandy soil feels gritty in the hand and does not clump together when you squeeze it. This soil does not retain moisture or nutrients well.

Clay soil holds together when squeezed and feels heavy and sticky when wet. It holds nutrients well but is prone to waterlogging.

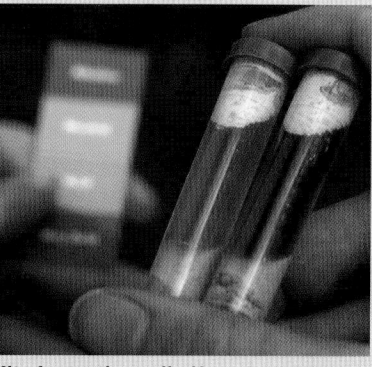

Kits for testing soil pH are inexpensive and usually reliable. Most involve the simple process of checking a soil solution against a colour scale.

Clay soils retain nutrients well but can easily become waterlogged, while sandy soils drain freely but quickly lose nutrients and dry out. If drainage is very poor and water pools on the surface, the cause could be deeper. Dig down and check for a compacted "hard pan" layer that will need to be broken up to allow water through.

Soil pH level

The pH, (acidity) of your soil affects which crops will grow well on your plot, so check it before planting. Simple-to-use kits to measure pH are widely available; just follow the instructions given.

Soil is considered neutral at pH 7.0; acid below this figure; and alkaline above it. A slightly acid pH of 6.5 is ideal for most fruit and vegetables, although in general they tolerate all but the extremes. If you intend to grow brassicas on acid soil, try applying lime the autumn before planting to raise the pH level, which helps prevent clubroot disease, see page p.241.

Improving soil

Digging and preparing beds may seem like a chore, but once you see the difference it makes to yields of fruit and vegetables it's easier to motivate yourself. If you do only one thing, add as much well-rotted manure or compost to the soil as you can. Mix it with grit on heavy, clay soil in autumn to improve drainage and reduce stickiness. Work manure into light sandy soil in spring to improve water-retention and add nutrients. Unless the ground is very compacted, single digging to one spade's depth, adding the organic matter and backfilling, is enough. Avoid standing on the soil whenever possible, and use a plank to work from if it is wet.

Defining the beds with paths in between improves access. Mulch the paths with a weed-suppressing material and concentrate on improving the soil in the beds.

Rotate your crops

Separate beds make it easier to practise crop rotation, where related crops are grown in different areas every season to prevent soil-borne pests and diseases building up. Some plant groups have their own nutrient requirements, and can deplete the soil of these, if grown repeatedly. Plan a three-year rotation where the hungry cabbage family (brassicas) follow nitrogen-fixing peas and beans, which follow potatoes and root vegetables.

(above) **Worth all the hard work,** this flourishing plot, supporting a variety of healthy crops, begins with soil improvement and preparation.

(below) **Dividing your growing areas** with mulched paths reduces the need to walk on the soil to reach the plants. Defining beds also makes it easier to organize your crop rotation schedule.

Keeping plants well fed and watered

If you expect your plants to grow rapidly they must have adequate nourishment and water. Their roots take up water, as well as three main nutrients (nitrogen, phosphorus, and potassium) from the soil, along with a range of trace elements such as manganese, copper, and iron. It makes sense to improve the soil every year, to ensure that these needs can be met without you having to give your plants continual extra help. As long as the soil isn't excessively acid or alkaline, it is likely that most nutrients will be made available to plants from the soil's own mineral content or the breakdown of organic matter into humus by micro-organisms. So there is another reason to keep digging in plenty of well-rotted manure and compost.

Big eaters

Although many plants in good soil may not need feeding, "hungry" crops, like tomatoes and brassicas, benefit from additional fertilizers, as do container-grown crops.

Concentrated fertilizers such as organic blood, fish and bone, or inorganic Growmore, often come in powder or granular forms that are easy to apply to open soil. Liquid fertilizers just need diluting and are ideal for feeding container plants.

Watering is not as simple as it seems. A plant that is wilting in dry soil will benefit quickly from a good soaking, but plants can also look sickly growing in waterlogged soil, so check first.

Plants under cover and in containers need regular watering; every day in the height of summer. Those growing in open soil are less dependent on you, unless they are newly planted or there is a drought. Here it is better to water thoroughly, soaking the soil to a good depth occasionally, rather than wetting the surface every day. Check by digging down after watering if you are unsure how much water is needed.

(far right) **Sprinkle a top-dressing of fertilizer** around the base of your plants to deliver nutrients close to the roots.

(right) **Seep hoses** are an efficient way of irrigating rows of crops without wastage of water.

(below) **Regularly digging** in mature, homemade compost is the best way to improve the structure and fertility of your soil.

(left) **Hoverflies**, like many beneficial insects, not only pollinate flowers but also prey on crop-damaging pests.

(below) **Spray chemical pesticides** carefully. Check the label to ensure they are safe to treat food crops and only spray late in the evening.

Organic or not?

Many people grow their own to ensure their crops are produced organically, but every gardener has to decide whether to use artificial chemicals or not.

Organic gardening relies upon establishing a balance, where plants grow strongly thanks to the addition of organic matter to the soil (ideally homemade garden compost), and pest numbers are controlled by beneficial wildlife. It takes time to achieve this balance, and there will be occasions when pests and diseases win the day, but there are easy steps you can take to swing the odds in your favour.

Planting fruit and vegetables with ornamental plants is a great way to maximize productivity and colour in smaller gardens, but it also helps protect them from pests. While a large patch of cabbages or carrots is an obvious target, the same plants scattered through a flower border will be harder for pests to spot. In a similar way, planting strongly scented flowers, such as French marigolds, among vegetables helps distract insect pests and attracts their predators; a practice known as "companion planting".

Planting flowers alongside your fruit and vegetable also attracts pollinating insects that will visit the crops, improving their yield.

If pests do get the upper hand, biological control, which involves introducing an organism to kill your chosen pest, can be effective if used properly. The conditions must be right however, and at times when your crops are under severe attack, the use of chemicals is hard to resist – turning to a selective insecticide to target a heavy infestation, for instance.

When using sprays on or near food plants, always check the label carefully to see that it is safe to use. It will also say how soon your crops will be safe to harvest. Also, only spray insecticides late in the evening, after beneficial insects have stopped flying, so you kill the target pests, not allies like bees and hoverflies (see pages 104–105 on organic pest control).

Natural allies such as birds, hedgehogs and beneficial insects play a vital role in keeping pest numbers under control. Try to attract them into your garden by providing cover and water.

Tools and equipment

A small range of good-quality tools makes gardening a pleasure, and it's worth investing in the best you can afford, and looking after them, so they last. Exactly what tools you will need depends on the space to be cultivated. If you grow only in pots, you can do without the large tools required to cultivate open soil, but otherwise their needs will be much the same as someone with a generous plot.

Wherever you grow, find yourself a sturdy trowel for planting and an ergonomic hand fork for weeding in tight spots. Secateurs are essential for fruit pruning, but will also save your kitchen scissors being blunted on many other occasions when things need to be cut or chopped.

A good watering can, with detachable fine and coarse roses, is indispensable, particularly if you grow crops from seed.

Choose tools the right size and weight for your stature and strength to make heavy work as manageable as possible. In a larger garden a wheelbarrow is also useful.

You'll find that you collect seed trays and pots, all sorts of plant supports, and possibly a shed, as you go along, but don't forget that it's useful to have sundries like potting compost, labels and string, before the season starts.

(clockwise from left)
Fork – Ideal tool to use when incorporating organic matter into the soil, and for lifting crops and plants.

Rake – Used to clear stones and debris from the soil surface, and to create a fine tilth for sowing seeds.

Spade – Can be used in place of a fork on light, sandy soils. Also useful for moving dry materials, like compost.

Trowel – An essential hand tool for planting out and removing weeds.

Hoe – Used for killing annual weeds among crops, severing them off at the root so they wither.

To sow or buy?

Raising plants from seed is by far the cheapest way to fill your plot, and allows you to choose from an enormous range of varieties. But seed is not the only option.

Potatoes and onions are grown easily from tubers and bulbs, and an impressive range of vegetables, fruit trees and bushes are available to buy as young plants.

Seed selection

You can buy seeds from garden centres, mail order from seed catalogues (see pp.246–247), or collect your own from previous year's crops (see pp.172–173).

Select varieties that suit your particular needs. For instance, consider dwarf or trailing cultivars if you garden in small beds or containers; pick those that mature early if you live in a colder area; and select varieties bred for good disease resistance if you garden organically.

When buying seeds, some are labelled 'F1 hybrid' or have 'F1' in their name. These are modern varieties, specially selected to be uniform, vigorous, and often more disease resistant than standard varieties. They are more costly, and won't come true-to-type if you save your own seeds. Some cheaper varieties are described as 'F2' or 'open pollinated'.

Plants grown from this seed will be more variable but are perfectly good for most gardeners.

Only buy as much seed as you need for the coming season. If you have any left over, keep it cool and dry; most (except parsnip and carrot) will still germinate after several years in storage. You will find information on how to sow seed indoors and out on pages 42–43, and specific advice on crops within the monthly chapters.

(far left) **Seeds are an** economical way of raising vegetables, such as this sturdy young sweet corn.

(left) **Seed sown directly** outdoors in the right conditions often produces gratifyingly quick results.

(below) **You can start things** off earlier with seeds; all you need is a small propagator or a warm windowsill.

(above) **Buying a few trays** of ready-grown seedlings is the quickest and easiest way to start off a vegetable plot, although probably not the cheapest. Reputable garden centres and nurseries will offer healthy plants.

(left) **Young container-grown fruit trees** can be bought and planted all year round. Make sure they look well tended.

Young plants

Tubers for crops such as potatoes and Jerusalem artichokes, and the small bulbs, known as sets, from which onions and shallots are cultivated, are available from late winter into spring. Ensure that you buy disease-free stock from a reputable nursery, garden centre, or mail order supplier.

You can also buy young plants from the same sources. Buying plants is more expensive than growing from seed, and you don't get the same choice of varieties, but for those with limited time or outdoor space for seed sowing, this is a good option. Look for sturdy, dark green plants and acclimatize them gradually to outdoor conditions before planting out. Beware of buying tender plants, such as tomatoes and courgettes, too early if you have nowhere frost-free to grow them on. Plants delivered by post should be opened immediately, watered, and potted up as soon as possible. (For details on planting individual crops, see the planting pages that follow for each month.)

Fruit bushes and trees

Container-grown bushes and trees are available all year round, and because their roots are left relatively undisturbed, they can be planted at any time of year – although high summer is best avoided. Don't buy old stock, which may be pot-bound and often goes unpruned in garden centres, and steer clear of bulging, weedy pots, and poorly shaped plants, even if sold at reduced prices.

Bare-root plants, lifted from nursery fields when dormant, are normally available early to late winter. Specialist fruit nurseries stock the widest range, offering many different varieties and rootstocks, often by mail order. Look out for "maidens", which are one-year-old trees that establish quickly, can be pruned as you wish, and cost less than larger specimens.

Once out of the ground, the exposed roots must not be allowed to dry out, and planting should be done as soon as possible. See pages 202–203 for information on choosing and planting fruit trees.

Month-by-month guide

Growing year-round crops needs a bit of planning, so use this calendar guide to track all your sowing, planting, growing, and harvesting, month-by-month. Remember that climates vary, even from one garden to the next, so keep an eye on the weather, and treat sowing and planting dates as approximate. For a summary of each crop, see the planners on pages 230–235.

January: ready to eat

Enjoy freshly unearthed parsnips, celeriac, and Jerusalem artichokes in soups and stews, along with potatoes, carrots, and swedes from your stores. Cut the first spears of sprouting broccoli this month.

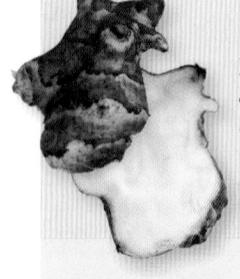

Dig up some **Jerusalem artichokes**

Brussels sprouts are sweet and nutty

The first tender spears of **purple sprouting broccoli** are ready now

Dried **herbs** from last year's crop are still full of flavour

Cut **endive** grown under cover for winter

Raid your stores of **onions**, **shallots**, and **garlic**

Use **stored vegetables** to make **soup** *pages 226–227* and freeze any left over for later

Pick tasty young leaves of **spinach beet**

Use frozen **beans** and **peas** from last summer *pages 148–149*

Enjoy the unusual taste of newly lifted **salsify**

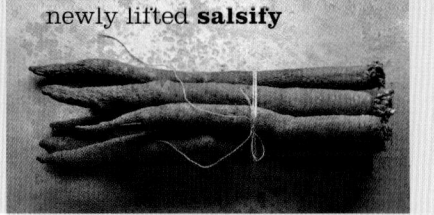

Winter cabbage should be doing well – use some for pickling *pages 176–179*

Leeks will taste good for some weeks yet

Braise some stored **trench celery** or add it to casseroles

Use dried or frozen **chillies** in spicy dishes

Kale is a good winter standby

*If you planted late **potatoes** for winter, eat any that are left*

There may be greenhouse **citrus fruit** pages 222–223 to pick – if you're lucky

Cut-and-come-again salads will supply fresh new leaves

Pick bright heads of **red chicory**, grown under cover for winter salads

Make pies and crumbles using **frozen soft fruit** *pages 150–151*

Grate **winter radishes** into your salads

Eat **pickles** prepared last autumn *pages 176–179*

Bring **winter squashes** out of store for a splash of colour

Try **sprouting seeds** *pages 36–37* on your kitchen work top
• alfalfa
• beansprouts
• broccoli
• fenugreek

Boost your fruit intake with crunchy **stored apples** *pages 194–195*

Lift overwintering **celeriac** or take it from your stores *pages 210–211*

It's harvest time in January with the first of the forced **Witloof chicory**

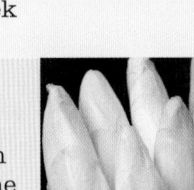

Parsnips should be keeping well in the ground

Use stored **root crops** *pages 210–211* for winter meals
• swede
• potatoes
• carrots
• beetroot

Pull up pungent **spring onions** overwintering under cloches

Toast the New Year with a glass of **homemade wine** *pages 180–181*

January: what to sow

EARLY-SEASON LEEKS

Early varieties of leek, such as 'King Richard' (p.225) and 'Jolant', are best sown in January. They need a soil temperature of at least 8°C (46°F) in order to germinate, so a heated propagator in a greenhouse, or a cool room indoors, is essential for success. Sow seed thinly, about 1cm (½in) deep, into trays or modules filled with compost. Grow them on indoors, and the young plants will be ready to harden off and plant out later in spring.

HARVEST: **SEPT–APR**

TASTY SUMMER ONIONS

Maincrop onions need an early start, especially in colder areas where spring growth can be slow. Sow them indoors this month in a heated propagator at a temperature between about 10–15°C (50–59°F) and get them off to a flying start. Sow thinly, 1cm (½in) deep in trays and prick them out as they grow. Alternatively, sow about five seeds to a module and grow them on as little space-saving clusters of mature bulbs.

HARVEST: **JUL–OCT**

SOW

BROAD BEANS
LEEKS
LETTUCE
ONIONS

BROAD APPEAL

For early crops of broad beans, sow seed 5cm (2in) deep in modules or small pots, this month. Keep them under cover in a greenhouse or cold frame and they will be ready to plant out in early spring. Sow your beans outside only in a mild winter, with a temperature of at least 5°C (41°F), and give them some protection, such as garden fleece.

HARVEST: **MAY–AUG**

LETTUCE BEGIN

In mild areas, lettuces sown now under frames or cloches can be planted out in early spring for a really early supply of sweet salad. Sow thinly, 1cm (½in) deep, either in modules or in drills, 10cm (4in) apart. Look for early cos, butterhead, and loose-leaf salad-bowl varieties (p.81).

HARVEST: **APR–OCT**

CUT AND COME AGAIN

If you crave some fresh baby salad leaves, then try sowing a variety of cut-and-come-again crops under cover, either in the greenhouse or cold frame in beds, or in compost-filled boxes or seed trays. The best to try at this time of year are cress, salad rocket, sugar loaf chicory, or winter mixes, such as 'Oriental Saladini'. Scatter the seeds thinly, 1cm (½in) apart and cover with about ½cm (¼in) of soil before watering well. The leaves will be ready to harvest in a matter of 5–6 weeks.

HARVEST: **ALL YEAR**

SALAD RADISH

Sow small-leaved radish, such as 'Saxa', in your unheated greenhouse borders or in large containers this month. Slow-growing, these varieties crop in winter, although may need extra protection with fleece or cloches on cold nights. Sow thinly, 1cm (½in) deep, in drills, 10cm (4in) apart. Thin the seedlings to 2cm (¾in) apart.

HARVEST: **APR–NOV**

SALADS

RADISHES

PEAS

See SOWING UNDER COVER page 42

DON'T FORGET

Windowsills are ideal for raising seedlings but they can become cold at night. To keep your plants safe, bring them into the room on frosty nights, then return them to their sills in the morning.

EARLY PEAS – THE EASY WAY

HARVEST: **JUN–OCT**

Peas, which you can sow indoors this month, hate root disturbance, so sow them in deep modules or a length of guttering to make transplanting easier.

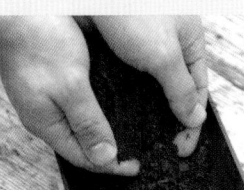

1 PREPARE THE GUTTER
Cut plastic guttering into lengths that match the peas' final planting space. Block both ends, then fill them with seed compost.

2 SOW THE SEED
Choose dwarf early varieties and sow the seed 2cm (¾in) deep, 5cm (2in) apart. Standard gutter will accommodate two rows.

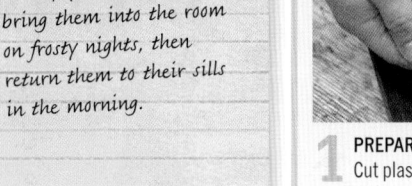

3 PLANT WHEN READY
When the seedlings are ready and hardened off, dig a gutter-sized trench and gently ease the entire length of compost into position.

Cut-and-come-again salads

Baby salad leaves are tasty, nutritious, and one of the quickest crops you can grow. The great thing is that they re-grow after being cut, not just once, but two or three times, giving a bumper harvest from a small space. They are ideal for small plots and containers, and can be grown under cover for salad throughout winter.

Winter leaves

Anyone with a greenhouse, cold frame, or even a bright windowsill in a cool room, can successfully grow cut-and-come-again salads, to crop right through the lean winter and early-spring months. Not all leafy crops grow well when daylight is short and conditions are cool. If you are sowing under cover from mid- to late winter, choose peppery salad rocket and oriental mustards, mild mizuna, colourful loose-leaf lettuces, and crisp sugarloaf chicory and pak choi, for a range of interesting textures and flavours. At this time of year it usually takes 5–6 weeks to grow baby leaves that are ready to cut, whereas in summer they can reach a good size in 3–4 weeks. For a crop ready to harvest earlier in winter, sow the same selection of seeds under cover from early- to mid-autumn.

Summer crops

From early spring, you can sow cut-and-come-again salads directly outdoors, in rich, well-weeded soil, or into patio containers or windowboxes. Most of the winter crops listed above will now grow well outdoors. Increase the variety by adding baby spinach and kale, if you like the taste. Normally,

early spring is too soon to sow salad crops if you want mature plants, because they bolt – rapidly run to seed – due to the cool weather. Since the plants suggested here will be cut as baby leaves, there is no need to worry about them going to seed. For a continuous supply of salads, keep sowing successively every 3–4 weeks until mid- to late summer, and cut batches of baby leaves regularly so that more re-grow to take their place.

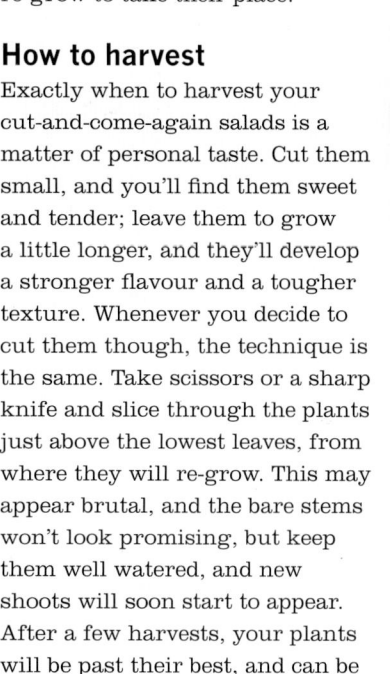

How to harvest

Exactly when to harvest your cut-and-come-again salads is a matter of personal taste. Cut them small, and you'll find them sweet and tender; leave them to grow a little longer, and they'll develop a stronger flavour and a tougher texture. Whenever you decide to cut them though, the technique is the same. Take scissors or a sharp knife and slice through the plants just above the lowest leaves, from where they will re-grow. This may appear brutal, and the bare stems won't look promising, but keep them well watered, and new shoots will soon start to appear. After a few harvests, your plants will be past their best, and can be composted. Grow on new sowings.

1 Land cress has a peppery taste that is delicious in salads and can be used instead of watercress. It is ready for harvesting 6–8 weeks after sowing. It grows well under cover during winter.

2 Corn salad is also known as lamb's lettuce, and produces a steady supply of small leaves, even during winter. Wash well before use to remove grit that can build up between the stems.

3 Wild rocket has a stronger taste than normal garden rocket. Its serrated leaves also look more attractive and make a better garnish. Peppery to eat, it gives a welcome kick to salads.

4 Oriental mustards are usually cooked when fully grown, but can also be eaten raw when harvested as baby leaves. The plants grow well, even in the coldest areas, and also look quite decorative.

5 Mizuna has a mild mustard flavour, and makes an attractive and tasty addition to salads when picked as baby leaves. Let summer crops grow a little longer for larger leaves to stir-fry.

6 Pak choi is more commonly grown in summer as a mature crop, although the baby leaves can be picked when just a few weeks old in spring. It has a mild flavour and a good crisp texture.

7 Mibuna is similar in taste to mizuna. Its narrow, spear-shaped leaves grow in clumps, but are slow to appear in spring, so it is best grown as a summer crop. Try adding the leaves to soups.

8 Baby lettuce leaves are loose-leaf varieties cropped at an earlier stage. Sow a large batch in spring, using some as cut-and-come-again crops and letting some mature for summer salads.

Other varieties to try:
Chervil (p.50)
Endive (p.51)
Rocket (p.50)
Tatsoi (p.50)

CUT-AND-COME-AGAIN SALADS

January: what to do

STOCK UP

When bad weather keeps you indoors, spend some time comparing the catalogues of mail order seed suppliers. These offer a huge range of varieties to choose from, and you can shop around for competitive prices. Also take the opportunity to stock up on spring essentials such as pots, compost, seed trays, labels, stakes, and twine.

SOIL MAKEOVER

Double digging and incorporating manure is the best way to improve your soil before planting. It can be done in autumn (p.204) or now, providing the soil isn't frozen.

1 DIG TRENCH ONE
Mark out the area being dug, dig out a trench two spades deep, and put the soil to one side.

2 DIG TRENCH TWO
Dig a second trench next to the first, turning the upper layer of soil into the base of the first trench.

3 ADD MANURE AND MIX
Add manure to the part-filled first trench, then the rest of the soil from trench two. Repeat.

TEND

GARDEN ESSENTIALS

FORCED FRUIT

BRASSICAS

DOUBLE DIGGING

EARLY WARMING

To encourage some of your plants, such as strawberries, to crop earlier than normal, in May instead of June, cover them now with cloches. The extra heat will allow them to flower and fruit earlier. This is also the time to place a rhubarb forcer over your plants to promote earlier stems that are sweeter and more tender. Remove the forcer in March and allow the plants to recover. Only force established plants.

STAY TIDY

As winter progresses, most hardy brassicas, including winter cabbages, sprouting broccoli, cauliflowers, and kales, tend to drop their more mature lower leaves. These can accumulate around the base, harbouring pests and diseases, and also start to smell. Pick up and compost fallen leaves regularly.

BAD APPLES
One bad apple can spoil all the rest, so check through your stored fruit (pp.194–195) for signs of brown rot fungus, damage from mice and other pests, or problems caused by fluctuating temperatures. Discard any diseased or spoiled produce, even if the damage is minimal. Make sure your store is well ventilated and insulated.

NEW FRUIT TREES
Most tree and bush fruits planted in late autumn need pruning as soon as they are in the ground (pp.206–207). Cut blackcurrants right back so that all shoots have one bud above soil level. Redcurrant and gooseberry stems should be cut back by half, and raspberry and blackberry canes cut to 30cm (12in). On young, feathered maiden apple and pear trees, cut back the leading shoot and select lateral shoots to form the first branches. Don't prune cherries, plums, peaches, and apricots until spring (p.86).

FRUIT STORES

FRUIT PRUNING

WINTER PRUNING

WINTER PRUNING
Free-standing mature apple and pear trees need some winter pruning now to keep them fruiting well and to maintain an open, balanced shape. Your aim should be to remove any weak, congested, or damaged branches that are likely to be unproductive.

1 PRUNE TO SIDE BRANCH
To prune back to a side branch, undercut with a saw to about halfway through the stem. Make the final cut from above, to meet the undercut.

2 SHORTEN THIN BRANCHES
To encourage the formation of flowers in spring, cut back long spindly growth to a short branch, using sharp secateurs.

3 REMOVE WEAK GROWTH
If you have pruned your tree in previous years, check the old pruning sites and remove any weak stems growing round the cut areas.

4 PREVENT CONGESTION
Take out branches that are crossing over others, or growing towards the centre of the tree. This prevents congestion and disease.

See PRUNING FRUIT IN AUTUMN pages 206–207

Preparing a seedbed

Plants are at their most vulnerable as seeds and tiny seedlings. At this stage they need as near-perfect conditions as possible in which to germinate and grow quickly. Providing your seedlings with well-drained, weed-free soil that has been worked to a fine texture, will get them off to a good start. Time and effort spent on your seedbeds now will be well rewarded later with strong, healthy young plants.

Creating a tilth

Although seedlings do not need the most fertile soil, they are unlikely to thrive unless their environment has been prepared carefully beforehand. Creating what gardeners call a "fine tilth", where the soil surface is raked into fine crumbs, is important for successful germination, but this is easier on some soils than others. All soil types will benefit from the addition of a good organic compost. On heavy clay soils, working in a layer of sand helps to reduce stickiness and improve structure and drainage.

Jo's **tips**

If you want to create a nursery seedbed in which to raise young plants, such as brassicas, for transplanting, then choose a good open site rather than a neglected corner at the back of the garden.

Seedlings require sunshine, plenty of rain, and a soil that holds some moisture. Keep them away from the shade, shelter, and competing roots of tall trees and hedges as much as possible.

1 CLEAR WEEDS
Thoroughly weed the seedbed, taking care to remove whole perennial roots, like those of dandelions, which will regrow if left in the soil. Remove any large stones, too.

2 IMPROVE THE SOIL
Add a layer of well-rotted compost, as well as sand, to help drainage if you are working heavy clay. Dig the soil over lightly with a fork to break up the surface and work in the compost.

3 RAKE TO A TILTH
Firm the soil gently with the back of your rake, then move the rake backwards and forwards across the bed, removing stones, until you have a good, even, crumbly tilth.

4 MARK OUT A DRILL
Once you are happy with the soil texture, you can start sowing. Draw the pointed edge of a hoe through the soil to make a tidy drill at the correct depth for your chosen seeds.

Making a raised bed

Raised beds offer a low-maintenance way to grow your own crops, and suit busy lives and small spaces. They can be made from a range of materials, to heights and sizes to suit any plot. Because the beds can be constructed where there is no soil, or where the soil is poor, any bright spot can become a miniature allotment. They can provide temporary growing spaces, and be dismantled easily if you need the space.

Benefits

Raised beds make life easier: the paths between them mean you only have to dig, weed, and cultivate the area used for growing, and they can be filled with quality bought-in soil or compost, which reduces how much routine soil preparation you need to do. Where drainage is a problem they help lift plants clear of cold, wet earth. They also allow the soil to warm up more quickly in spring so that seeds can be sown sooner, giving your crops a useful head start.

Easy access

Avoid having to stand on your raised bed, compacting the soil with your feet, by making sure they are not too wide. Unless you are very tall, build your beds no more than 1.2m (4ft) across, so you can reach to the centre without over-stretching. Of course, beds can be narrower if you choose, and they can be whatever length and height you like. Taller beds are ideal for those who need plants in easy reach.

To provide a sound footing to work from when tending your bed, leave a wide path all the way around, preferably covered with weed-suppressing mulch.

OLD RAILWAY SLEEPERS
Lengthy sleepers make an excellent material for raised beds because you can build them up layer by layer to suit your needs. They are very heavy, so get help when moving them.

BRICKS
You can make beds any size and shape using bricks. They are also durable and maintenance-free. Brick beds must have drainage channels to prevent waterlogging.

RECYCLED MATERIALS
Many different materials can be used for beds, including wooden pallets, old water tanks, or even old tyres. Whatever you use, make sure it can support the weight of the soil safely.

January: what to harvest

TENDER BUDS
Early varieties of sprouting broccoli, such as 'Rudolph', sown last May, should start sending forth tender stems, topped with tight purple or white buds, this month. Be sure to cut or snap off shoots before they get too long and the flowers open, and each plant could keep cropping for up to 8 weeks. Sprouting broccoli is delicious lightly steamed or stir-fried, and has a sweet flavour. The shoots must be cut before the flowers open, so freeze any that you can't eat within 2–3 days, as they soon go past their best (pp.148–149).

GRATE RADISH
Try to bite into one of these large hardy radishes in the same way that you would a summer salad variety, and you may be disappointed with their rather tough texture. Instead, these unusual vegetables are a treat when grated into salads, or cooked in hearty winter stews. Sown in July, they keep their flavour best when left in the ground, but if the weather turns bad, lift and store them in sand, like carrots (pp.210–211).

HARVEST

SPROUTING BROCCOLI

WINTER RADISH

CELERIAC

APPLES

TWO CROPS IN ONE
This gnarled root vegetable, first sown in February, will survive in the soil through most winters, and can be pulled when required. Usefully, you can also cook and eat the leaves, which have a potent celery flavour. Try them added to soups or mixed with cabbage. To protect the roots in cold regions with regular hard frosts, cover the roots with fleece or a layer of straw.

IN STORE NOW
Not all apples will keep past Christmas, but in ideal storage conditions (pp.194–195) some dessert varieties, such as 'Pixie', and late culinary varieties, like 'Bramley's Seedling' and 'Howgate Wonder', will still be good to eat. Don't forget the sliced and stewed supplies squirrelled away in the freezer.

COUNT YOUR CHICONS

About 3–4 weeks after being plunged into darkness (p.216) tasty, pale chicons, the forced new shoots of Witloof chicory, should be ready to harvest. Cut them about 2.5cm (1in) above the root with a sharp knife and eat the crisp, slightly bitter leaves raw in salads or braised. Chicons will keep in the fridge, but wrap them to exclude light and prevent them turning green. The cut root may re-sprout, giving a second crop, so don't forget to put it back in the dark. If it doesn't, discard the old root and start again.

SPRING GREENS

Cut-and-come salads can be sown throughout the year (pp.28–29), and will crop through winter under cover, especially if you grow hardier varieties, such as corn salad. Pick regularly but sparingly, and try to alternate the plants you pick from, so they have time to re-grow. Only harvest healthy growth and discard any leaves damaged by frost.

WITLOOF CHICORY

CUT-AND-COME-AGAIN SALAD

GARLIC

CHECK YOUR STORED GARLIC

Planted in autumn or early spring and lifted the following summer, stored garlic bulbs start to sprout as spring approaches. Check your bulbs and roast them before they show green shoots.

SIGNS OF GROWTH
Discard any soft bulbs. Once one bulb shows signs of green shoots, the rest will quickly follow. Roast the bulbs to store for longer.

ROAST WHOLE
Remove any green shoots, drizzle olive oil over the bulbs and roast them in the oven at 180°C (350°F/ Gas 4) for about 30 minutes.

BACK IN STORAGE
Allow the garlic to cool before you store in jars under olive oil. Use the sweet-tasting cloves to flavour soups and stews.

DON'T FORGET

Keep a close eye on your stored crops, especially if they're still outside or in the garage or shed. Mice, birds, and many insects will be active in warmer spells, looking for something to eat.

Try also MAKING SOUP pages 226–227

HARVESTING IDEAS

Growing sprouting seeds

Packed with protein, vitamins, and minerals, sprouting seeds add a healthy fresh crunch to salads, sandwiches, and stir-fries all year round. They are incredibly quick and easy to grow – just add water – and in only a few days your crop will be ready to eat. All you need are some recommended seeds and a large jar with a perforated lid.

1 **Wash the jar well**, add the seeds and rinse them thoroughly with cold water. Only fill the jar about a third full to allow room for the seeds to grow. Fill with water and leave seeds to soak for 6–12 hours.

2 **Drain the jar thoroughly** and put it in a well-ventilated place out of direct sunlight. Rinse the seeds with cold water and drain completely twice daily. This keeps them fresh and will stop them from drying out.

3 **After 2–4 days** for peas and beans, or 4–6 days for other seeds, the crop should be ready to eat. Try the sprouts at various stages to see which you prefer. Allow them to dry for a few hours before storing in the fridge.

4 **Make your own** sprouting jars by stretching muslin over the neck of a jar with an elastic band. Tiered trays are ideal for sprouting several types of seeds simultaneously. Sprouting bags are perfect for larger beans or peas.

Jo's TIPS

Only white mung beansprouts need to be kept in the dark. All other seeds will sprout in daylight, out of direct sun, and are less likely to go mouldy in a well-ventilated position than a stuffy cupboard.

TRY THESE

Use only seeds sold specifically for sprouting to ensure that they are suitable and that they have not been treated with chemicals such as artificial fertilizers.

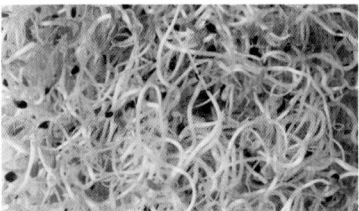

Aduki beans – Slightly sweet, these red-skinned beans produce short white sprouts. Ready to eat in 2–4 days.

Alfafa – Always a favourite with its mild, nutty flavour and crisp shoots, this small seed sprouts in 4–6 days.

Broccoli – High in antioxidants, with a bold brassica taste. Best sprouted in seed mixes that take 3–6 days to crop.

Mung beans – Sprout in the dark for traditional Chinese beansprouts, or enjoy shorter shoots in 2–4 days.

GROWING SPROUTING SEEDS

February: ready to eat

There are plenty of treats this month. Think of luscious roast garlic in oil, or stored berries and apples made into winter pies and crumbles. If it's frosty, brussels sprouts will be at their sweetest and best.

Raid the cupboard for the last pots of summer **jam**
pages 128–129

Leeks should be lasting well, so make the most of them

Spring onion bulbs are swelling nicely under cover

Make some hearty **parsnip** soup

Hardy **winter cabbage** is usually reliable

There may be a few **apples** left in your store

Brussels sprouts taste best after frost

Stored **winter squashes** give a glow to gloomy days

Use up stored **winter radishes** while they're good to eat

Purple sprouting broccoli is getting into its stride – freeze some for later on

Make pies and crumbles using frozen **soft fruit**

Cook **Swiss chard** in the same way as spinach

Uncover stored **swedes** and use them in soups and stews

Keep cutting **red leaf chicory**

Use **salsify** as soon as you lift it – this root dries out quickly

No need for a supermarket trip if your **root vegetable** stores are lasting out

Kale tastes delicious boiled or used in stir-fries

Always something green with **cut-and-come again salads**

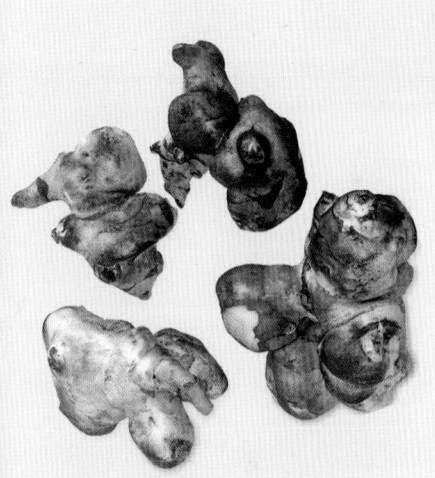

Harvest **winter cauliflower** when the curds reach a good size

Never a dull meal – if you use last autumn's **pickles** *pages 176–179*

Sprouting seeds *pages 36–37* make a crunchy salad topping

Endive should still be cropping well under cover

Don't forget any **Jerusalem artichokes** still in the ground

Shrubby **herbs**, such as bay, sage, and rosemary, can still be cropped sparingly

Newly lifted **celeriac** makes a good alternative tomashed potato

Use the homemade pesto put in the freezer last year *page 147*

Enjoy roast **garlic**, stored under oil in January *page 35*

Use up stored **onions** and **shallots**

February: what to sow

CRUNCHY CELERY
Celery and celeriac need a long growing season, so should be sown indoors at 10–15°C (50–59°F). Sow celeriac, 1cm (½in) deep in modules or seed trays, to crop autumn to spring. Sow celery on the surface of damp compost, to enjoy from summer to winter. Grow both on indoors, to harden off and plant out later in spring.

HARVEST: **VARIOUS**

CHILLI START
These heat-loving plants need a long, hot season to ripen well, and benefit from being sown early. Sow the seed indoors, 1cm (½in) deep, into pots or trays standing in a heated propagator, or on a warm windowsill. Keep them moist and warm, at around 21°C (70°F).

HARVEST: **JUL–OCT**

SOW

CELERY & CELERIAC

CHILLIES

BROAD BEANS & PEAS

GLOBE ARTICHOKES

SOW PEAS AND BEANS
HARVEST: **VARIOUS**

If your soil isn't frozen or sodden, sow early broad bean outdoors, such as 'Super Aquadulce', to pick in May, plus early peas, like 'Feltham First', for a June crop.

1 SOWING BEANS
Sow broad beans in drills, 25cm (10in) apart, using a dibber to bury them 5cm (2in) deep, and at 20–25cm (8–10in) intervals.

2 SOWING PEAS
Peas prefer warm soil and germinate better if cloched. Sow 4cm (1½in) deep, 8–10cm (3–4in) apart, in 20cm (8in) wide drills.

3 STILL TOO COLD?
If outdoor conditions aren't suitable for sowing, start beans off in modules, and sow peas in guttering (p.27), under cover.

GOURMET VEG
Globe artichokes are gourmet vegetables that are expensive to buy, so it makes sense to grow your own. If you have space, and want plenty of these statuesque plants, the most economical way is to grow them from seed. Sow them 1cm (½in) deep in modules or trays in a propagator, or on a windowsill. Seed-raised plants can be variable, so only grow on the strongest seedlings.

HARVEST: **JUN–SEPT**

GROW BRASSICAS
Sow Brussels sprouts and kohl rabi (p.208) 1cm (½in) deep in modules or trays in a heated propagator, or on a bright windowsill, to give them an early start. Choose early varieties of Brussels sprouts to sow now, for a tasty crop from winter to spring. Kohl rabi, sown in a propagator this month to crop in early summer, need planting out before the plants are 5cm (2in) tall to reduce the risk of bolting. This fast-growing vegetable can also be sown successively outdoors from early spring to late summer.

● HARVEST: **VARIOUS**

SPEEDY SPINACH
Spinach is a fast-growing crop that can be prone to bolting when sown early. To help prevent this, sow the seed under cloches or in cold frames this month and next, using special 'short-day' varieties, such as 'Triathlon'. Sow the seed 1cm (½in) deep, in drills spaced about 30cm (12in) apart, thinning the seedlings 10–15cm (4–6in) apart.

● HARVEST: **APR–NOV**

BRUSSELS & KOHL RABI

SPRING SPINACH

PARSNIPS

EARLY PARSNIPS
HARVEST: **NOV–APR**

If you live in a mild area, sow parsnips early for a long growing season, warming the soil with cloches or plastic to help improve germination.

1 MARKING OUT Rake the seedbed to a fine tilth, removing any large stones. Make drills with a hoe, 2cm (¾in) deep and 30cm (12in) apart.

2 SPACE THE SEED Sow three seeds per station, spaced 10cm (4in) apart. Cover the seed and water well. Parsnips are slow to germinate.

3 GROW THEM ON Cover early sowings with cloches for best results, and thin seedlings to one per station. Protect plants from carrot fly.

DON'T FORGET
If you live in a colder region, this may be your first opportunity to sow leeks, lettuce, onions (all p.26), cut-and-come-again salad, radish, peas (all p.27).

Indoors, grow sprouting seeds (pp.36–37).

See SOWING UNDER COVER page 42

SOWING FEATURE

Sowing under cover

Even if you are new to vegetable growing, you will probably want to sow some crops under cover, and the advantages are undeniable. Sowing early, and providing additional warmth and shelter, gives tender plants a useful head start, allowing them to crop sooner and for longer. Seedlings raised under cover also often show stronger growth than those sown directly outside – and give better harvests.

A protected environment

There is nothing complicated about sowing seeds under cover, and it is not necessary to have a greenhouse. You simply need to give your plants a protected environment, whether you sow them in trays, or individual pots, or modules. The protection you provide could consist of a cold frame, a cloche, or just a sunny windowsill indoors.

Seedling plants under cover can be highly susceptible to diseases. You should constantly monitor their conditions to ensure that warmth and humidity are maintained at the correct levels.

1 PREPARE SEED TRAYS
Fill seed trays to about 1cm (½in) from the top with a good multipurpose compost. Firm lightly, using the base of another tray or your fingers. Water well and allow to drain.

2 SOW SEEDS
Sow small seeds thinly over the surface, shaking them carefully from the packet or your hand. Plant larger seeds deeper, using a dibber or pencil to make a hole for each seed.

3 ADD TOP LAYER
Use a sieve to distribute a fine layer of compost over the seeds. Larger seeds may need soil pushed over them with a dibber. If your seeds are very small, try not to disturb them.

4 WATER GENTLY
Damp down the compost, using a watering can with a fine rose and taking care not to overwater. You should maintain this level of watering throughout germination.

5 COVER THE TRAY
To create a warm, moist atmosphere for germination, place the seed tray in a heated propagator. Alternatively, you can cover the tray with a plastic lid or sheet of glass.

Pricking out seedlings

As soon as your seeds have germinated, turn down the heat in the propagator or remove the lid from the tray, to help prevent fungal diseases. When the seedlings are large enough to handle, prick them out to grow on in individual pots.

6 LIFT SEEDLINGS
Holding each seedling very lightly by either of its first leaves, use a dibber or pencil to ease the plant out of the compost. Take care not to pull on the fragile roots.

7 PLANT INDIVIDUALLY
Fill individual pots or multi-celled seed trays with new compost and transfer the seedlings one at a time. Grow them on until they are sturdy enough to be planted out.

Sowing outside

Sowing directly into the soil is the simplest and cheapest way to raise vegetables. Preparing your seedbed well, sowing at the right depth, and getting the timing right can make the difference between a lush row of healthy plants and a frustratingly patchy harvest.

Good preparations

It is much easier to distinguish germinating vegetables from weed seedlings if they come up in a straight line. To achieve this, mark out your row by running string between pegs pushed into the ground at either end.

Sow larger seeds deeper than smaller ones. As a rule, make your drill three times as deep as the seed. When you have sown your seeds (as illustrated below), carefully pull the soil across the drill to cover them, using a hoe or rake, or your hands.

Label the row clearly before removing the string line, because it is all too easy to forget what you have sown and where. Water the seeds in thoroughly, using a can fitted with a fine rose to avoid washing them away.

Jo's **tips**

Never sow into cold, wet soil as seeds may rot, or if they do come up, they're likely to bolt. Delay sowing until the weather improves or cloche the soil to warm it. Always protect seedbeds from mice, birds, or cats.

1 SOWING IN A DRILL
To make a drill run the point of a hoe, or a bamboo cane, along the string line at a consistent depth. Pour seeds into the palm of your hand, take a pinch and sprinkle them thinly.

2 STATION-SOWING
To reduce the need for thinning out, try 'station-sowing'. Mark the row and use a dibber to create stations at the right depth and spacings for your crop. Sow three seeds in each station.

SOWING INSIDE AND OUTSIDE

February: what to plant

CHOOSE RHUBARB   HARVEST: **MAR–JUL**

Although rhubarb is best planted in autumn, when newly dormant (p.198), you can also plant now when the new stems are about to sprout.

'CHAMPAGNE'
This variety produces long, vibrant red stems with a sharp, sweet taste. It is good for cooking.

'TIMPERLEY EARLY'
Is an early variety, ideal for forcing in spring, that giving a heavy crop of long, thick, juicy stems.

'VICTORIA'
A late variety, suitable for colder areas where early growth could be damaged by spring frost.

PLANT

JERUSALEM ARTICHOKES

SPRING GARLIC

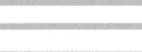
RHUBARB

TASTY ARTICHOKES
Before planting these knobbly tubers, bear in mind that they grow up to 3m (10ft) tall. The plant tolerates all but the worst soil and some shade, and can be planted in under-used corners. Artichokes also make a good screen because of their height. Plant the tubers 10cm (4in) deep, about 30cm (12in) apart, and leave 90cm (36in) between rows for maximum harvests. These plants can be invasive.

HARVEST: **NOV–MAR**

LATE GARLIC
If you have heavy soil and find that over-wintered garlic rots in the ground, plant a spring variety such as 'White Solent'. Split the cloves and push them into the soil, flat end down, tops covered. Cloves planted in autumn under cover (p.184) should be planted out now. Position 10cm (4in) apart, in rows with 25cm (10in) between them.

HARVEST: **JUL–AUG**

SHALLOTS AND LOTS OF ONIONS

Sets are small bulbs to plant now for an earlier crop than from seed-raised plants. Plant into well-prepared soil 2cm (¾in) deep.

HARVEST: **JUL–OCT**

Space onions 10cm (4in) apart, shallots 15cm (6in) apart, in rows spaced 30cm (12in). Delay planting onion sets if the weather is cold.

'RED BARON'
A productive onion with firm, dark red bulbs. Like all red varieties, it is mild enough to be eaten raw.

'STURON'
This is a maincrop onion, producing large, fleshy, brown-skinned bulbs. It has good resistance to bolting.

'LONGOR'
Described as a 'banana' shallot due to its elongated shape, this variety is easy to chop when cooking.

'RED SUN'
This is a red shallot, with white flesh and a mild flavour that can be eaten raw. It is good for pickling.

SHRUBBY HERBS

FRUIT TREES

ONIONS & SHALLOTS

HERBS IN POTS

HARVEST: **ALL YEAR**

Plant shrubby and evergreen herbs, such as bay, sage, and thyme in pots now to establish before summer.

1 PICK A POT
Choose a large enough container for the plant, make sure it has plenty of drainage holes, and part-fill it with soil-based compost.

2 POSITION THE PLANT
Position the plant at the same depth as in its own pot, 5cm (2in) below the rim of the container. Fill with more compost and water well.

FRUIT TREES

This is a good time to plant bare-root fruit bushes and trees (pp.202–203), while they are still dormant. Before planting, improve the soil, digging in well-rotted manure or compost. Dig a hole deep and wide enough so the roots can be spread out fully. Drive in a stake for trees. Plant to the same level as the soil line on the stem. Backfill the hole, firm in well, and water thoroughly.

HARVEST: **VARIOUS**

Try COLD & HOT PICKLING pages 176–179

February: what to do

PROTECT BLOSSOM
Apricot and peach blossom opens so early in spring that it's highly vulnerable to damage from even relatively minor frosts. Damaged flowers will not set fruit. To protect your crop, cover the flowers with horticultural fleece draped over the branches. Protect wall-trained trees with a covered frame. Remove the fleece on warmer days to allow insects in for pollination – see below.

WALL-TRAINED FIGS
In cool regions, fig trees crop once a year, forming embryonic fruit near the tips of their summer shoots. These are carried through winter to ripen the following summer. Prune trees now to encourage new fruit-bearing growth on fan-trained trees in spring, cutting back half the shoots that carried fruit last summer to one bud. Tie the unpruned fruit-bearing shoots to the horizontal wires, filling in spaces in the framework.

TEND

APRICOTS

FIGS

BERRY CANES

PEACHES

PRUNE CANE FRUIT
Autumn raspberries will fruit on canes produced this year, so cut all the canes back to the base now, before new growth appears. Summer raspberries and blackberries crop on last year's canes; these can be battered by harsh winter weather. Check your plants and cut any damaged tips back to a healthy bud. Secure any loose canes to their supports.

BE A BEE
Peaches and apricots come into flower this month, and must be pollinated if they're to produce fruit later in the year. If the weather remains cold, there will be few insects around to do the job. To ensure a crop, use a small, soft paintbrush to transfer pollen between flowers. Don't forget any trees covered against frost.

WINTER PRUNING

This is the last chance to prune your currant and gooseberry bushes while they are still dormant. Prune up to a third of the older shoots at the base from your blackcurrant bushes. Also trim back by half the leading shoots of gooseberries; red- and whitecurrants, cut back sideshoots to two buds, and remove any dead or overcrowded wood to open up the centre of the bush. You can also prune cobnuts now by shortening long sideshoots, which you may have "brutted" last summer (p.157), to three or four buds.

TURN COMPOST

This is a quiet month in the garden so take the opportunity to turn your compost heap. All heaps need to be turned at least once. Using a fork, break up any matted lumps, and move drier, uncomposted material from the top and edges of the heap, to the centre. If the contents are mostly composted, empty the heap now and start again (pp.190–191).

FRUITS & NUTS

COMPOST

EARLY POTATOES

CHIT POTATOES

To give your early potatoes a head start and produce a better crop, start the tubers into growth indoors — chitting. This isn't necessary with maincrops.

1 CHECK TUBERS
To plant out in 6 weeks' time, check through your seed potatoes now and discard any that are shrivelled or diseased.

2 STAND IN BOXES
Take each tuber and find the end with the most buds or eyes. Stand it, this end up, in a box in a cool, light, frost-free place.

3 PLANT OUT
Stocky shoots should develop from each eye. When these are about 2.5cm (1in) long the tubers are ready for planting out.

DON'T FORGET

Take care when clearing fallen leaves and other debris, or turning the compost heap, as at this time of year they may be sheltering beneficial animals, such as frogs, toads, and hedgehogs (pp.104–105).

See START A COMPOST HEAP pages 190-191

Potatoes

Potatoes are easy to grow, and a good choice for new plots because they tolerate and help to break up recently cultivated soils. Maincrop varieties have large, leafy tops and sprawling roots, and require lots of room for a family-size crop. If space is limited, get a decent harvest of new potatoes by growing them in containers or bags.

Early or maincrop?

Choosing from the enormous range of varieties on offer is a hard task, even for experienced growers, but understanding the terminology is the first step to finding the right potato for you. Varieties are grouped as 'earlies', 'second earlies' and 'maincrops', according to the amount of time it takes them to mature. As you might expect, early varieties grow fastest and are ready in about 90 days, while maincrops can take up to 150 days before they are ready to harvest. Many gardeners choose to grow early varieties because they can be planted closer together, and produce a crop of baby new potatoes by early summer. They do give lower yields than maincrop varieties, which are also a better choice if you want tubers to lift and store.

Eating qualities

When deciding between varieties, you'll also want to consider the texture, flavour, and even the colour of varieties, before you select what to plant. Perhaps the most important factor is whether the flesh has a waxy or floury texture. Waxy potatoes stay firm when cooked and are ideal for boiling, which makes them a good choice as salad potatoes. Varieties with a drier, floury texture have an annoying habit of disintegrating when boiled, but are wonderful baked, roasted, or chipped. Flavour is subjective, but there's no doubt that some varieties have a distinct nutty taste, while others are extremely mild. The colour of both the skin and flesh can also influence your choice. Red-skinned varieties are irresistible baked, while yellow-fleshed types make appetizing salad potatoes.

Disease resistance

Like other crops, potatoes are susceptible to a number of pests and diseases, which rarely destroy the plants, but can often adversely affect the quantity and quality of tubers. Although not immune to them, early varieties tend to be less seriously affected by diseases, such as potato blight (p.242), and pests such as potato cyst eelworm (p.238), because they are not in the ground as long as maincrop varieties. If you are aware of a particular problem in your garden or area, then choose varieties that have some in-built resistance to the pest or disease. Blight-resistant potatoes include 'Lady Balfour', 'Sarpo Mira' and 'Valor'.

EARLIES

1 'Foremost' is a tasty variety with firm white, waxy flesh that holds together well when boiled. It gives a good yield, stores well, and resists common scab.

2 'Red Duke of York' is a red-skinned variety with floury flesh that is good eaten boiled, baked, roasted or chipped. This is a highly rated all-rounder.

3 'Accent' is a heavy-cropping variety, producing white-skinned potatoes with firm waxy flesh – best boiled. It has good resistance to eelworm and scab.

SECOND EARLIES

4 'Charlotte' matures later than most second earlies, and has firm yellow, waxy flesh, with a good flavour. It also has some blight and scab resistance.

5 'Belle de Fontenay' is an early, white-skinned, waxy variety, often grown for salad potatoes. It has a good flavour; later tubers store well.

MAINCROP

6 'Yukon Gold' produces large tubers, with golden skin and flesh. It has a good flavour, and is best baked, roasted or fried. It keeps its attractive buttery, colour after cooking.

7 'Pink Fir Apple' is a waxy, red-skinned potato, with long nobbly tubers. It crops in October and stores well. Best boiled, but can be chipped.

8 'Ratte' is usually grown as a salad potato. With a waxy texture and a delicious nutty flavour, it is highly versatile in the kitchen.

Other varieties to try:
'Epicure' – early
'Highland Burgundy' – maincrop
'Nadine' – second early
'Orla' – second early
'Salad Blue' – maincrop
'Swift' – early

POTATOES

February: what to harvest

HEEL IN PARSNIPS

These large roots take up a lot of space, which is needed now for new seedbeds. To make room for spring planting, lift your remaining parsnips and store them in another part of the garden. Using a fork, carefully ease out the parsnips, taking care not to damage the roots, and heel them in elsewhere. Heeling-in simply involves digging a shallow-angled trench, where the roots can be laid close together and covered with soil. They will take up far less space and can be unearthed as required.

LAST CHANCE FOR SWEDES

If you left part of your swede crop to overwinter in the ground, now is the time to dig up any remaining roots. Even if they survive for longer without rotting or pest damage, they will become increasingly woody and inedible. This is your last chance to make use of the crop, and a good moment to clear ground that will soon be needed for new plantings. It's also worthwhile checking swedes in storage for pest damage or decay.

HARVEST

PARSNIPS

SWEDES

WINTER SALAD

WINTER CUT-AND-COME-AGAIN

Winter salads needn't be dull. Many leafy crops can be grown under cover as cut-and-come-again salad (pp.28–29) at this time of year.

Once the leaves are the size you prefer, cut them with scissors 2cm (¾in) above the soil and a new crop should regrow in a few weeks.

CHERVIL
This is commonly grown as a herb, and has a mild, parsley-like flavour. It can also be harvested as young leaves to spice up your salads.

TATSOI
This salad leaf has a mild, mustard flavour and a crisp texture, and can be eaten raw or cooked. The plants are very hardy, ideal for cold areas.

ROCKET
A few leaves of peppery tasting rocket can transform a salad. Cut the leaves when they are new and fresh, as they turn bitter when older.

PERPETUAL SPINACH
The tender new leaves are delicious either in salads or cooked. Cut them from alternate plants to leave room for new growth along the row.

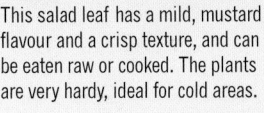

INDOOR HERBS

It's a real treat to have fresh herbs to pick throughout winter. Container-grown herbs, such as marjoram, mint, thyme, and parsley, will continue to thrive on the windowsill or in the conservatory with minimal attention. As long as you ensure that the plants are warm and watered, they should keep new growth coming until it's time for them to go back outdoors in spring. Use scissors to snip off the fresh tips when required.

LIFT ARTICHOKES

Jerusalem artichokes don't store well, so it's best to dig them up as required. Unearth the tubers with a fork, being careful not to spear any. Remove even unusably small ones, because they will regrow in spring if left in the soil. Scrub the tubers with a brush, peel them, and use quickly for soups and side dishes before they discolour.

HERBS

LEEKS

ENDIVE

JERUSALEM ARTICHOKES

LATE LEEKS

Late-season leek varieties are very hardy and will stand in the ground until spring without spoiling their texture or flavour. Lift them as required with a fork. Their roots can hold on tightly, so loosen the soil to a good depth, to allow the leek to pull away without breaking. To avoid carrying a lot of soil into the kitchen, cut off the roots and drop them on the compost heap.

CUT ENDIVE

Endives growing under cover should resprout after cutting, so never uproot a plant when harvesting. Instead, cut the base of a mature endive head with a sharp knife and trim off any damaged leaves. Endives will keep for several days somewhere cool, as long as they are not stored damp.

March: ready to eat

As the days begin to lengthen, pick new leaves from windowsill herbs and cloched leafy crops, such as Swiss chard. Sprouting broccoli will be cropping profusely; freeze extra spears for later.

Keep picking your **sprouting broccoli**

Eat **sprouting seeds**
- alfalfa
- beansprouts
- broccoli
- fenugreek
pages 36–37

Windowsill herbs are coming into growth

This month, dig the last **Jerusalem artichokes**

Make hot desserts from **frozen fruit**
pages 150–151

Brussels sprouts are finishing, freeze some for later *pages 148–149*

Eat stored **onions** and **shallots**

Pick fresh **cut-and-come-again** leaves

Use cubes of frozen **herbs** and **pesto**
page 147

Winter cabbage will soon be over – keep harvesting

Use stored **beetroot**, **potatoes**, **carrots**, and **swedes**

Unearth the last fresh **celeriac** roots now

Covered crops of **Swiss chard** and **spinach beet** will see you through until spring

New season **forced rhubarb** is deliciously sweet and tender

Use up fruit jams, made last year, ready for your new crops

Chutneys and **pickles** taste better as they mature

Kale is still cropping

Forced chicory – end of season

This is your last chance to lift or use stored **winter radish**

Lift more **leeks**

Crop **winter cauliflowers** while the heads are tightly closed

Drink **homemade wine**, made in summer
pages 180–181

Covered crops of **endive** finish this month – enjoy them in salads

Use the last **leaf chicory**, grown under cover

Salsify, freshly lifted, is a real culinary treat

Eat **roast garlic** prepared in January
page 35

Crop undercover **spring onions**

Dig sweet **parsnips** while you still can

Eat up late **frozen vegetables** to make space for new harvests

March: what to sow

TWO ROOTS
To prevent them bolting, sow summer beetroot and turnips in soil warmed under cold frames or cloches or in a greenhouse. Try bolt-resistant 'Boltardy' beetroot or turnip 'Purple Top Milan'. In drills 20cm (8in) apart, sow seed 1cm (½in) deep. Thin beetroot to 8cm (3in) apart, and leave 10cm (4in) between turnips.

HARVEST: **VARIOUS**

CALABRESE
Unlike other brassica crops, calabrese does not transplant well from seedbeds. So, either sow directly outside at its final spacing of 30cm (12in) each way, or sow into modules outdoors or in a cold frame. You can then plant the seedlings out at the same spacing.

HARVEST: **JUN–OCT**

SOW

BRASSICAS

BEETROOT & TURNIPS

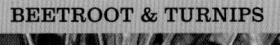

SPRING ONIONS

CALABRESE

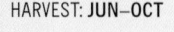

BRASSICA BASICS
Sow summer cabbage and cauliflowers now to crop in summer and autumn. Sprouting broccoli sown this month will produce spears in winter and early spring. To make more of your space, sow them in 1cm (½in) deep drills in a seedbed, and transplant to their final spacing 5–6 weeks later. Net the young plants to keep pigeons off.

HARVEST: **VARIOUS**

NON-STOP ONIONS
For a constant supply of full-flavoured salad onions throughout the year, start sowing outdoors now, and continue making further successional sowings every 2–3 weeks all summer. Weed the bed thoroughly first and make narrow drills about 10cm (4in) apart. Sow the seed very thinly, about one seed every 2cm (¾in), to reduce the need for thinning out later on.

HARVEST: **ALL YEAR**

AUBERGINES – BLACK MAGIC

HARVEST: **AUG–OCT**

Sow seeds 1cm (½in) deep, prick out, and pot them on once the seedlings reach 5cm (2in). Keep the seeds at a minimum temperature of 20°C (68°F).

'MONEYMAKER'
This is a reliable, early variety, that produces large, deep purple fruit. Suitable for growing indoors or out, and also in patio containers.

'CALLIOPE'
Almost free of spines, this compact variety produces an abundance of small, 10cm (4in) long fruit. Pick often to ensure a sustained crop.

'BLACK ENORMA'
As its name suggests, this variety produces exceptionally large pure black fruit. Just two or three plants should keep you going.

STILL TIME TO SOW

In warm areas, sow outside: broad beans, onion, leeks, (all p.26), peas (p.27), rocket (p.29), parsnips and spinach, (both p.41). Inside sow: radish, lettuce (both p.27) celeriac, celery, globe artichoke (all p.40) Brussels, and kohl rabi (both p.41).

TOMATOES, PEPPERS & CHILLIES

CARROTS

AUBERGINES

CROPS FOR SALSA

For indoor crops of tomatoes, peppers and chillies, sow now at about 20°C (68°F), in a heated propagator or on a warm windowsill. Sow about 2cm (¾in) deep in modules or seed trays, and make sure seedlings get plenty of light to stop them getting tall and leggy. Prompt pricking out and potting on will give plants plenty of space, and ensure strong specimens. For outdoor crops, only sow when frosts are less severe, so the plants won't be ready too early to plant out.

HARVEST: **JUL–OCT**

COSY CARROTS

Carrots won't germinate in cold soil, so sow them now under cloches, and remove them as the weather warms. Choose early varieties like 'Early Nantes' and 'Parmex'. Rake the seedbed to a fine tilth and sow thinly in drills 1cm (½in) deep, 15cm (6in) apart. Early crops usually miss the worst carrot fly attacks.

HARVEST: **MAY–DEC**

TAKE YOUR PICK

Peppers

Heat-loving peppers are easy to grow under cover or on a sunny patio. Sow now, or buy young plants later in spring to give them a long season to grow and mature.

1 'Gypsy' is an early variety, maturing from greenish-yellow to orange or red 2 weeks sooner than standard crops. The thin-skinned fruits reach up to 10cm (4in) long and are ideal in salads.

2 'Marconi' produces 15cm (6in) long, attractive, thick-walled fruits that are delicious eaten cooked or raw. Peppers can be harvested when green or left to sweeten as they turn red.

3 'Californian Wonder' produces 12cm (5in) long, bell-shaped fruits, that mature from green to deep red, and are perfect for stuffing. It is heavy cropping and is ideal for growing in containers.

4 'Gourmet' is an early-ripening variety that produces a large crop of bright orange fruits, which are excellent cooked or eaten raw. It is compact and ideal for growing in containers.

5 'Tasty Grill' produces tapered red or yellow fruits up to 25cm (10in) in length, which, as the name suggests, are perfect for grilling. This is a sturdy plant and very early cropping.

6 'Ingrid' is an unusual variety that matures dark brown, and makes a change from familiar-looking peppers. The think-skinned fruit have a mild flavour and ripen best in warmer areas.

Other varieties to try:
'Bell Boy'
'Canape'
'Jingle Bells'
'New Ace'
'Red Knight'

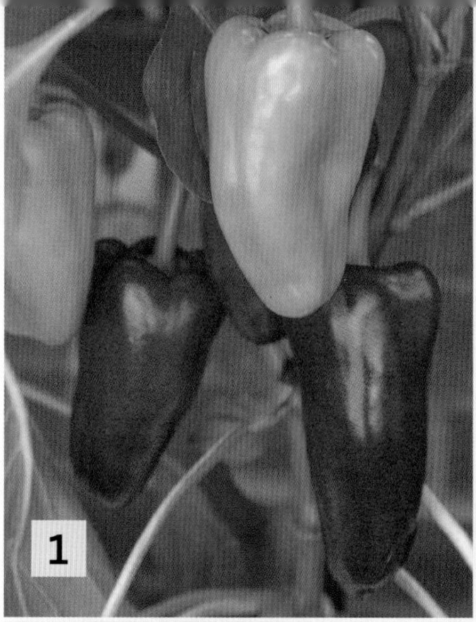

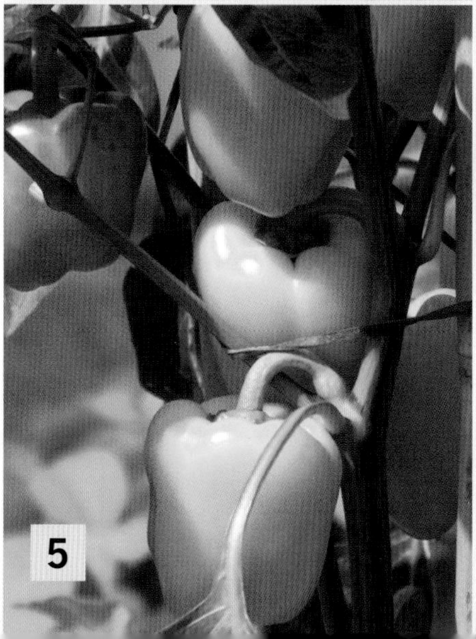

Chillies

Compact and colourful, chillies are perfect for the greenhouse or a windowsill. The crop from just a few plants will spice up your cooking for a whole year.

1 'Aji Amarillo' is native to, and incredibly popular in, South America. It produces long, thin fruits that are medium-hot and especially useful for making sauces and salsas.

2 'Padron' produces 5cm (2in) long fruits, which can be eaten when young, green, and relatively mild, or left to heat up as the skin turns fiery red.

3 'Prairie Fire' produces masses of fast-growing, extremely fiery-tasting chillies. Fruits are only 3cm (1¼in) in length, and mature from cream to yellow and finally to a rich, bright red.

4 'Cherry Bomb' produces high yields of round, thick-walled fruits that ripen from green to red. Chillies are medium-hot, and good for salsas or salads.

5 'Alma Paprika' fruits grow to around 5cm (2in) long, maturing from cream colour through to red. They have a warm, sweet flavour and are perfect for grinding for use as paprika or eaten raw.

6 'Apache' is a compact plant, growing to 45cm (18in) high, so is ideal for growing in a container. Fruits are medium-hot and 4cm (1½in) in length.

Other varieties to try:
'Anaheim' – mild
'Dorset Naga' – hot
'Habanero' – hot
'Hungarian Hot Wax' – mild

PEPPERS AND CHILLIES

TAKE YOUR PICK

Beetroot

A breeze to grow in good soils, try successional sowings of white, yellow, striped, and red varieties, for a summer and autumn of technicolour salads.

1 'Red Ace' is heavy-cropping and produces round to oval roots that are dark red in colour. It is tolerant of a variety of soils, and also keeps well.

2 'Chioggia Pink' is rich dark pink on the outside with a striking pattern of pink and white circles inside. It is sweet and tender, and the young leaves can be used in salads or cooked like spinach.

3 'Pablo' produces high yields of round, smooth, dark red roots that are sweet and tasty, and can be grown as baby beets. The young leaves can be cooked like spinach or used in salads.

4 'Bulls Blood' is often grown as an ornamental, or as a cut-and-come-again salad crop, but its roots are a striking rich colour and tender when young.

5 'Forono' produces 18cm (7in) long, cylindrical, red-purple roots, which are full of flavour. They have dark red flesh, and are particularly good for pickling, or for eating young in salads.

6 'Boltardy' is a popular choice, with globe-shaped, sweet, red roots. Both the leaves and the roots can be cooked or eaten raw in salads. It is high- yielding and very resistant to bolting.

Other varieties to try:
'Albina Vereduna'
'Burpee's Golden'
'Cylindra'
'Detroit Globe'
'Pronto'

Broccoli

For summer and autumn crops, sow calabrese from now into summer. Sow thin-stemmed sprouting broccoli in mid-spring for a delicious late winter treat.

1 'Bordeaux' is a heavy cropping sprouting variety with an usually long harvesting season – July into winter. It produces very tender, tasty spears and is ideal to grow as an early crop.

2 'White Star' produces attractive creamy white spears in April and May. It can be cooked or eaten raw as it has a delicious, sweet flavour.

3 'Fiesta' is a calabrese that produces large, domed heads. Once the main head is harvested the plant will produce sideshoots, which can also be eaten.

4 'Romanesco' is excellent eaten raw or cooked as it has an exceptional, nutty flavour and a good firm texture. Worth growing for its attractive heads formed of distinctive, vivid green spirals.

5 'Late Purple Sprouting' produces an abundance of hardy, tender spears ready to harvest from March onwards. Heads are packed with flavour and turn bright green when cooked.

6 'Claret' is a vigorous plant that produces large yields of thick, succulent, vividly coloured spears, which are ready to harvest from April onwards.

Other varieties to try:
'Belstar' – calabrese
'Cardinal' – sprouting
'Green Magic' – calabrese
'Kabuki' – sprouting
'Rudolph' – sprouting

BEETROOT AND BROCCOLI

Tomatoes

Home-grown tomatoes taste so superior plucked ripe from the plant that it's hard to go back to bought fruits when the crop is over. They are easy to grow outside in a warm spot and, depending on variety, will also flourish in sheltered pots and on sunny windowsills. In cooler areas tomatoes may be more reliable grown in a greenhouse.

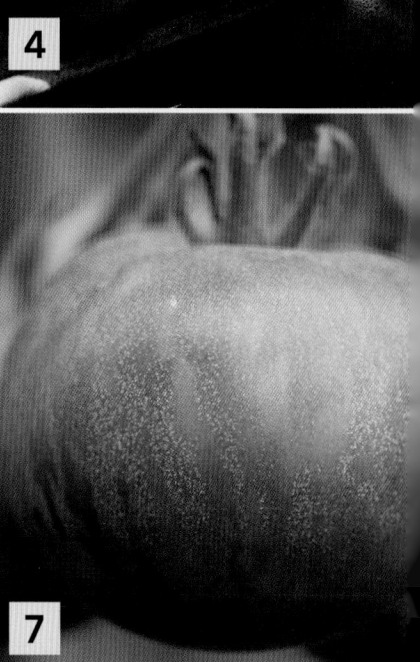

Right plant, right place

Before you buy tomato seed or young plants, consider where they will be growing. If you want a bumper crop from your greenhouse, you'll probably want to train tall plants to the roof apex to maximize your space. Whereas, if you plan to grow them on your windowsills or in hanging baskets, miniature bushy plants will be more suitable. Perhaps you want fruit that will ripen reliably outdoors, or would love to grow tomatoes like those you ate in France? There is a variety to suit every gardener's needs, but you have to know what you're looking for to find what's right for you.

Cordon or bush?

Tomatoes are only divided into two main growth habits, but confusingly more than one name is commonly used for each. Tall 'cordon' or 'indeterminate' varieties have a main stem that will grow to more than 2m (6ft) long in ideal conditions. They are usually trained up supports in greenhouses, and their growing tip needs to be pinched out when they reach the desired height (p.103). Any sideshoots between the leaves and main stem are also removed to re-direct the plant's energy from leaves to fruit production. In contrast 'bush' or 'determinate' varieties need no pinching out, because it is their sideshoots that develop and spread out over the soil carrying the fruit. These varieties often mature earlier, which makes them better suited to outdoor cultivation, and also perfect for growing under cloches or in patio containers.

Choose your favourite fruit

Anyone who thinks that tomatoes are exclusively red and round is in for a shock – some varieties ripen to orange, yellow, purple, or pink, and they can be found in an extraordinary array of shapes and sizes. Cherry tomatoes are small, often sweetly flavoured types that are the easiest to grow and ripen outdoors in cooler climates. Standard, round salad tomatoes are usually good greenhouse performers, and will also do well outdoors in warmer areas. Boxy plum tomatoes are fleshy, solid, and later maturing, so will only ripen outside where summers are warm. Large, ribbed beefsteak and marmande-types are well know for their meaty flesh and excellent flavour, but they need a long, hot growing season in order to do well.

TOMATOES

BUSH

1 'Tumbler' has a trailing habit, making it ideal for baskets and containers. Keep basket-grown plants very well watered and fed for a good crop.

2 'Tumbling Tom Yellow' is a trailing variety that produces long trusses of small, golden orange fruit. Best grow outdoors in a sheltered position.

3 'Totem' is a compact variety, ideal when space is limited, as it can be grown in containers and windowboxes, and gives a good crop of sweet fruits.

CORDON VINES

4 'Gardener's Delight' produces a heavy crop of intensely-flavoured, bite-sized orange-red fruit. This cordon variety is suitable for growing in a greenhouse or a sheltered site outside.

5 'Sungold' matures golden-orange, giving a bright splash to salads. This tall cordon variety produces small, abundant fruit, which is reputed to be the sweetest available.

6 'Sweet Olive' produces small, fleshy, olive-shaped fruits with a rich flavour. The tall plants grow well inside and out, and require no side-shooting.

7 'Tigerella' is an early variety that gives a good crop of tangy fruit, with distinctive yellow-striped, red skin. It can be grown indoors or out.

8 'Marmande' produces large, fleshy, ribbed fruits with a distinctive rich flavour. These plants should be stopped at three trusses to allow fruit to ripen.

9 'Moneymaker' is a reliable variety that gives a good crop of tasty, mid-sized fruit. It can be grown inside or out, and is suitable for beginners.

Other varieties to try:
'Alicante' – cordon
'Balconi Red' – bush
'Black Russian' – cordon
'Minibel' – bush
'Suncherry' – cordon
'Sweet Million' – cordon

March: what to plant

A BUNCH OF CAULIFLOWERS
Early summer cauliflowers, sown in autumn and overwintered under cover (p.184), are now ready for hardening off and planting out into their final positions. Choose good, firm soil, with a pH of 6.5–7.5, avoiding beds manured the previous autumn or those where brassicas have recently been grown. Plant each cauliflower about 50cm (20in) from the next, because they will develop into large plants. Place collars round the base of each to protect against cabbage root fly and net against pigeons, if necessary.

HARVEST: **JUN–AUG**

SPRING SPINACH
Spinach plants sown under cover last month (p.41) should be planted out now, after hardening off, to be ready for cropping later in spring. Plants can reach a good size, so space them 15cm (6in) apart with a distance of 30cm (12in) between rows, and protect them again with cloches if conditions turn cold. The lushest growth is produced on plants growing in rich, moist soil in full sun, so site plants accordingly.

HARVEST: **APR–NOV**

PLANT

CAULIFLOWERS

SPINACH

PEAS

GRAPES

SUMMER PEAS
Harden off young peas, sown in January, and plant in fertile soil and full sun. Dig a shallow trench for those sown into guttering (p.27), and slide the plants into it in one go, to reduce root disturbance. Module-raised peas should be planted 5–8cm (2–3in) apart. Insert supports, such as pea sticks, or canes and netting (pp.88–89).

HARVEST: **JUN–OCT**

GROW GRAPES
On a sheltered site in full sun, fix horizontal support wires to a wall or to sturdy wooden posts – a south-facing wall is ideal. Improve the soil with compost. Plant vines 1.2m (4ft) apart and 25cm (10in) from the support base, and firm in well. Ensure the graft union scar is above soil level.

HARVEST: **OCT–NOV**

BUDDING BROAD BEANS

After a short period of hardening off, plant out broad bean seedlings, sown in February, 15cm (6in) apart with 23cm (9in) between rows in full sun and good rich soil. In sheltered spots dwarf varieties like 'The Sutton' may not need support, but if in doubt a simple system of stakes along each side of the row, with string or wire fastened between them will be enough to keep mature plants standing. Remember not to plant broad beans where they, or other peas or beans, have recently been grown.

HARVEST: **MAY–AUG**

PLANT BERRIES

Blackberries are tough plants and will tolerate slightly poor drainage, some shade, and even late frosts, but such hazards are best avoided. Improve the planting area with plenty of compost, and plant each cane to the depth it was in its pot, spaced 4m (12ft) apart. They require post and wire supports to keep the growth manageable.

HARVEST: **JUL–OCT**

BROAD BEANS

BLACKBERRIES

FIRST EARLY POTATOES

PLANT POTATOES

HARVEST: **JUN–SEP**

Plant first earlies if the ground isn't frozen. Their roots help to break up newly cultivated earth and they like a sunny site, with deep, fertile soil.

1 CHITTING
Chitted tubers give a quicker crop than unchitted. Dig 15cm (6in) deep drills, at least 38cm (15in) apart to give them plenty of room.

2 PLANTING
Carefully place a potato 'rose-end' up in the bottom of the drill every 30cm (12in), trying not to damage the shoots.

3 COVERING
Rake soil over to cover the row. If the weather is cold, a thick mulch of compost or well-rotted manure will help protect the tubers.

DON'T FORGET

Frosts may be less severe this month but keep cloches, fleece, and even sheets of newspaper handy to protect emerging crops on cold nights. Also protect young plants from slugs and snails.

See FREEZING FRUIT pages 150–151

Herbs

If you grow only one edible crop, make it herbs. It's easy to buy culinary herbs, but picked fresh from the garden they have a more intense flavour. Many need little attention and with their colourful, aromatic foliage, and sometimes attractive flowers, they are ideal not just in dedicated herb gardens, but also in flower beds and pots.

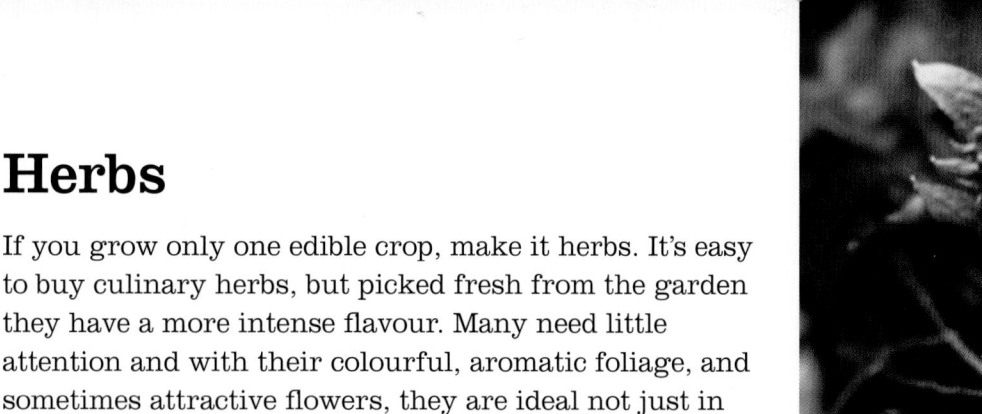

Where to grow herbs

A number of favourite garden herbs, such as rosemary, thyme, and marjoram, come from the Mediterranean, and love growing in free-draining soil in full sun. These plants have evolved to cope with dry conditions and relatively poor soil, where many other plants would struggle, so they are perfect for placing in awkward spots, such as the base of a sunny wall. There are also herbs that prefer moister conditions and will tolerate some shade. Parsley, mint, and chives all fall into this group and produce the lushest growth in soil that has been improved with plenty of organic matter. Whether you are planning a herb garden or simply experimenting with one or two varieties, these requirements are worth bearing in mind.

Containers

Herbs do well in containers. In fact, if you have heavy soil they are likely to grow better in free-draining compost than they do in the ground. Make sure that the pots have plenty of drainage holes and add a layer of crocks at the base of the pot to further improve the drainage. Pots can be placed close to the kitchen door, so that when you want to add an aromatic flourish to your cooking, you can step straight outside and pick what you want.

Planting and maintenance

The simplest herbs to grow in the garden are perennials, such as sage and marjoram, which are usually bought as small plants. Once in the ground, they flourish year after year with minimal attention. Most perennials benefit from cutting back in summer, after flowering, as this helps to keep the plant compact and encourages a fresh flush of growth that is ideal for picking.

Mint, another perennial, has shoots that spread just below the soil surface, which allows it to rapidly become invasive. To help prevent this, plant mint in sunken pots and regularly remove any escaping shoots.

Basil and coriander are annuals, which flower in their first season and then die. They must be grown from seed each year. Sow every 3–4 weeks from spring onwards, so that you have a succession of plants to pick through the summer. Biennial herbs, such as parsley, flower in their second year, but any biennials that you use frequently are best sown every year in the same way as annuals.

1 Basil – Deliciously sweet with a hint of aniseed, basil is a tender annual that can be sown between mid-spring and midsummer, in full sun and heat.

2 Coriander – Perfect for dishes with Asian flavours, this annual should be sown successively from early spring until late summer, because it often goes to seed quickly.

3 Mint – A vigorous perennial, mint comes in many varieties, all of which can be invasive. Grow it in well-watered pots or a container sunk into the soil.

4 Rosemary – Easy to grow, this perennial Mediterranean shrub looks good in flower beds. To keep plants bushy, cut them back after their light blue spring flowers have died down.

5 Parsley – Curly or flat-leaved, this hardy biennial herb grows well in pots and tolerates some shade. Sow it at regular intervals from spring into summer.

6 Marjoram – Loved by butterflies and bees, perennial marjoram has pink summer flowers and grows best in full sun, although the attractive golden-leaved varieties appreciate a little shade.

7 Thyme – This low-growing perennial is available in a huge range of varieties, all of which thrive and develop the fullest flavour in dry, sunny conditions.

8 Sage – A beautiful perennial garden plant that thrives in sunny conditions, sage benefits from being pruned in late spring after its blue flowers have finished, to keep it compact.

9 Chives – Easy to grow from seed or as divisions from existing plants, chives appreciate a moist soil. They make a lovely edging plant with pink pompon flowers in spring, and sometimes a second flush of flowers in summer.

Other varieties to try:
Dill – annual
Fennel – perennial
French tarragon – perennial
Lovage – perennial

HERBS

March: what to do

CLEAR FOR CULTIVATION

Mulches help suppress weeds in beds where crops are growing or in areas being cleared for cultivation. Black landscaping fabric (see left) is permeable to rain, so is useful for growing crops through, but you might need to irrigate beneath it. You could also cover large weedy areas for a few months with old carpet to kill off perennial weeds before cultivation. Organic mulches, such as compost or straw, should be laid at least 5cm (2in) thick. As well as discouraging weeds, they add organic matter to the soil.

WAR ON WEEDS

Weeds compete with seedlings for light, moisture, and nutrients, so give your vegetables a head start by removing all weeds from seedbeds and planting areas. Annual weed seedlings can simply be hoed off and the debris raked up. Perennial weeds need to be dealt with more rigorously. Dig them out with a fork and make sure you remove every scrap of their roots. If you don't, most of them will regrow in a short time.

TEND

SUPPRESS WEEDS

DIG OUT WEEDS

HERBS

MULCH

HELP FOR HERBS

Encourage a fresh flush of fragrant leaves on perennial herbs such as rosemary, marjoram, sage, and thyme, by pruning them back before growth starts. This treatment also helps keep plants compact and an attractive shape. With perennials that die right back, such as mint and fennel, clear away any of last year's dead stems to make way for new shoots.

IMPROVE SOIL

To get the best from your fruit trees and bushes it's important to keep their soil in good heart, particularly if you garden on a light sandy soil. Lay a generous mulch of compost or well-rotted manure, at least 5cm (2in) thick, at the base of each plant, allowing space around the canes or trunk to avoid the risk of rot.

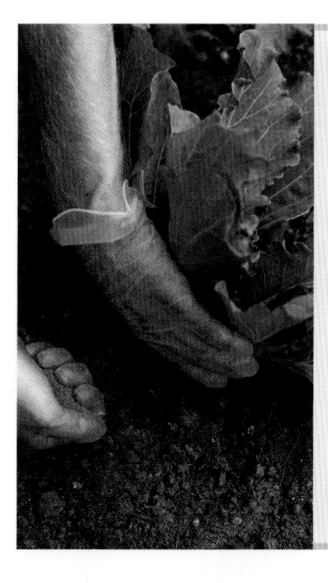

SPRING BOOST

Crops that have come through a hard winter can look distinctly the worse for wear at this time of year. If your cabbages, purple sprouting broccoli, kale, or overwintered onions have yellowing leaves, it's a sure sign that they could do with an early spring boost. To perk them up, apply a balanced fertilizer this month.

BEDS FOR BEANS

Climbing beans and celery grow best on a rich soil that retains plenty of moisture. To encourage strong growth, prepare their beds in advance of planting. A traditional way to provide the right conditions involves digging a trench about 30cm (12in) deep and 45cm (18in) wide. Work in plenty of well-rotted manure or household compost as you backfill the trench. Beans are legumes and supply their own nitrogen, so if manure and compost are scarce, use kitchen peelings to help retain moisture.

FEED

PREPARE THE SOIL

SEEDLINGS

PRICK OUT SEEDLINGS

If your propagator (p.42) or windowsill is full of tomato, pepper, celery, or other seedlings, start pricking them out into individual pots.

1 REMOVE FROM TRAY
Using a small dibber or pencil, loosen the roots of each seedling and lift it from the compost by the first pair of leaves, not by its stem.

2 REPOT
Plant out in separate modules. Make a hole with the dibber and replant the seedling. Gently firm the compost and water in.

3 HARDEN OFF
To acclimatize the seedlings to outdoor conditions, harden them off in a cold frame with a lid that can be opened and closed.

DON'T FORGET

Pests are beginning to emerge this month, so look out for snail trails and signs of marauding insects. Decide how you want to approach pest control (pp.104–105) and be ready to take action.

See START A COMPOST HEAP pages 190–191

Growing mushrooms

Mushrooms are an unusual crop but once you've grasped the basic technique, they're easy to grow and can provide a worthwhile harvest from unused spots outdoors, or in a dark corner inside. The familiar white and brown cap mushrooms are the quickest and easiest, but you can also grow more exotic species, like oyster mushrooms.

1 It's simple to grow your own white cap mushrooms from a kit at any time of year, as long as you have the correct growing conditions. Pour the specialist compost into the tray or container provided. Break up lumps.

2 Moisten the compost thoroughly. Carefully open the packet of mushroom spawn and scatter it evenly over the compost. Gently mix it into the surface using your hand or a hand fork. Don't mix the spores in deeply.

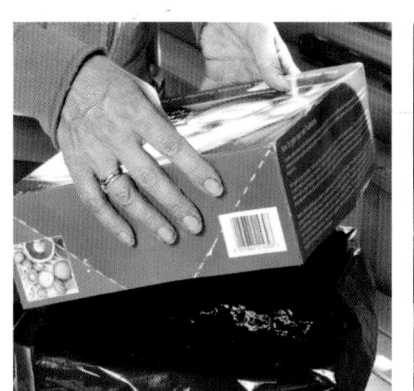

3 Cover the container with the lid or use layers of damp newspaper. Place it somewhere at around 15°C (59°F) and keep it moist. Mushrooms don't need to be in the dark, just out of direct sunlight; a shed would suit.

4 After about 14 days, web-like mycelium should be visible on the surface. Remove any newspaper and cover the mycelium with 2.5cm (1in) of compost, keeping it moist. The first mushrooms will appear in 10 weeks.

GROWING MUSHROOMS

TRY THESE

There are many different types of mushroom and growing kits to try at home. Some are more complicated than others – just follow the instructions given.

White cap mushrooms – Much tastier when home-grown, these are quick and easy to grow throughout the year.

Oyster mushrooms – Grown outdoors on logs, you'll need patience until these bear fruit in spring and autumn.

Shiitake mushrooms – These are grown on logs, shocked into fruiting by soaking in cold water for 48 hours.

Brown cap mushrooms – Also known as chestnut mushrooms, these are grown in the same way as white caps.

March: what to harvest

TASTY FLORETS
After a May sowing and the winter spent outside, hardy cauliflowers, such as 'Winter Aalsmeer', should start developing their large, white curds this month. Cauliflowers are best cut while the curds are still firm and healthy, or else the heads can yellow and open. They do, however, have a tendency to all come at once. Split into florets and freeze surpluses (pp.148–149) or pickle them (pp.176–179).

RED STALKS
In good weather, rhubarb will start sending up tasty red-tinted stems. Only harvest from mature plants over 2 years old, picking what you need by gripping them near the base and pulling. Don't cut the stems as the stump left can encourage rot to set into the crown.

HARVEST

CHICORY

WINTER CAULIFLOWER

CABBAGE & SPROUTS

RHUBARB

THE BITTER END
Bitter-leaved, red and sugarloaf chicory, sown in late summer and grown under cover through the winter, will be coming to an end this month. Red-types, such as 'Palla Rossa Verona', can either be harvested by cropping individual leaves, or cutting the whole head with a sharp knife just above ground level. Cut the heads whole of sugarloaf varieties, like 'Pan de Zucchero'. Even at this late stage both types may re-sprout to provide further harvests, so if their space isn't needed for another crop, leave them in the ground to grow on for now.

LAST BRASSICAS
New spring crops may be just around the corner, but don't be tempted to overlook the last of your hardy winter brassicas. Having started at the bottom, you'll probably be picking near the tops of the stems of late sprout varieties, such as 'Exodus' and 'Trafalgar', by now. When the sprouts are finished, remember to cut the delicious leafy tops, too. You should also pull up or cut winter cabbages as required, trimming away any weather-damaged outer leaves. After harvesting, dig up the roots. If there are any signs of disease, such as clubroot, burn them – don't compost them.

GROW BETTER BEET

Swiss chard and spinach beet sown in late summer (p.154) survive most winters outdoors and come into growth again this month, with fresh leaves to crop. Cut back old battered growth and pull bright new leaves away at the base. The succulent stems are good to eat.

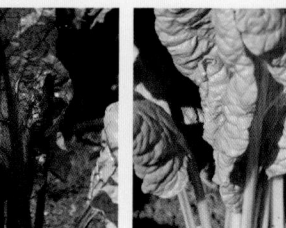

'RHUBARB CHARD'
As its name suggests, this variety has ruby-red stems and purple-flushed foliage, much like rhubarb. It is also good for winter colour.

'LUCULLUS'
This is a prolific chard that gives a good crop of white-stemmed leaves. Like all beet, its stems can be cooked and served like asparagus.

'BRIGHT YELLOW'
All beet comes into crop early in spring, providing tender new leaves. Use this variety raw to add a cheery splash of colour to your salads.

PERPETUAL SPINACH BEET
Easy to grow, this thin-stemmed variety is hardier than true spinach, and gives a reliable, tasty crop. It is a good choice for drier soil.

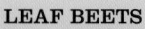

LEAF BEETS

STORED ROOTS

SPRING ONIONS

ROOT CHECK

Any lifted and stored winter root crops (pp.210–211), like carrots and beetroot, will need using up in soups and stews as soon as possible. Check through them and discard any that are showing signs of decay. Don't be tempted to bring what's left indoors to keep in the fridge, because they will shrivel up and spoil much faster there than in their original stores.

EARLY ONIONS

Start harvesting hardy varieties of spring onions, such as 'White Lisbon' and 'Ramrod', sown in late summer or early autumn, and overwintered outside. If the soil has become compacted around the bulbs, loosen it with a hand fork before picking – the onions can easily break if pulled too hard.

April: ready to eat

Enjoy a wintry feast and finish up the vegetables such as Brussels sprouts and leeks that have fed you during the lean winter months. Pea shoots, spinach, and other spring crops will begin to take their place.

New **lettuces** grown under cover can be harvested as loose leaves

Last year's **jam** is still useful for pies or puddings *pages 128–129*

Colourful **Swiss chard** is both good to eat and ornamental

Purple sprouting broccoli will finish cropping this month

Whatever the season, there are always **cut-and-come-again crops**

Check your stores for any **pickles** *pages 176–179* that need to be eaten up

Pick the last **Brussels sprouts** and also harvest the tops as an alternative to cabbage

Shallots, onions, and **garlic** are handy to have in store

It's end of season for **kale**, so freeze any surpluses for later

Mushrooms *pages 68–69* grown earlier this year should be popping up now

End of winter means the last of the fresh **leeks**

New season **spinach** – a welcome spring crop

If you haven't finished your **celeriac**, pickle what's left for later in the year *pages 176–179*

Spring cabbage comes in as winter cabbage bows out

Sprouting seeds *pages 36–37* are the easiest crop of all

Homemade white wine *pages 180–181* matures rapidly. Open a bottle of last year's now.

Make some fresh **mint** sauce to go with spring lamb

There are plenty of delicious recipes for **winter cauliflower**

If you've no fresh herbs to snip, use dried ones in your cooking

Summer radishes are just coming in – sample them at their youngest and freshest

Eat **frozen vegetables** *148–149* from last year to make room in the freezer for new harvests

Too early for peas, but not for picking **shoots** from early pea sowings

It's now or never for eating the last few **Jerusalem artichokes**

Spring onions – pick some, leave some for later

Use the last **parsnips**; cut up and freeze any that you don't need right now

Tender new season forced **rhubarb** has an exquisite flavour

Winter cabbage gives way to wonderful spring leaf crops

Stored **swedes** are still on duty in the kitchen

Salsify will keep going for a little longer

Windowsill **herbs** are coming into new growth

April: what to sow

SOW ON CUE
Sow cucumbers, courgettes, and summer squash at the end of the month to give them a head start, especially those you plan to grow under cover. Sow them 2cm (¾in) deep in small pots and put in a heated propagator, or on a warm windowsill. Keep cucumbers at 20°C (68°F) and the courgettes and squash at 15°C (59°F).

HARVEST: **JUL–OCT**

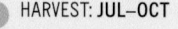

BEAN FEAST
For an early start for French and runner beans, warm the soil with cloches and sow beneath them, or sow into modules or pots under cover, 5cm (2in) deep, and plant out later. If sowing outside, space climbing beans 30cm (12in) apart, and dwarf beans, 20cm (8in) apart.

HARVEST: **JUL–OCT**

SOW

CUCUMBER & COURGETTE

BEANS

MELONS

FENNEL & ENDIVE

TRY MELONS
HARVEST: **AUG–SEP**

Sow two seeds, 2cm (¾in) deep in small pots at 18°C (64°F). Once germinated, thin the weakest, water sparingly and grow the plants on a few degrees cooler.

'BLENHEIM ORANGE'
This is a traditional variety, with netted, green skin and orange-red flesh. It has a good flavour, and is suitable for cooler regions.

CANTALOUPE
This is a type of melon, not just a variety, and produces small fruit with yellow skins and flesh. Good in cooler areas, even outdoors.

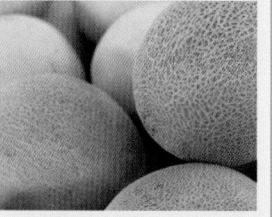

'ANTALYA'
This is a galia-type melon, with netted, yellow skin and sweet, green flesh. Grow under cover as it prefers warmer conditions.

LUXURY VEG
Sow Florence fennel and endive to crop during the summer. Raise plants in modules under cover to transplant later, or sow seed directly outdoors if the soil is above 10°C (50°F) – Florence fennel may bolt in colder soil. Sow seed 1cm (½in) deep. Outdoors, sow thinly in drills 25cm (10in) apart for endive, 30cm (12in) apart for Florence fennel. Thin the seedlings promptly.

HARVEST: **VARIOUS**

GROW GREENS

Sow kale this month, such as 'Black Tuscan', to harvest in autumn and winter, plus summer and autumn cauliflowers. Sow them outdoors into drills or modules, 1cm (½in) deep, thinning those sown in the soil to 8–10cm (3–4in) apart. Grow the plants on and transplant them into their final positions in June. Space kale plants 45cm (18in) apart, and the cauliflowers 60cm (24in), and water well. Cover the seedlings and young plants with nets in areas where pigeons can be a problem.

HARVEST: **VARIOUS**

LETTUCE SEASON

You can sow lettuce seed almost all year but now is peak season. Sow seed thinly, 1cm (½in) deep, either directly in rows, 20–35cm (8–14in) apart, depending on variety, or in modules to plant out later. The latter method is ideal for plants to pop into odd gaps or pots. Be vigilant, because slugs will find young lettuce seedlings quickly.

HARVEST: **MAY–NOV**

KALE & CAULIFLOWERS

SUMMER LETTUCE

SWEET CORN

SWEET CORN FOR SUMMER

HARVEST: **AUG–OCT**

Sweet corn prefers warm growing conditions, but if you live in a mild area, sow it outdoors under cloches once the soil temperature is above 13°C (55°F).

1 MARKING OUT
Sweet corn make tall plants, so give them space. Station sow seeds 35cm (14in) apart, in rows with 60cm (24in) between them.

2 BLOCK PLANTING
The flowers are pollinated by wind, which is essential for the cobs to form fully. Plant in blocks to help ensure good pollination.

3 SOWING INDOORS
If you live in a cooler area, sow seed singly, 4cm (1½in) deep, in modules or pots, under a cold frame or in a greenhouse.

STILL TIME TO SOW

Outside sow: leeks, onion (p.26), peas (p.27), parsnips, Brussels, kohl rabi, spinach, (p.41), cabbage, turnips (p.54), carrots (p.55). Indoors: celeriac (p.40), calabrese (p.54), tomatoes, peppers, and aubergines (p.55).

French and dwarf beans

Easy to grow, these beans can be picked young for their pods, or allowed to grow for a crop of haricots, to eat fresh or dried.

1 'Rocquencourt' is an unusual yellow-podded dwarf bean that can be grown without support. The flowers and pods make this variety attractive enough to grow in a patio container.

2 'Delinel' produces a large, reliable harvest of pencil-thin, stringless pods when regularly cropped. Growing to only 45cm (18in) tall, it is suitable for containers. Water and feed well.

3 'The Prince' gives a good crop of flattened pods, similar to young runner beans. This dwarf variety has a delicious flavour, especially when young, and is a good choice for freezing (pp.148–149).

4 'Blue Lake' is a climbing variety that produces a heavy yield of sweet-tasting, stringless pods when cropped regularly. When allowed to develop, it gives a good crop of tasty haricots.

5 'Purple Teepee' is a dwarf variety that gives a good harvest of distinctive purple pods, which turn green when cooked. Young beans can be eaten raw and added to salads for extra colour.

6 'Cobra' is a climbing bean that gives a plentiful supply of slender, stringless pods. Its purple flowers are especially attractive, allowing it to be grown in mixed borders – ideal for smaller plots.

Other varieties to try:
'Borlotto Lingua di Fuoco' – climber
'Hunter' – climber
'Limka' – climber
'Safari' – dwarf
'Valdor' – dwarf

TAKE YOUR PICK

Runner beans

Eaten as pods, sliced or whole, runner beans are a must for every vegetable patch. Grow them from seed or buy plants in late spring.

1 'White Lady' gives a good crop of thick, succulent pods. The white flowers are not as attractive to birds, which make them less prone to damage. The plant sets beans in hot, dry conditions, unlike many others.

2 'Polestar' is a stringless variety, making the beans easier to prepare in the kitchen. If picked regularly, it gives a good crop until the end of summer. The smooth beans freeze well.

3 'Painted Lady' has very attractive bicoloured flowers, and is almost as good to look at, as it is to eat. It produces delicious beans, and is a good choice to grow in mixed garden borders.

4 'Desiree' produces a heavy crop of fleshy green pods, making it a good choice for where space is limited. You'll only need a few plants to keep you supplied with beans all summer.

5 'Lady Di' gives a very heavy crop of long, stringless pods. The beans inside are slow to develop, which means the pods can be left to grow for longer without becoming too tough.

Other varieties to try:
'Enorma'
'Hestia' – dwarf variety
'Red Rum'
'Scarlet Emperor'
'White Apollo'

BEANS

Courgettes

Just two or three of these vigorous plants will supply you with plenty of tender fruit in a wide variety of shapes and colours. You can harvest the flowers too.

1 'Zucchini' is an early variety that matures 2 weeks sooner than standard crops. The dark-skinned fruits are best picked when 15cm (6in) long.

2 'Jemmer' is a free-fruiting variety. The long golden courgettes are easy to spot among the leaves, meaning fewer will be accidentally left behind.

3 'Venus' is a compact variety that produces dark green fruits from July until the first frosts. Harvest regularly to encourage a sustained crop.

4 'Defender' produces a very high yield, making it a good choice if you only have room for a few plants. It is resistant to cucumber mosaic virus (p.241).

5 'Parador' is a golden-fruited variety that matures early, and will crop prolifically through summer. Harvest young for salad-sized courgettes.

Other varieties to try:
'Black Forest' – climbing
'Eight Ball' – round
'Patriot' – bush
'Supremo' –bush
'Tondo di Toscana' – round

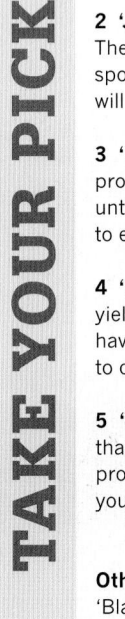

TAKE YOUR PICK

1

2

3

4

5

Sweet corn

These tall plants look good in a border as well as in the vegetable bed. Other crops will also grow between the stems, making this a useful crop in smaller plots.

1 'Lark' produces, sweet-tasting kernels that are thin skinned and tender enough to eat raw or cooked. It is a mid-season variety that performs well in cool areas.

2 'Indian summer' produces white, yellow, red, and purple kernels, giving its cobs a multi-coloured appearance. This sweet-tasting variety performs best in warmer areas.

3 'Swift' is a dwarf sweet corn that produces thin-skinned, sweet-tasting cobs that reach up to 20cm (8in) long. This variety matures early and performs well in cooler climates.

4 'Sundance' is a good choice for cooler regions, and reliably produces an early crop of 18cm (7in) long yellow cobs. The kernels are sweet and creamy.

5 'Butterscotch' is as early-maturing variety with tender kernels that stay sweet even after freezing. It grows to just 1.5m (5ft) tall, shorter than many.

Other varieties to try:
'Conqueror'
'Honey Bantam'
'Mirai White'
'Sunrise'
'Sweet Nugget'

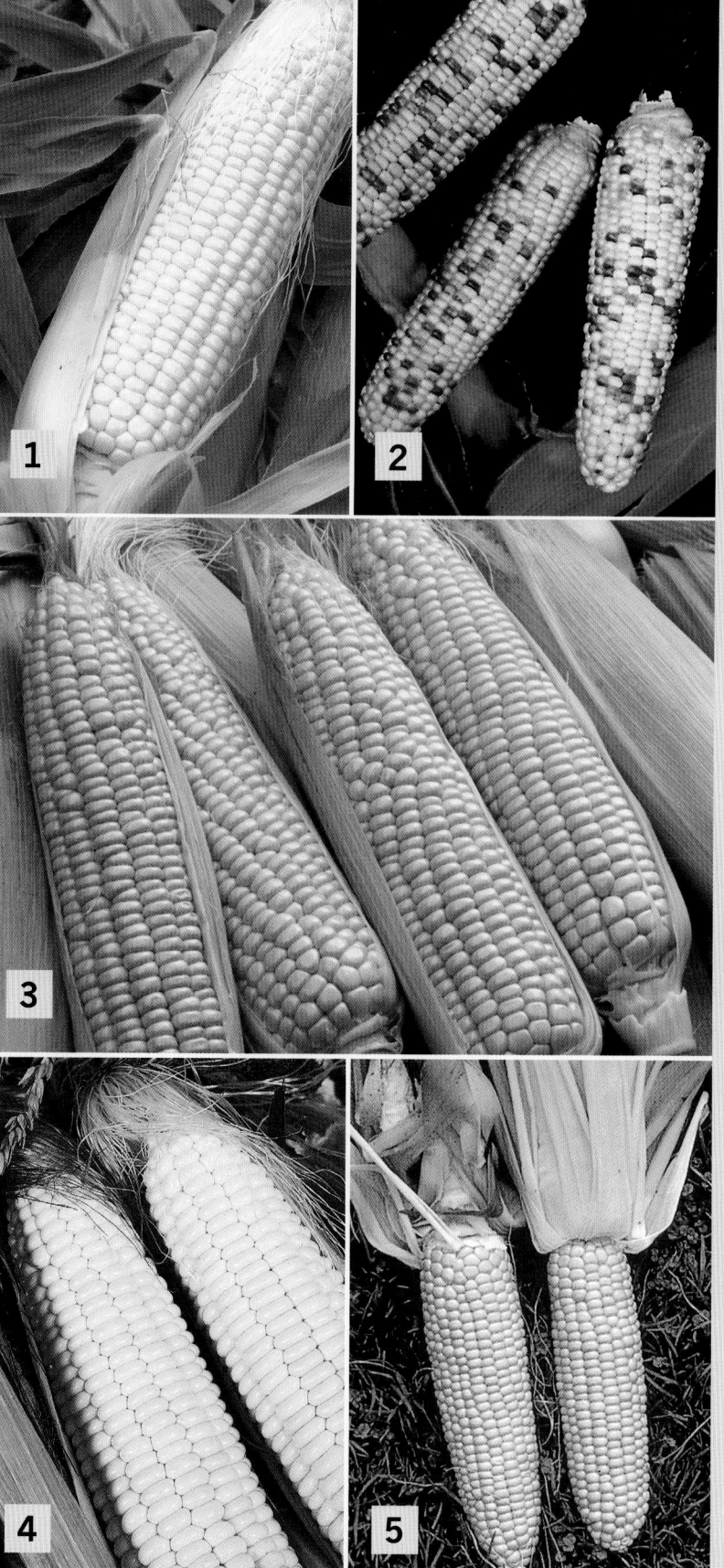

COURGETTES AND SWEET CORN

Cucumbers

Home-grown cucumbers are so much better than those bought from shops. Most require a warm greenhouse to succeed, but ridge-types will grow reliably outside.

1 'Marketmore' is an outdoor variety, and gives a prolonged crop of fruits, each measuring up to 20cm (8in) long. It is resistant to both downy and powdery mildew (p.241 and p.243).

2 'Crystal Apple' can be grown outside, and has pale yellow-green fruit the size of apples. These are sweet and juicy, and appeal to children. They're also suitable for pickling (pp.176–179).

3 'Masterpiece' is a ridge cucumber that produces a steady supply of slightly prickly, dark green fruit. These are best harvested at 20cm (8in) long. Plant two or three for a summer-long harvest.

4 'Carmen' is an all-female greenhouse cucumber that produces long green fruit throughout the summer. It is disease-resistant, making it a good choice for organic gardeners.

5 'Burpless Tasty Green' is an outdoor variety, with crisp, tasty fruit that can be harvested at 25cm (10in) long. As its name suggests, the fruit won't cause indigestion. It is very easy to grow.

6 'Passandra' is a miniature, indoor variety and bears fruit, half the normal size, on every flower. It is resistant to downy and powdery mildew, as well as cucumber mosaic virus (p.241).

Other varieties to try:
'Cetriolo Marketer' – ridge-type
'Cucino' – indoors or out
'La Diva' – greenhouse
'Telegraph Improved' – greenhouse
'White Wonder' – greenhouse

TAKE YOUR PICK

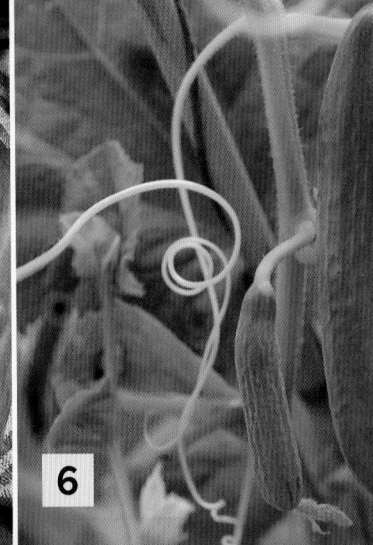

Lettuce

Some types of lettuce have dense hearts, others do not. All grow fast from seed, and can be sown under cover in winter or outside from spring onwards.

1 'Tom Thumb' is a butterhead variety, and quickly forms a solid head of soft, ruffled, tasty leaves. It is a compact plant and can be grown closely packed together. It is suitable for containers.

2 'Winter Density' is a hardy cos lettuce, that in mild areas, can be sown outside in autumn (p.166) ready to harvest in spring. It is also suitable for spring and summer sowing.

3 'Lollo Rosso' is a highly attractive loose-leaf lettuce. Its frilly leaves are flushed with red, and look good in mixed beds or containers. Cut the leaves as you need them, or the whole head.

4 'Sioux' is an iceberg lettuce, and forms a dense head of red-tinted leaves that become brighter into summer. It is good in smaller gardens as it can be treated as an edible bedding plant.

5 'Pinokkio' is a cos variety that produces small, neat heads of sweet-tasting, dark green leaves. Single leaves can be cut 6 weeks after sowing, or the plant can be left to heart-up for another 4 weeks.

6 'Freckles' is a cos lettuce with bold, red-splashed leaves. It is very attractive in the garden and in salads. Grow it in containers for colour and a handy crop. Water well, especially in dry spells.

Other varieties to try:
'All Year Round' – butterhead
'Clarion' – butterhead
'Green Salad Bowl' – loose-leaf
'Little Gem' – cos
'Saladin' – crisphead

CUCUMBERS AND LETTUCE

April: what to plant

SPEEDY STRAWBERRIES
If you're looking for a quick crop from plants put in between now and early summer, then cold-stored plants are the answer. Often available by mail order, these unpromising looking specimens will quickly put on new leaves, send out flowers and should fruit within 60 days of planting. Plant in soil improved with plenty of compost where strawberries haven't recently been grown, or in large pots.

HARVEST: **JUN–SEP**

GROW GLOBES
Harden off and plant out winter-sown kohl rabi before the plants get too big. This decreases the likelihood of bolting; plant out and cover with cloches rather than delay. Space plants 23cm (9in) apart and leave 30cm (12in) between rows.

HARVEST: **JUN–NOV**

PLANT

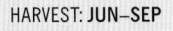
STRAWBERRIES

KOHL RABI

HERBS

LETTUCE

HERB PLANTING
HARVEST: **VARIOUS**

Few jobs in the garden are as rewarding as planting up a herb patch. They grow in all shapes and sizes, so pick the right ones for where you want them.

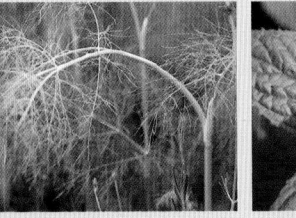

UPRIGHTS
Plant taller, upright herbs, such as bronze- and green-leaved fennel, towards the back of your planting scheme to give it height.

SPREADERS
Some herbs, such as mint, spread quickly and may over-run slower growers. Plant these in sunken pots to restrict their spread.

LOW CREEPERS
Plant a mixture of low, spreading herbs, like thyme and marjoram, at the front of your scheme to create a carpet of summer colour.

SUMMER SALAD
Lettuces raised from seed under cover (p.26) will be ready to plant out now, either spaced 30–35cm (12–14in) apart in beds or in large pots and growing bags on a sheltered patio. Young plants may also become available in nurseries and garden centres this month, which are ideal for filling gaps before other crops get going. Cover with a cloche if the weather turns cold.

HARVEST: **MAY–NOV**

PLANT OUT ONIONS

Now is the time to plant out onion seedlings, sown in spring (p.26), positioning them 15cm (6in) apart using a dibber. Any sets not sown earlier (p.45) can also be planted now at the same distances. Avoid planting larger sets, which are prone to bolting, and only plant them out when the soil is warm and workable. Rake the soil lightly to loosen it and make a shallow drill about 2.5cm (1in) deep, the length of your row. Push each set gently into the ground so that its tip is just level with the soil surface.

● HARVEST: **JUL–OCT**

PLANT MAINCROP

Buy certified disease-free seed potatoes, which can be chitted, but there is thought to be little benefit to maincrop yields. Make 15cm (6in) deep drills and place a potato, bud-end up, every 38cm (15in). Cover with soil and space further rows 75cm (30in) apart. Maincrop potatoes are below ground longer than early varieties but store well over winter.

● HARVEST: **SEP–OCT**

ONIONS

POTATOES

ASPARAGUS & ARTICHOKES

PLANT OUT PERENNIALS

HARVEST: **VARIOUS**

Spring asparagus and summer globe artichokes need fertile, well-drained soil in full sun. Buy artichokes as young plants; asparagus as 1-year-old crowns.

1 DIG FOR ASPARAGUS
Dig a 30cm (12in) wide and 20cm (8in) deep trench for asparagus and make a 10cm (4in) high ridge down the middle of it.

2 COVER ASPARAGUS
Place crowns on the ridge, about 30cm (12in) apart, spread their roots and cover with soil. Fill in the trench as the stems grow.

GLOBE ARTICHOKES
Plant artichokes at a depth of about 5cm (2in), allowing about 1m (3ft) between plants. Cover with fleece if the weather turns cold.

DON'T FORGET

Crop rotation helps prevent the build up of pests and diseases in the soil. Plan to grow related crops, such as peas and beans, together and find a different bed for them next year.

PLANTING IDEAS

Patio fruit and vegetables

Don't be deterred if the only area you have for your kitchen garden is a paved patio or courtyard, because these are often designed to make the most of sunny, sheltered spots that are ideal for growing fruit and vegetables. Many crops thrive in containers, and although the harvests will be smaller, they're no less rewarding.

Container cropping

Growing fruit and vegetables in containers has many advantages over gardening in open soil. For a start there's no heavy digging to do, and you can select the perfect compost for every plant. Weeding should be minimal and less back-breaking because the pots raise the soil surface; this makes picking crops easier too. Containers can also be moved to take advantage of summer sun or winter shelter, as required.

Herbs and salads are great for beginners, but tomatoes, chillies, aubergines, and even root crops in deep pots, should all thrive, especially dwarf and patio varieties. Even fruit trees and bushes will crop well in large containers, once established, so don't feel you have to miss out if you're gardening in a small space.

ENSURE GOOD DRAINAGE
Before planting, check there are adequate holes in the bottom of the container. If not, carefully drill some or use another pot. Place broken polystyrene or shards of clay pot in the bottom to improve drainage.

USE THE RIGHT COMPOST
Single-season crops, such as lettuce, can be planted into potting compost. Trees, shrubs, and perennial crops such as rhubarb, are best planted into a longer-lasting, soil-based compost, such as John Innes No.3.

Jo's tips

Routine feeding and watering of fruit and vegetable plants in pots is vital if you want a good harvest. Water them generously once or twice a day during summer, and apply a balanced liquid feed to root and leaf crops, or a high potash feed to fruiting crops, weekly during the growing season.

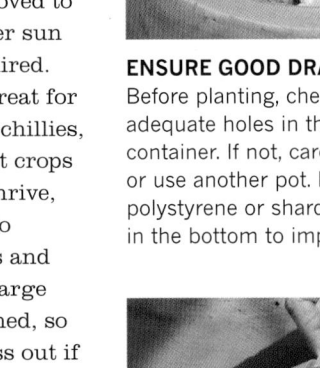

FOOD AND MOISTURE
To help prevent your crops drying out, and to keep them well fed, incorporate water-retaining gel crystals and slow-release granular fertilizer into the compost before planting.

CLIMBING CROPS IN POT
To grow climbing vegetables, such as peas and runner beans, insert canes into the compost to form a wigwam (p.88). Plant seedlings or direct sow seed at the base of each cane.

TRY THESE

Almost any large, durable container with good drainage is suitable for crops, so be creative. Try recycling old cans, tin baths, crates, and sacks.

Windowboxes are ideal for herbs and low-growing crops that you might want to pick from the kitchen window.

Growing bags are incredibly versatile, and can be used inside or out for a huge range of fruit and vegetables.

Recycled containers can be as varied as your crops. Try growing potatoes in old bins and leeks in builder's bags.

Clay and concrete pots look good on the patio, although they can be heavy and prone to frost damage.

Summer fruit growing in containers can be attractive as well as productive. Even if you have a vegetable bed, plant up containers to bring crops closer to the kitchen.

April: what to do

GIVE THEM AIR

It's easy to neglect plants when they are hidden away beneath cloches, but being under cover means they do need extra care. Remember to open the lid of the cloche on sunny days to give your plants ventilation, otherwise they will overheat. Be sure to tuck them up again every evening to keep out the cold, because nights can still be chilly this month. Weeds grow well under cloches too, so remove them regularly and check for pests while you are at it. Cloches also keep out the rain, so watering is essential.

PRUNING STONE FRUIT

Prune now to fan-train young peach, apricot and cherry trees. After planting and fixing support wires to the wall or fence, cut the vertical leading shoot back to two branches, about 30cm (12in) from the ground, one growing to the left and one to the right. Prune them to about 38cm (15in) and tie to bamboo canes attached to the wires. In the second spring, cut back all new growth by one third, and in the third spring by a quarter.

TEND

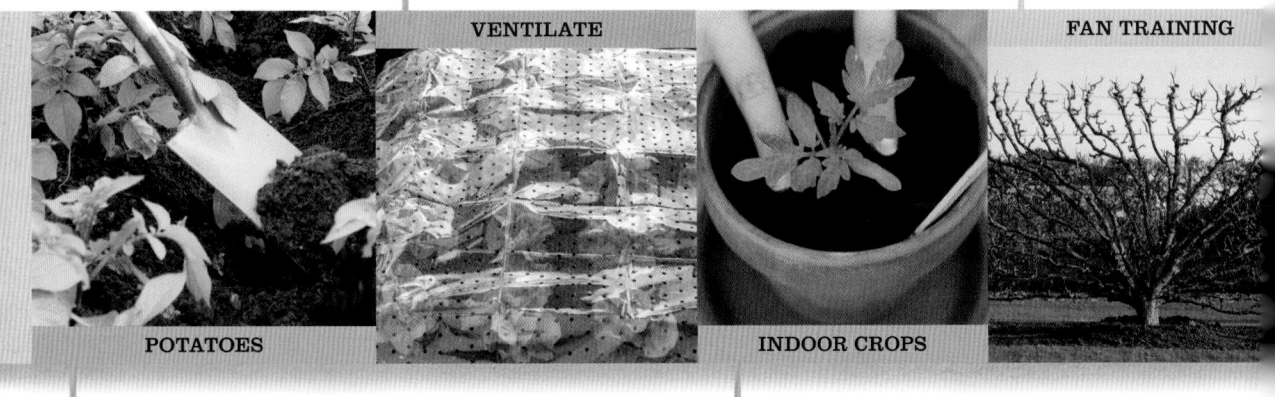

POTATOES   VENTILATE   INDOOR CROPS   FAN TRAINING

EARTHING UP

Pulling earth up around the stems of growing potatoes stops the tubers turning green and poisonous on exposure to light. Do this once the plants are about 15cm (6in) tall. If they are growing in open ground, pull up the soil into a mound to cover the lower leaves, leaving the tops exposed. Earth up container-grown plants in the same way by adding more compost.

MOVING ON

Young plants destined to be grown in large containers are best potted on in stages, in progressively larger pots. Water a plant well before knocking it out of its pot, part-fill the new pot with compost and position the plant. Fill the pot to about 1cm (½in) below the top with compost, firm gently, and water in.

HARDENING OFF

Seedlings raised under cover (p.42) need to be acclimatized to cooler, breezier, conditions before they are planted outdoors. Do this gradually over about 2 weeks. The first step is to increase the amount of ventilation. Then move your plants into a sheltered position outside for longer periods each day. Eventually they will need protection only on cold nights and will be ready to plant out. Check that all danger of frost has passed before you move young plants into their permanent outside position.

CITRUS CARE

Although citrus trees (pp.222–223) need protection in winter, they don't do well in a hot conservatory or greenhouse all summer. As the weather warms up, move them to a sheltered site outdoors. Apply a general fertilizer that contains trace elements, such as iron, copper, and zinc, and repeat every 14 days until autumn.

SEEDLINGS

CITRUS

PESTS

WATCH OUT FOR PESTS

A vegetable plot full of tender new shoots will tempt in all kinds of pests (pp.236–239). Be vigilant and deal with them before an entire crop is ruined.

BRASSICA COLLAR
Cabbage root fly maggots feed on brassica roots, causing plants to wilt. Collars prevent adult flies laying eggs near young plants.

SLUG PELLETS
Unless you garden organically (pp.104–105), protect seedlings and young crops with a light sprinkling of slug pellets.

PHEROMONE TRAP
Hang pheromone traps in your apple and pear trees as an organic method to protect your fruit against codling moth caterpillars (p.237).

DON'T FORGET

You might want to net your fruit bushes now, even though they are a long way off fruiting. Some birds love the flower buds of fruits such as gooseberries and currants and can do a great deal of damage.

See CITRUS
pages 222–223

Providing support

Supporting climbing or sprawling plants not only allows them to make healthy, upward growth, but has the advantage of making the most of valuable vertical space in small gardens. Peas, beans, cucumbers, tomatoes, and small-fruited winter squashes all look great scrambling skywards, keeping the crops off the soil.

Choosing supports

Many different materials make perfect plant supports, so take your pick from canes, trellis, netting, sticks, or whatever else you can find. Whichever you choose, make sure that it is strong enough to take the weight of fully grown plants, especially if your garden is exposed to the wind. Also check that the support suits the way that your crops climb, with plenty of places to take hold of, or gaps to grow through.

Climbing plants have different ways of gripping onto supports, all of which suit some materials better than others. Peas and squashes have curling tendrils

(left to right) **Twining beans** twist their stems around supports but need tying in when first planted. **Pea tendrils** look delicate, but hold on to netting or branched sticks very securely. **Cordon tomatoes need tying** into their supports regularly.

that wrap around supports, allowing them to make their own way skywards, so they need lots of little places to grasp, provided by well-branched pea-sticks or netting. Beans, on the other hand, twine their stems around the

supports, so do best twisting up a smooth cane, although the young plants may need tying in to get started. Cordon tomatoes have no means of holding on, so need to be tied in regularly to canes or taut vertical strings.

Cane wigwams

Cane wigwams are simple and effective supports, made by pushing up to eight canes firmly into the soil and angling them to a point at the top. To allow climbing beans to reach their full potential, use 2.4m (8ft) canes, leaving space at the base of each for plants to grow. Willow and hazel wigwams can be bought or made, and their more rustic appearance suits many gardens. Climbing beans are the traditional wigwam crops, but there's no reason why outdoor cucumbers, and other climbers including sweet peas, shouldn't scramble over them as well.

1 SECURE WITH STRING
Fully laden wigwams may support a considerable weight, so tie them firmly at the top where the canes cross, and again lower down to stop the canes buckling outwards.

2 TIE CLIMBERS IN
It's a good idea to tie young bean plants into their canes with string to get them growing the right way. This also helps prevent them merging into each other and becoming tangled.

GROWING FEATURE

TRY THESE

Using a variety of different supports keeps the full range of climbing crops happy, and helps makes the best use of your growing space.

Plastic netting gives effective support to most climbing or sprawling plants. Stretch it between posts or on fences.

Pea sticks are traditionally cut from hazel trees, but any branched sticks, as tall as needed, will do.

Garden fences and trellises provide shelter and support to taller crops. Attach wires for plants to cling onto.

Vertical strings tied to frames or inside greenhouses are ideal for cucumbers, cordon tomatoes, and melons.

Finished wigwams are ideal for climbing crops, like peas and beans, and make good use of a small space. You can even make them in large containers for patio crops.

April: what to harvest

FIRST SUMMER SPINACH
Start picking the first baby salad leaves now, from spinach plants sown under cover in early spring (p.41). Pick them regularly to encourage further crops, but leave some plants to develop unmolested, to give you a harvest of full-sized plants for cooking later in summer. Cooked spinach freezes well, but the baby leaves growing now are best eaten fresh. Give time to re-grow.

KALE HEARTS
The kale season is about to close but the plants will soon be producing fresh young leaves at their centres, which are far more appetizing than the winter-worn, outer ones. Crop these leaves, then uproot and compost the plants as they finish.

HARVEST

RADISHES   SPINACH   ROCKET   KALE

RAPID RADISH
Hot and peppery, these feisty roots can be ready to eat just 3 weeks after sowing (p.27). They soon spoil quickly, so pull them as soon as they're ready.

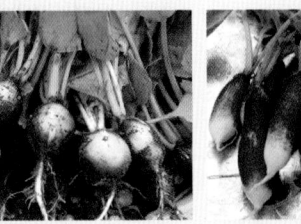

'CHERRY BELLE'
This is a quick maturing variety that produces small, rounded radish that are sweet and mild. They are delicious whole in salads.

'FRENCH BREAKFAST'
This variety takes about a month to mature from sowing, and produces mild, crunchy roots that are just long enough to eat sliced.

'SCARLET GLOBE'
This is a quick-growing variety with bright red skin and crisp white flesh. It is ready to harvest after 6–8 weeks; sow successionally.

ROCKET SPEED
These delicious, peppery leaves are ready to pluck in as little as 3 weeks from sowing (pp.28–29). Pick leaves individually or use scissors to cut entire rows of plants, 2.5cm (1in) above the soil surface. Feed and water to encourage new growth, then re-harvest at least once more. If you then let them run to seed, you can use the creamy flowers to decorate salads. The leaves and flowers are best eaten fresh.

SPRING GREENS
If you've plenty of spring cabbages, sown last July (p.132), harvest some now as spring greens before they heart-up, leaving others to develop. If you don't need the space for other crops, cut the cabbages above their lowest leaves, rather than uprooting the plant. The stalks often re-sprout to produce a second crop of small heads.

EARLY STRAWBERRIES
Early varieties of strawberries, brought under cover in January (p.30), should be coming into fruit by the end of this month. Wait until the fruit has turned completely red before picking it with the stalk intact. If you just have a few plants, the berries will be a treat to eat while you're out gardening. If you have a larger crop, they should still be eaten as soon after picking as possible to be at their best. Failing that, use them for early jam (pp.128–129).

SHOOTS & LEAVES

SPRING CABBAGE

STRAWBERRIES

TASTY TIPS
With so much fresh growth around it's worth taking a tour of your vegetable and herb patch for pickings to perk up a plain salad. Most crops won't miss a few leaves and shoots, just pick sparingly so you don't check the later development of your mature crops.

SWISS CHARD
The baby leaves of Swiss chard add colour to the vegetable patch with their bright stems. They have a sweet, earthy flavour.

PEA SHOOTS
Peas benefit from being pinched out, which is handy as the shoots have a delicious sweet flavour. Just snip off the topmost leaves.

HERBS
The young leaves of many herbs often have the most intense flavour. Try picking the new shoots of basil, coriander, and marjoram.

BEETROOT
Beetroot gives two crops in one. Pick a few red-veined leaves for salads, and enjoy eating the earthy-tasting roots a couple of weeks later.

Try MAKING FRUIT CORDIALS pages 144–145

May: ready to eat

Pick the first irresistible broad beans, peas, beetroot, carrots, and turnips while they are tiny and sweet. Savour delicious new asparagus and strawberries, and use up last year's jars of jams and pickles, too.

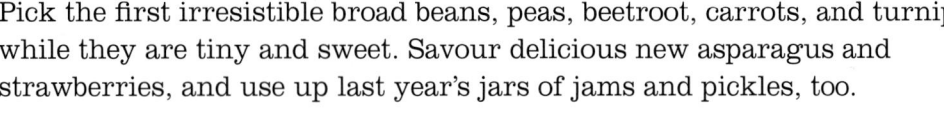

Ready now – tiny **baby beetroots**

If you have a good crop of **spinach,** preserve some as spinach **pesto** *page 147*

New season **peas** and **mangetout** couldn't be fresher or sweeter

Harvest the young leaves of **spring cabbage** now, or leave them to form hearts

Check your mushroom compost *pages 68–69* every day for fresh crops

No need to peel new baby **turnips,** just trim and cook them whole

Eat the last homemade **jam** *pages 128–129* and keep the empty jars for this year's preserves

New season **gooseberries** will appear late this month

It's the last of the **winter cauliflower**, but summer varieties will soon be ready

Snip a few sprigs from your perennial **herbs**

Hardy **onions** planted last autumn can now be harvested

Pull up some finger-sized early **carrots**

Harvest **spinach beet** and **Swiss chard,** taking leaves from alternate plants down the row

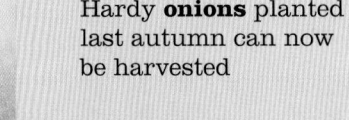

Crispy **summer radishes** add bite to your salads

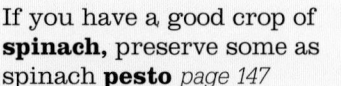

Pick some **broad beans** while small and cook the pods whole

Cut-and-come-again salads – keep cutting and the leaves will keep coming

Cut new **asparagus** spears every few days and freeze the surplus

Early maincrop **lettuce** can be cut now

The distinctive flavour of **rocket** adds interest to green salads

Fresh **sprouting seeds** *pages 36–37*, such as mung beans, are tasty and healthy

Lift the very last of the **salsify** – it's already time to sow a new crop

Enjoy the last taste of roast **garlic** stored in oil *page 35*

Finish up last year's homemade **pickles** *pages 176–179*

Summer comes early if you have **strawberries** indoors under cover

Pinch out **pea shoots** and **tips** to use in salads

Harvest young **beetroot** leaves as well as the roots

Pick some slender young **spring onions**

Eat the leeks lifted and frozen last month

Drink leftover homemade wine *pages 180–181* because you'll need the bottles

Pick stems of **rhubarb** for pies, crumbles, and fools

May: what to sow

READY FOR WINTER
Maincrop carrots, such as 'Autumn King' and 'Flyaway', are slower to mature than early varieties. Sow them now until midsummer for crops to store. Sow seed thinly into 1cm (½in) deep drills, spaced 15cm (6in) apart, then thin to 5–8cm (2–3in). Choose well-dug soil in full sun that is not stony or recently manured.

HARVEST: **JUL–DEC**

SOW SQUASH
Summer and winter squash can be sown outside next month but it's worth giving crops a head start in cooler areas. Sow seed 2cm (¾in) deep into small pots or modules, in a heated propagator or on a warm windowsill. Water lightly to prevent damping off.

HARVEST: **VARIOUS**

SOW

SWEDES & TURNIPS

MAINCROP CARROTS

SALSIFY

GARDEN SQUASH

ROOTS TO SUCCESS
HARVEST: **VARIOUS**

Sow swedes and turnips 1cm (½in) deep in drills, into good soil that stays moist to help prevent them becoming tough.

SWEDES
Slower-maturing and larger growing than turnips, thin the developing swede plants to 25cm (10in) apart. Harvest in autumn.

TURNIPS
Fast-growing, sow early varieties now for a midsummer crop. Sow maincrop varieties in midsummer for an autumn and winter crop.

CURIOUS SALSIFY
This unusual root crop has an earthy, nutty flavour, and can be boiled or steamed. It grows in any soil that is not too stony. On heavier soil, dig a trench to a spade's depth, and fill it with sandy soil or compost to help the long roots develop. Rake the soil to a fine tilth and sow seed thinly in rows 30cm (12in) apart. Germination can be slow, but thin seedlings to about 15cm (6in) apart.

HARVEST: **NOV–MAY**

STILL TIME TO SOW
You can still sow most crops from last month, indoors and out, if you've had a slow start. Now is your last chance to sow sprouting broccoli (p.54), French and runner beans (p.74), and sweet corn (p.75).

YEAR-ROUND LEAVES

The closely related leaf crops Swiss chard and leaf beet are very easy to grow, and can be enjoyed raw in salads or cooked. They are a good choice for smaller gardens. Protect the plants during winter, and you can look forward to fresh greens even in the coldest months.

HARVEST: **ALL YEAR**

1 PREPARE THE SITE
Neither crop is fussy about the site, but they both prefer soil that has been improved with plenty of well-rotted manure.

2 SOW IN DRILLS
The seeds of these crops are large and easy to handle. Sow them thinly in drills 2cm (¾in) deep and spaced 38cm (15in) apart.

3 COVER AND WATER
Carefully cover the seeds and water them well. Swiss chard can also be sown singly in modules and planted out later.

4 THIN SEEDLINGS
As they grow, thin individual plants to 30cm (12in) apart. Don't waste the thinned young plants, use them in your salads.

SWISS CHARD & LEAF BEET

CABBAGE & CAULIFLOWER

WITLOOF & SUGARLOAF CHICORY

WINTER BRASSICAS

Now is the time to sow your winter cabbages and spring cauliflowers, so they have time to grow before the cold, frosty weather comes. Sow outdoors into a seedbed, 1cm (½in) deep in drills. Grow them on, thinning the young plants to 8–10cm (3–4in) apart, then transplant them into their final positions in July. Avoid planting cauliflowers on freshly manured soil, which promotes excess leafy growth.

HARVEST: **VARIOUS**

CHIC CHICORY

For Witloof chicory to force in winter (p.216), and summer and autumn crops of sugarloaf varieties, sow from now to early summer. Witloof chicory prefers poor soil, sugarloaf-types need rich soil. Sow both 1cm (½in) deep, in drills 30cm (12in) apart, thinning to 25cm (10in). Sugarloaf can also be sown into modules for transplanting.

HARVEST: **VARIOUS**

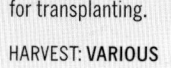

TAKE YOUR PICK

Winter cabbage

Winter cabbage is hardy enough to crop and look attractive throughout the coldest weather. Where space is limited, grow some in your flower borders.

1 'Savoy Siberia' is a very hardy variety, ideal for areas where the winters are particularly cold. The heads are packed with sweet-tasting, textured leaves that last well once mature.

2 'Tarvoy' is a useful variety as its heads stay in good condition in the garden for many weeks when mature. It is a good choice if you plan to grow a large crop to cut over a longer period.

3 'Tundra' is a reliable variety that produces sturdy heads of tightly packed green leaves. It is late to mature and very hardy. The heads stay in good condition for weeks until harvested.

4 'January King' is a very hardy variety that produces large heads of blue-green leaves that develop a red flush in cold weather. Quick-maturing, young, small heads can be cut in autumn.

5 'Jewel' is a hardy variety that produces loosely-packed heads of dark green, smooth leaves. It is slow to mature and resists bolting, so can be left in the ground until needed.

Other varieties to try:
'Brigadier'
'Celtic'
'Marabel'
'Ormskirk'
'Savoy King'

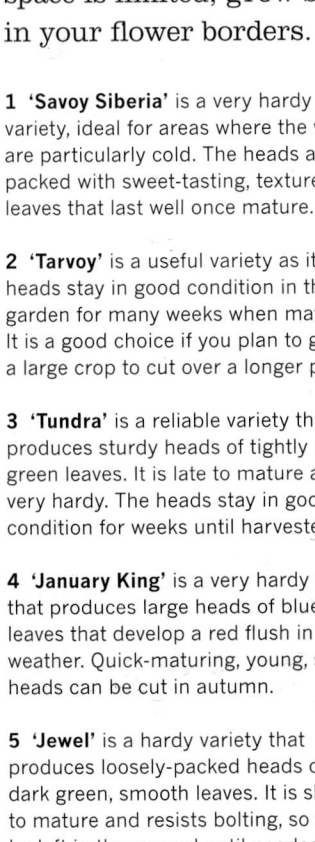

Chicory

Often expensive or difficult to buy, chicories are crisp, slightly bitter salad crops. Sow them from now to late summer, and enjoy fresh leaves until next spring.

1 'Treviso Precoce Mesola' is a versatile, quick-growing red chicory – also known as a radicchio. It can be harvested throughout summer as salad leaves or left to develop into full heads.

2 'Pan di Zucchero' is a sugarloaf chicory that produces tall, upright heads of loosely-packed green leaves that mature in autumn. Plants grown under protection will crop through winter.

3 'Palla Rossa' is a red chicory with a delicate flavour. It can be harvested as salad leaves in summer or as whole heads in autumn. It develops its best leaf colour as the weather cools.

4 'Variegata di Castelfranco' is a colourful variety that can be harvested as salad leaves or full heads, or forced like a Witloof chicory (p.216). It is a tasty crop with a delicious, crunchy texture.

5 'Zoom' is a Witloof chicory, grown to be forced and eaten as "chicons" (p.216). The forced heads have a strong, bitter taste, and can be eaten cooked or raw. This is a useful winter vegetable.

Other varieties to try:
'Cesare' – red
'Lightning' – Witloof
'Orchidea Rossa' – red
'Trevi' – red
'Variegata di Chioggia' – red

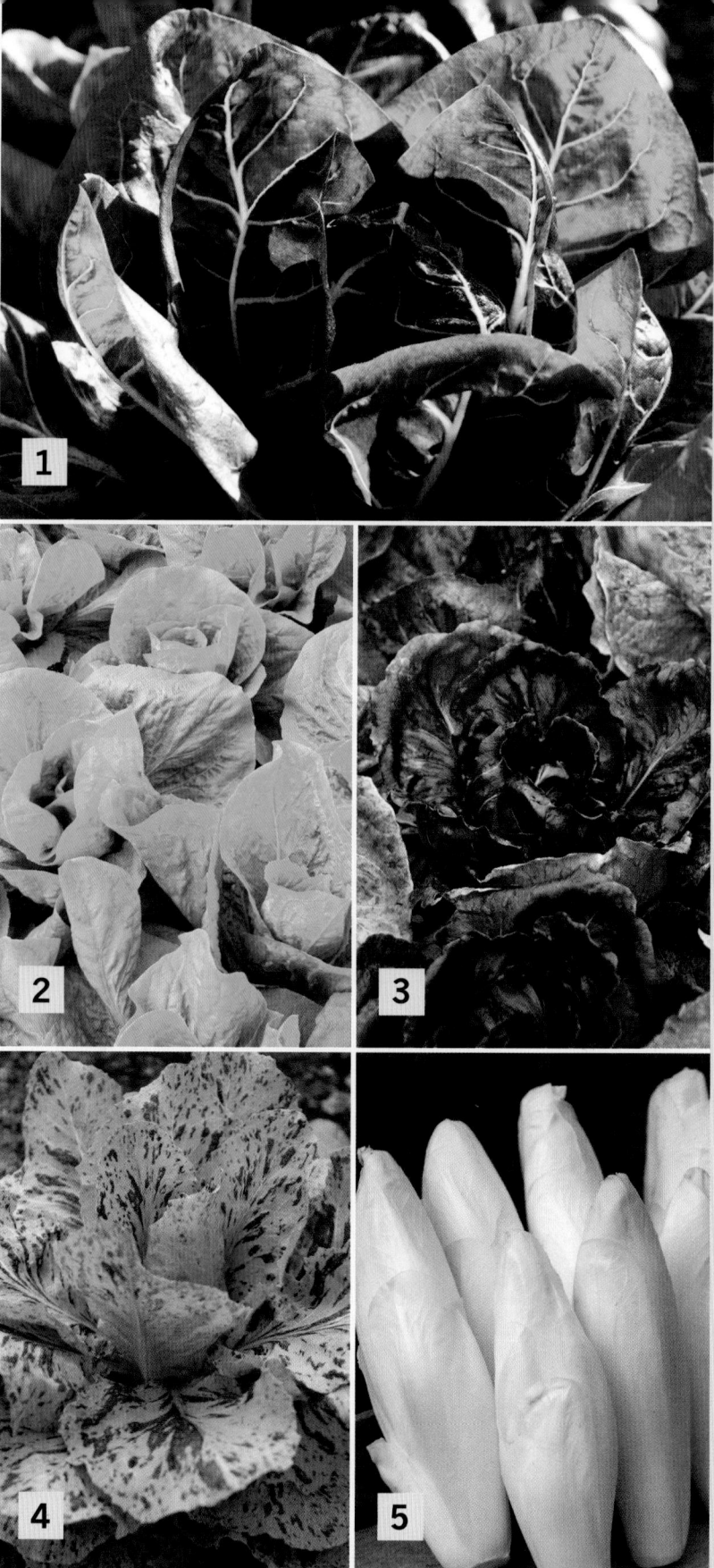

WINTER CABBAGE AND CHICORY

May: what to plant

YOUNG CELERY

Young self-blanching and trench celery plants, sown in February (p.40), can now be hardened off and planted out, once the risk of frost has passed. Celery needs rich, moist soil in full sun to do well. Self-blanching types are often planted in blocks to keep the stems upright, so space plants about 20cm (8in) apart. For trench celery, work manure or compost into a 30cm (12in) deep and 45cm (18in) wide trench and fill in to leave a 5cm (2in) dip along the length to retain moisture. Plant the celery in the dip about 30cm (12in) apart.

HARVEST: **AUG–DEC**

FLORENCE FENNEL

Florence fennel, sown earlier in April (p.74), should now be full of feathery foliage, ready to be hardened off and planted out. If the weather is still chilly wait a little longer, or the plants will bolt (run to seed). Florence fennel needs a good moist soil, so work in plenty of compost before planting. Allow space for the swelling stems: about 30cm (12in), between each plant. Water them in well and watch out for snails and slugs.

HARVEST: **JUN–OCT**

PLANT

CELERY

BROCCOLI

LEEKS

FLORENCE FENNEL

BIG BRASSICAS

Brussels sprouts, which crop autumn to winter, and sprouting broccoli, to pick in spring, are tall, wide plants and need to be planted in a firm soil to give their roots a good hold and stop them toppling over. Transplant them from their seedbed when the plants are 8–10cm (3–4in) tall. Space broccoli and dwarf Brussels sprout varieties 60cm (24in) apart and tall sprout types 90cm (36in) apart.

HARVEST: **VARIOUS**

LARGE LEEKS

If you want large leeks, dig in plenty of compost before planting. Seedlings sown under cover (p.26) should be hardened off and planted out when they are 15–20cm (6–8in) tall. Space them 15cm (6in) apart and allow 30cm (12in) between rows. To plant, make a 15cm (6in) deep hole with a dibber, pop in a leek and water each row as you finish.

HARVEST: **SEPT–APR**

PLANTING PLUGS

Many vegetable varieties can be bought as small plants from garden centres or as plug plants from mail order nurseries. These are a great way to fill your vegetable plot if you have limited time or no space to raise tender crops indoors. Choose stocky, dark green plants.

1 UNPACK THE PLUGS
If you bought your plug plants through mail order, you should unpack them, plant, and water them as soon as they arrive.

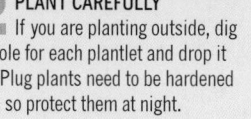

2 PLANT CAREFULLY
If you are planting outside, dig a hole for each plantlet and drop it in. Plug plants need to be hardened off, so protect them at night.

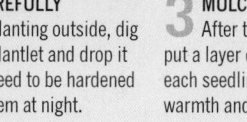

3 MULCH AROUND
After the first watering, put a layer of mulch around each seedling. This helps to hold warmth and moisture in the soil.

4 KEEP WELL WATERED
Keep the young plants well watered for 2 weeks or so, while they establish, and protect them against slugs and snails.

SQUASH & PUMPKINS

TOMATOES

PLUG PLANTS

WINTER SQUASH & PUMPKINS
HARVEST: SEPT–OCT

These vigorous trailing plants need 3–4 months of warm weather to produce a worthwhile crop.

1 SLIDE FROM POT
Squash and pumpkin seedlings are ready when they have three or four true leaves. Ease the plants gently out of their pots.

2 DIG LARGE HOLE
Plant in rich soil at least 1m (3ft) apart, using a trowel to dig a fairly large hole for each seedling. Firm them in and water well.

START TOMATOES

Plant up tomatoes into the greenhouse border, growing bags, or large containers. Bush varieties are attractive for windowsills and conservatories. Tall cordon varieties can be grown indoors, too, if there is enough space and light. Plant them 45cm (18in) apart, or two per growing bag, and add canes or twine supports to the apex of the greenhouse immediately, because growth is rapid.

HARVEST: **JUL–OCT**

May: more to plant

SUN-LOVING AUBERGINES

Aubergines love warmth and are difficult to grow in temperate climates. The plants are best kept under cover, either in a greenhouse or conservatory, or on a windowsill. Pot them up into 20cm (8in) pots in potting compost, or plant them in the greenhouse border 30–40cm (12–16in) apart, allowing them as much light as possible. If you live in a very mild area and have a sheltered spot outdoors, a dwarf variety of aubergine such as 'Bambino' will fruit successfully in a good summer.

HARVEST: **AUG–OCT**

YOUNG CELERIAC

Although mature celeriac plants are extremely hardy, seedlings will bolt (run to seed) if exposed to low temperatures. Don't harden them off until the weather is mild. Plant out celeriac seedlings 30cm (12in) apart in soil that has been enriched with organic matter so that it retains plenty of moisture. Water the young plants well after planting and continue to water them regularly to help swell the roots.

HARVEST: **OCT–MAR**

PLANT

CABBAGE   AUBERGINES   COURGETTES   CELERIAC

PLANT OUT CABBAGE

When your summer and autumn cabbages, sown in March (p.54), are about 8cm (3in) tall, transplant them into their final positions. Ideally, choose a sunny bed with firm soil. Space summer cabbages about 35cm (14in) apart and autumn-types (20in) 50cm apart. Make holes using a dibber, and lift plants into them gently by the leaves not the stem. Firm the soil around the roots and water well.

HARVEST: **AUG–NOV**

COURGETTES

If you have enough space in a greenhouse or polytunnel, plant courgettes into soil improved with compost or well-rotted manure for an early crop. These plants are large and very hungry and thirsty, so space them at least 90cm (36in) apart. A fabric mulch helps to retain moisture.

HARVEST: **JUL–OCT**

LATE EARLIES

Maincrop potato varieties are usually planted at this time of year, but if you have limited space and are looking for a quicker crop, then there's nothing to stop you planting an early variety, as long as you can find seed potatoes this late in the season. Make drills 15cm (6in) deep and plant maincrops 38cm (15in) apart with the chitting end pointing upwards, leaving 75cm (30in) between rows. Allow 30cm (12in) between earlies, with rows at least 38cm (15in) apart. Cover over with soil and water if it is dry.

HARVEST: **AUG–SEP**

CLIMBING CROPS

Once melon and indoor cucumber plants, sown in April (p.74), have two or three leaves, plant them into a greenhouse border, 45cm (18in) apart, or two per growing bag. Don't plant deeply, because stems are prone to neck rot. Water well, keep moist, and shade the leaves from hot scorching sun. Provide support (pp.88–89).

HARVEST: **VARIOUS**

POTATOES

MELONS & CUCUMBERS

PEPPERS

PLANT OUT PEPPERS

HARVEST: **JUL–OCT**

Peppers and chillies thrive under cover, giving earlier, larger crops than plants grown outside. Plant in pots, growing bags, or ideally in a greenhouse border.

1 WHEN AND WHERE
Peppers and chillies are large enough to plant into a border once they have their first flowers. Make sure the bed is free-draining.

2 SETTING OUT
Ease plants from their pots, handling the rootball not the stem or leaves. Position them in rows, 30–45cm (12–18in) apart.

3 FIRM IN AND WATER
Bury the plants at the same depths as in their pots, and firm them in gently. Water them well, and don't allow them to dry out.

TAKE NOTE

On bright, sunny days, greenhouses and cold frames can become very warm. Open vents and windows, and ensure your plants and seedlings don't dry out.

See PROVIDING SUPPORT pages 88–89

May: what to do

DOUBLE FRUIT CROP

Removing every other fruit from your gooseberry bushes in the second half of this month will give you a crop of smaller berries to cook now and allow the remaining fruit to develop to an impressive size for harvesting in June. This practice is worthwhile only for dessert gooseberries that are going to be eaten uncooked.

SPOTLESS STRAWBERRIES

As the fruit begins to swell on strawberry plants, apply a mulch around them, tucking it right under the berries to keep them clean and away from the soil.

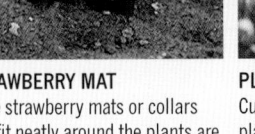

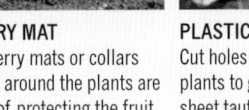

STRAWBERRY MAT
Fibre strawberry mats or collars that fit neatly around the plants are an easy way of protecting the fruit.

PLASTIC SHEET
Cut holes in plastic sheeting for the plants to grow through. Keep the sheet taut to avoid water pooling.

STRAW BEDDING
The traditional strawberry mulch is a thick layer of straw. Pack it carefully beneath each plant.

TEND

GOOSEBERRIES

RASPBERRIES

YOUNG PLANTS

STRAWBERRIES

CUTTING CANES

Raspberries are vigorous plants that send up new canes from their base each spring. Summer-fruiting types can become overcrowded, which may lead to a poor and possibly diseased crop. Thin them out by removing the weakest of this year's shoots, leaving five or six strong new canes per plant. Pull out new canes that spring up away from the row, to check unwanted spreading.

STILL DELICATE

Even when hardened off (p.87), seedlings are vulnerable to late frosts. If there is a cold snap, plant out under cloches or tunnels covered with fleece. Old newspapers make good overnight cover if frost is forecast. Soft new growth is also vulnerable to pests: keep bugs out with barriers such as netting, fleece, or brassica collars.

PINCH OUT TOMATOES

Tomatoes grow rapidly once planted in their final positions and if you have chosen tall cordon (indeterminate) varieties, such as 'Gardener's Delight' or 'Shirley', they will soon need some support. As they race upwards, regularly tie the main stems loosely on to their canes or stakes with twine. At the same time, remove any sideshoots that are developing where the leaves branch from the main stem. Vigorous shoots are often sent up from the base of the plant and these should be removed, too.

BEAT THE BUGS

Cover crops with fleece or net immediately after planting to keep out pests such as carrot fly (p.237). Buy or make rigid wire hoops to support the netting. and push them into the soil, covering the row, every 30cm (12in). Lay the netting over the hoops and anchor it into the soil with metal pegs or weight it down with lengths of wood.

GREENHOUSES

TOMATOES

PROTECT CROPS

SCORCHING HOT

In a greenhouse, intense summer sun can scorch the foliage of plants and raise the temperature far too high. Put up shading in late spring and remove it in early autumn as the sun's strength diminishes. Blinds are expensive, but there are many cheaper options.

PAINT-ON SHADING
Shading paint is cheap and is easy to apply to the outside of glass greenhouses. It will not wipe off some plastics, so check the label.

SHADING MESH
Shading fabric may not look particularly attractive, but when attached to the outside of the greenhouse it is highly effective.

EFFECTIVE VENTILATION
Leave doors and vents open all day if it is very hot. Automatic ventilators are available that open and close vents according to temperature.

DAMPING DOWN
Sprinkle water on floors and staging to stop the atmosphere becoming too dry. Shut doors and vents for a while afterwards to increase the humidity.

Organic pest control

Every garden, no matter how well tended, will have its share of pests and diseases to contend with. When you are growing your own food, you may prefer not to spray crops with pesticides. Instead, try for natural biological control by encouraging, or introducing, populations of beneficial creatures to prey on persistent pests.

Grow healthy plants

Regularly maintaining your kitchen garden helps minimize problems with pests and diseases. Constantly improving the soil with plenty of organic matter will improve its structure and fertility, and allow plants to grow stronger, making them more resistant to infection and damage. Keeping beds free of plant debris and weeds is also good practice, leaving pests and diseases with nowhere to hide or overwinter, so tidy the area you're cultivating regularly. Keep an eye out for the first signs of pests, such as aphids on shoot tips, and tackle them before you have an infestation on your hands. Simply squashing greenfly or small caterpillars can be remarkably effective.

Friendly predators

Providing food, water, and shelter for a wide range of wildlife will encourage them into your garden, where they will feed on pests and help keep their numbers under control. Feeders will bring in birds that also have a taste for aphids, caterpillars, snails, and other pests. Hedgehogs devour slugs, snails, and grubs of all kinds, so are worth encouraging with piles of logs and leaves. Where an insect pest does take hold, it's possible to introduce a biological control, such as nematodes, to combat them.

APPLY NEMATODES
Microscopic, parasitic nematode worms effectively control a range of pests, including slugs, snails, caterpillars, and weevils. They come in a powder, which is watered into the soil using a watering can.

GROW FLOWERS
Growing flowers among your crops not only adds colour, but also encourages pollinating insects to visit. These often feed on pests, too. The scent of flowers may also prevent pests locating crops.

CREATE HABITATS
Creating different habitats entices all kinds of beneficial creatures to take up residence. A pond will bring frogs, toads, and insects, as well as other hungry and thirsty animals and birds.

MAKE HIDING PLACES
Hiding places, such as log piles, pieces of old carpet, or propped up slates, provide shelter for beneficial creatures like hedgehogs and frogs. If you find pests sheltering too, just remove them.

BENEFICIAL BUGS

Many insects pollinate crops and some feed voraciously on common insect pests, so it's a good idea to make your garden attractive to them.

Lacewings – Larvae and adults feast on aphids and other insect pests. Attract them with nectar-rich flowers.

Ladybirds – Adults and larvae prey on aphids. Provide dry places, such as seedpods, for them to overwinter.

Hoverflies – These wasp look-a-likes devour aphids and pollinate crops. Encourage them with colourful flowers.

Centipede – At home in leaf litter and log piles, centipedes have an eager appetite for all kinds of insect pests.

Sacrificial planting – Grow plants that pests can't resist, to distract them from crops, or to alert you to the problem so you can control it. For example, blackfly love nasturtiums.

ORGANIC PEST CONTROL

May: what to harvest

PEAK TIME FOR HERBS

Annual herbs sown in April (p.82), and perennial ones planted last autumn (p.199), should be ready for the kitchen in the next few weeks. Many herbs need pinching out now to encourage bushy growth, so take advantage and use the shoots in your cooking. Most of the soft new growth should be tender enough to pinch off between your fingers, but scissors are better for woodier plants like rosemary and some thymes, and neater for chives. Pick the large leaves of basil as required and pinch out the flower shoots as they come.

SALAD SEASON

Sown outside in April (p.75), now is the start of the main lettuce season, with non-hearting, loose-leaf varieties, such as 'Green Salad Bowl' and 'Catalogna', ready first. To keep them cropping over several weeks, pick off the outer leaves as required, or cut the leaves with scissors about 2.5cm (1in) from the soil and allow them to re-sprout. Hearting types follow, which can be pulled up by the roots or cut at the base with a knife.

HARVEST

HERBS

LETTUCE

GOOSEBERRIES

GALLERY OF GOOSEBERRIES

Gooseberries (p.185) harvested this month are likely to be acidic, so perfect for cooking. Fruit left to ripen will soften and yellow, signalling that they are sweet enough to eat raw. Unless you have thornless variety, watch out for the fearsome spines when picking the fruit.

'HINNOMAKI RED'
Slow-growing variety that produces a heavy crop of large fruit that ripen red. It has good resistance to mildew. Good for small gardens.

'HINNOMAKI YELLOW'
A strong variety that bears a good yield of large, sweet, yellow fruit. It also shows good mildew resistance. Dessert variety, it's good eaten raw.

'INVICTA'
Widely available, this reliable dual-purpose variety can be eaten straight from the bush or cooked. It has good mildew resistance.

'CAPTIVATOR'
An almost thornless variety, good for gardens with children. It's sweet fruit ripen red and can be eaten from the bush. Good mildew resistance.

ASPARAGUS CROWNS

If you have planted asparagus crowns this year (p.83), patience is the order of the day. To allow plants to become established and build up strength, leave spears uncut in their first and second seasons. In subsequent years harvest the spears when they reach around 15cm (6in) tall, cutting them with a sharp knife, 5cm (2in) below the soil surface. Harvest them over a period of 6 weeks but leave at least six strong spears per plant to grow on. These will supply the all-important energy for the following year's crop.

ROOT TREATS

It's a real treat this month to be able to harvest the first salad beetroot and baby carrots, sown in March. Do this carefully, loosening heavy soils with a hand fork first to avoid damaging the roots, especially carrots. Twist rather than cut the leaves off your beetroot to prevent them bleeding. Remember, their leaves are good to eat, too.

ASPARAGUS

BEETROOT & CARROTS

TURNIPS

BROAD BEANS

TENDER TURNIPS

There's no denying that turnips are a quick crop to grow. Early varieties can be ready for harvest in just 6–7 weeks after sowing, so make sure you catch them at their best – while they're still sweet and tender. For perfect baby turnips, pull them when they are less than 5cm (2in) in diameter. If left to grow much larger, they soon become tough and unappetizing.

BROAD APPEAL

Broad beans sown in autumn or late winter should start to yield fleece-lined pods full of delicious, sweet beans this month. Pick frequently, because the beans are at their best when small and tender. If you've a glut, harvest the beans small and freeze them. Don't leave them to become big and starchy.

June: ready to eat

The summer bounty starts with waxy new potatoes, mild green garlic, and a dazzling array of just-picked salad leaves. Pounce on strawberries and gooseberries to eat fresh or to make into jams and desserts.

Pickle spare **globe artichoke** hearts in vinegar to enjoy later
pages 176–177

Eat super-sweet early **garlic** now

Rhubarb – rose-pink and succulent

Basil is ready eat and to preserve as **pesto**
page 147

Give salads some peppery punch with freshly pulled **summer radish**

Keep picking tasty spinach beet and Swiss chard

Spring onions are a summer-long staple – harvest them young, mild, and tender

Pick new **calabrese** while the heads are tightly closed

Mild tasting, pot-bellied **kohl rabi** are ready to eat now

Pull sweet, early carrots

Eat male **courgette flowers,** stuffed with cream cheese; leave the female flowers to bear fruit

Young herbs taste great

Use sweet-tasting **pea shoots** in your salads and stir-fries

Pick new season **cherries straight from the tree**

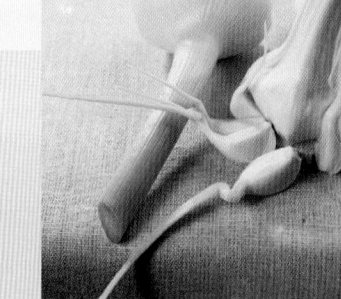

Fresh **asparagus**
– indescribable!

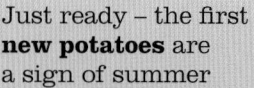

Just ready – the first
new potatoes are
a sign of summer

Pick
your first
**summer
cauliflower**

Full-sized **beetroots** are
ready now – add one to
your chocolate cake mix
for something special

Beetroot leaves
make a tasty and
colourful addition
to your salads

Enjoy
sweet heads
of **spring
cabbage**

Fresh **gooseberries**
are delicious; freeze
surpluses to enjoy
later in the year

The first
summer
turnips are
ready now
– ideal for
mashing

Keep **sprouting seeds**
pages 36–37, they're
packed with goodness

Give **peas**
a chance

**Jam made
with new
maincrop
strawberries**
is a highlight
this month

You won't go short on salads,
with **hearted lettuce** and
cut-and-come-again crops

Plenty of **broad
beans** to pick for a
few more weeks yet

Eat
aniseed-
flavoured
**Florence
fennel** now

Indoor **mushrooms**
provide a welcome
supply all summer,
so keep picking

**Perpetual
spinach**
will keep
you in
greens

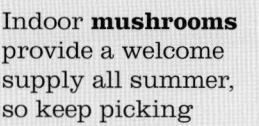

June: what to sow

LATER LETTUCE
Sow now for late-summer and autumn crops. Choose cos, butterhead, or crisphead-types for hearted lettuce; loose-leaf varieties to crop as cut leaves. In hot weather, lettuce might fail to germinate or wilt once growing. Sow in lightly shaded beds, and if the weather is very hot, sow in the evenings and cool the soil first with water.

HARVEST: **JUL–NOV**

SOW AND SOW
Don't forget to continue sowing cut-and-come-again salad crops for a constant supply. A range of baby leaf crops are suitable (pp.28–29). Weed the soil and sow seed thinly in drills, 10–15cm (4–6in) wide, to give a mass of foliage to cut in a few weeks time.

HARVEST: **ALL YEAR**

SOW

EDIBLE FLOWERS

LETTUCE

CHINESE GREENS

CUT & COME AGAIN

BLOOMING TASTY
Annual flowers are often overlooked in the productive garden, but many are edible as well as beautiful, and have their own distinct flavour. Direct sow now.

HARVEST: **JUL–OCT**

CALENDULA
Also known as pot marigold, this cheerful plant flowers in shades of yellow and orange. Use the petals to add colour to your salads.

NASTURTIUM
The leaves, flowers, and seed pods of this colourful, spreading plant have a delicious but strong peppery taste. It is best used sparingly.

FRENCH MARIGOLD
This summer bedding plant has a very pungent flavour. Use the flowers in salads, and add the petals to rice dishes for colour and a spicy kick.

FAR EAST FEAST
Chinese cabbage and pak choi like warmth, so wait until this month to sow, when they will be less likely to bolt. Both need moist, fertile soil, and will tolerate light shade. Sow seed thinly in drills 30cm (12in) apart for Chinese cabbage, 25cm (10in) for pak choi. Repeat sow, thin seedlings, and harvest in 6–8 weeks, when ready.

HARVEST: **JUL–NOV**

HURRY NOW FOR HERBS

HARVEST: **JUL–OCT**

This is the last chance to sow most annual herbs. If you leave it any later, they rapidly run to seed at the expense of the leaves you want for the kitchen.

1 SOWING OUTDOORS
Sow tougher herbs, such as dill, parsley, and coriander, directly into the soil outside in rows or patches. Space evenly.

2 GROWING ON
Keep the seed well watered and thin the seedlings to 20cm (8in) apart as they develop. Protect from slugs and snails (p.239).

SOWING INDOORS
In all but the mildest areas, sow basil indoors, grow it on undercover, and plant it out in a few weeks time.

STILL TIME TO SOW

Sow outside now: peas (p.40), kohl rabi (p.41), turnips, sprouting broccoli, beetroot, calabrese (p.54), Florence fennel (p.74), kale (p.75) carrots (p.94), sugarloaf and Witloof chicory, and chard (p.95).

SQUASHES & CUCUMBERS

FRENCH & RUNNER BEANS

ANNUAL HERBS

SQUASH FAMILY

With the last frosts now past, summer cucumbers and courgettes can be sown under cloches in their final positions outside, as can summer and winter squashes, and pumpkins. All need a sunny site, sheltered from the wind, and soil that has been improved with plenty of well-rotted manure or compost. Sow two seeds per station, 2.5cm (1in) deep, spaced 90cm (3ft) apart for cucumbers and courgettes, and at least 1.5m (5ft) apart for squashes and pumpkins.

HARVEST: **VARIOUS**

LATE BEANS

For late crops of French and runner beans, sow now, directly into soil prepared with plenty of rich organic matter. If you're growing climbing varieties, remember to put the supports in first (pp.88–89). Sow two seeds per station, 5cm (2in) deep, 15–20cm (6–8in) apart. Thin out the weaker plant.

HARVEST: **AUG–OCT**

Winter squash

Best grown where summers are warm, these vigorous plants produce late-summer fruit in a huge range of sizes, colours, and shapes. Most store well into winter.

1 'Uchiki Kuri' looks like a small pumpkin and produces an early crop of orange-red fruit. The flesh has a sweet, nutty flavour. Plants can be trained upwards where space is limited.

2 Butternut is a type of squash, rather than a variety, and is widely sold in supermarkets. Varieties include 'Harrier', 'Hunter', and 'Waltham Butternut', which all have, sweet, nutty fruit.

3 'Queensland Blue' produces large, heavily-ribbed fruit that mature to a distinctive blue-green colour. Best grown in larger plots, where the plants can be allowed to trail across the soil.

4 'Turk's Turban' is a smaller variety that produces highly attractive, edible fruit. Once peeled, there is little left to eat, so grow more than one plant to make up a worthwhile quantity.

5 'Sweet Dumpling' produces small, attractive fruit, the size of tennis balls, which are delicious roasted. This variety can be grown in containers, with the stems trained vertically up a wigwam.

6 'Crown Prince' is a blue-skinned variety with sweet-tasting, bright orange flesh. All squash keep well, but if stored properly, fruit of this variety will stay in good condition well into spring.

Other varieties to try:
'Bon Bon'
'Festival'
'Golden Hubbard'
'Golden Nugget'
'Hercules'

TAKE YOUR PICK

Pumpkins

Many pumpkins are grown for carving at Halloween, but sow a good culinary variety, and the flesh is fabulous cooked. Some also have tasty, edible seeds.

1 'Jack Be Little' is a miniature variety, with the plants each producing several palm-sized fruits. These are edible and delicious roasted, or they can also be used for decoration. This variety is suitable for pot-growing.

2 'Dill's Atlantic Giant' is among the largest of pumpkins, especially if fruits are thinned to one per plant. Pick young to eat, or allow the fruits to grow on for over-sized decorations.

3 'Rouge Vif d'Etampes' is an old variety with large, flattened, deep orange fruits that are heavily ribbed. Harvest when plate-size and enjoy them roasted, or grow them on for decoration.

4 'Baby Bear' produces bright orange fruit the size of a football. It is a good variety for smaller gardens as it doesn't need too much space. The thin-hulled seeds are especially good to eat.

5 'Hundredweight' is a giant variety that can be grown to eat or for decoration. Water and feed plants well for the largest fruit, although they may become too tough and heavy to cook.

Other varieties to try:
'Amazonka'
'Connecticut Field'
'Jack O'Lantern'
'Spellbound'
'Wee B Little'

WINTER SQUASHES AND PUMPKINS

June: what to plant

PLANT CAULIFLOWER

Spring-sown summer and autumn cauliflower should be ready to transplant from their seedbed now. Using a dibber, lift the seedlings carefully and transplant them into fertile soil that hasn't been manured recently. Space 60cm (24in) apart in each direction and water well and net them where pigeons are a problem.

HARVEST: **AUG–NOV**

PLANT GREENS

It's now time to plant out kale and sprouting broccoli, sown in spring. Both crops grow outside through winter, so give them shelter, and soil that hasn't been dug recently, to help their roots anchor securely. Transplant them from their seedbed in the same way as cauliflowers.

HARVEST: **DEC–APR**

PLANT

AUBERGINES

CAULIFLOWER

SUGARLOAF CHICORY

KALE & BROCCOLI

AUBERGINES, PEPPERS, & TOMATOES

HARVEST: **JUL–OCT**

Once plants raised indoors have been hardened off, and have their first flowers showing, these heat-loving crops can be planted outside in sunny, sheltered spots.

AUBERGINES
Aubergines give a better harvest when planted into large containers. Keep them well fed and watered. Harvest August – October.

PEPPERS
Plant in beds, containers, or grow bags, in full sun, and support with canes. They need good light and warmth to ripen fully.

TOMATOES
Suitable for beds, pots, or growing bags. All upright varieties require staking with canes. Grow cordon varieties under cover. Crop from July.

PLANT CHICORY

Sown last month (p.95), plant out your sugarloaf chicory seedlings now. This type of chicory forms dense heads that are larger than other forms, and they appreciate soil that has had compost dug into it recently, to encourage leafy growth. Harden off the plants and space them out evenly at 25cm (10in) intervals. Water in well.

HARVEST: **JUL–OCT**

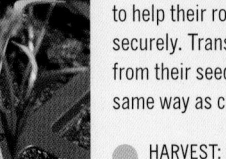

FAMILY FRUIT

HARVEST: **JUL–OCT**

These related crops are hungry plants, so work in plenty of compost when you plant out, once hardened off. Cover with cloches if the weather is cool and damp.

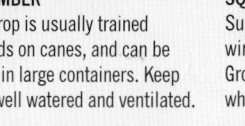

COURGETTE
These are large, quick-growing plants that need plenty of space. Position them 90cm (36in) apart. Can also be grown in large pots.

CUCUMBER
This crop is usually trained upwards on canes, and can be grown in large containers. Keep them well watered and ventilated.

SQUASH
Summer squash crop from July, winter varieties from September. Grow them vertically up canes where space is limited.

DON'T FORGET

When planting out, always water plants in well, and continue to keep them moist during dry spells.

Water under cloches regularly and prop them open to allow air to cool plants on sunny days.

CUCUMBERS, COURGETTES, & SQUASH

SWEET CORN

FRENCH & RUNNER BEANS

SWEET CORN

HARVEST: **SEP–OCT**

If your plants are hardened off, plant out now in a sheltered spot, into good soil that doesn't dry out.

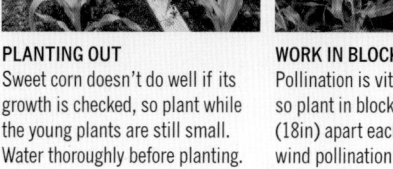

PLANTING OUT
Sweet corn doesn't do well if its growth is checked, so plant while the young plants are still small. Water thoroughly before planting.

WORK IN BLOCKS
Pollination is vital for full cobs, so plant in blocks with plants 45cm (18in) apart each way. This makes wind pollination more effective.

SUMMMER BEANS

Batches of French and runner beans, raised under cover in pots or modules, can be planted out as soon as their supports are in place (pp.88–89). Plant one per cane, or space them out 15–20cm (6–8in) apart along rows of netting or wire. Dwarf varieties require a similar spacing, but no supports. Try planting sweet peas to cling alongside runner beans to help attract pollinating insects.

HARVEST: **AUG–OCT**

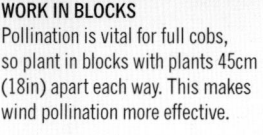

See PROVIDING SUPPORT pages 88–89

PLANTING IDEAS

Productive baskets

Hanging baskets are usually planted with flowering annuals but they can be just as attractive, and productive, when used to grow dwarf or trailing vegetables and herbs. This is not only a great way to make best use of a smaller plot, but it also allows you to bring your crops within easy picking distance of the kitchen.

1 LINE YOUR BASKET
To help retain moisture, line your basket with plastic, or a purpose-made liner, before filling the base with compost. Now add water-retaining crystals and slow-release fertilizer.

2 CHOOSE PLANTS
Position upright herbs and vegetables in the centre of the basket, with trailing varieties around the edge. In large baskets, add flowering annuals for extra colour. Plant closely together.

3 ADD COMPOST
Vegetables are thirsty plants; make sure there are no large pockets in the compost between plants and only fill to 5cm (2in) below the basket rim, so you can water it thoroughly.

4 WATER AND FEED WELL
Water the plants in well and position the basket in a sheltered, sunny spot. To encourage a good crop, water twice daily during summer, and apply a liquid feed every week.

TRY THESE

The best crops to grow in baskets are dwarf or trailing varieties, or those that you can either harvest quickly or pick while the plants are young.

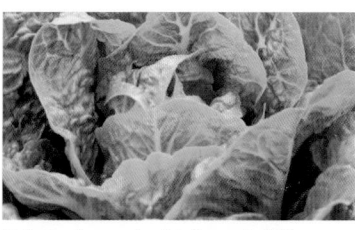

Salad – Loose-leaf lettuce (p.81), rocket and cut-and-come-again crops (pp.28–29) flourish in hanging baskets.

Peas – Dwarf, early peas, such as 'Sugarbon' grow well in baskets if kept watered and fed. Pick them frequently.

Tomatoes – Choose trailing bush varieties, like 'Tumbling Tom Red'. Most baskets will hold only one plant.

Herbs – Many compact herbs grow well in baskets. Try marjoram and thyme, which tolerate dry conditions.

PRODUCTIVE BASKETS

June: what to do

SUMMER PRUNING
This is a quick job that is worth carrying out after gooseberries, redcurrants, and whitecurrants have been harvested. Prune all of this year's new growth back to five leaves, cutting with sharp secateurs just above a leaf. Removing the tips of soft new growth stops the plants being colonized by aphids or infected with mildew and opens up the bush to improve airflow.

WATER AND HOE
Container-grown plants need frequent watering in hot weather, but so do plants in the soil. Keep an eye on plants that are prone to bolting and soak them well, perhaps once a week. Hoe between crops to remove weeds, leaving them to shrivel and die.

TEND

FRUIT BUSHES

MAINTENANCE

TOMATOES

SUMMER BERRIES

KEEP UP THE SUPPORT
Your tomatoes will still be heading skywards, so continue to tie them in to sturdy stakes or wires and pinch out sideshoots.

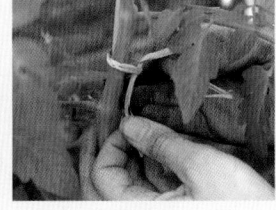

1 REMOVE SIDESHOOTS
Pinch out sideshoots that form where leaves join the main stem, because they will take energy away from flowering and fruiting.

2 TIE LOOSELY
When you attach the main stem of a tomato plant to its support, tie the twine loosely to allow the stem to expand.

CANE CONTROL
New canes sent up this year from the base of summer-fruiting raspberry and blackberry plants will now be getting long and unruly. Tie them in to keep them out of the way and prevent them getting damaged. The older canes that will fruit this year should be spread across the supporting wires, so keep the new shoots close together for now and spread them out once the older canes have been cut back.

WATCH THEM CLIMB
As they grow, climbing varieties of French and runner beans twist their stems around their supporting canes (pp.88–89). Once established, they can hang on tightly without your help. Sometimes, however, seedlings need a hand to get started, especially if they are getting tossed around in breezy conditions or flattened by heavy rain. Once the young plants are tall enough, tie each one loosely onto its support with garden twine, taking care not to damage the delicate stem, then watch them take off without tangling.

TRIM HERBS
Many shrubby and perennial herbs, such as rosemary, sage, and thyme, finish flowering during early summer, which gives you the opportunity to cut them back and keep them tidy. Trimming also encourages new growth that will quickly be ready to harvest. Use secateurs or shears depending on the size of the job.

RUNNER BEANS

HERBS

STRAWBERRIES

NEW PLANTS FROM OLD
Strawberry plants are easy to propagate from the long runners that they all produce. At no extra cost, you can increase your stock and replace old plants.

1 CHOOSE RUNNERS
Choose four or five strong runners and cut off the rest. Also remove runners from plants you don't want to use for propagation.

2 PEG DOWN IN POTS
Set the runners in buried pots of compost and peg down with wire. Once the plantlets have grown on, cut the runners and plant out.

3 PROPAGATE IN SOIL
You can also let the runners grow directly in the soil. Reposition the plantlet if necessary, peg it down and sever when established.

DON'T FORGET

The weeks that follow are likely to be hot and dry. If you haven't already laid an organic mulch around your plants to conserve moisture, do it now.

June: more to do

EARTH UP MAINCROPS

When maincrop potatoes reach about 20cm (8in) tall, earth them up by pulling soil around their stems, leaving the top leaves showing. This not only prevents tubers turning green and inedible in the light, it can help protect them from the spores of potato blight (p.243). This fungal disease thrives in warm, wet summers. Look for brown patches at leaf edges, and remove and destroy infected growth.

REGULAR MEALS

Whether your tomatoes, peppers, chillies, and aubergines are grown in the soil or in containers, they need regular feeding once the first fruit begins to set. Apply a high-potash tomato fertilizer every week. Use a sunken pot to help deliver the feed straight to the roots.

TEND

POTATOES

TOMATOES

FRUIT BUSHES

SOFT FRUIT

MILDEW ALERT

If powdery white patches appear on your gooseberry and blackcurrant bushes, it probably means they have been infected with American gooseberry mildew. This fungal disease particularly affects young growth, which becomes misshapen and dies. The mildew also appears on the fruits, which are still edible, though unappealing. Gooseberry mildew thrives in environments where air circulation is poor. The best control is to remove and destroy affected leaves and fruits, and prune the bushes (pp.140–141) to thin out growth and allow free air circulation.

PROTECT SOFT FRUIT

Birds love ripe, soft summer fruits as much as we do. To stop them feasting on your crops of berries and currants, protect the fruit with netting. The easiest way to do this is to plant bushes together and build a permanent fruit cage around them, but this is not always practical in smaller gardens. To net individual bushes, drive in four stakes around each one to hold up the net. Cover them over before the fruit ripens and changes colour. Ensure that the net is weighted down at the edges, because birds are adept at getting in and can easily become trapped.

SPOT CHECK FOR PESTS AND DISEASES

Spotting pests (pp.236–239) early, before they have a chance to multiply and damage crops, is key to keeping problems under control.

Check under leaves as you pass, and if plants are unexpectedly wilting, try digging one up to look for pests that attack the roots.

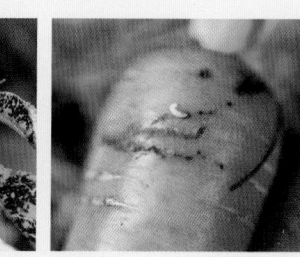

BLACKFLY
These aphids can rapidly smother foliage, sucking the sap and excreting a sticky substance that causes a black mould to develop.

CARROT FLY
The white maggots of this fly will destroy your carrot crop. Protect your plants with fine netting to prevent the female fly from laying her eggs.

ASPARAGUS BEETLE
Both the brightly coloured adult beetles and their dark grey larvae rapidly strip asparagus stems. Pick them off by hand and destroy them.

ONION FLY
The maggots feed on the roots and bulbs of onions. Signs are yellow, collapsing plants. Onion sets are less vulnerable than seedlings.

PESTS

APPLES & PEARS

BROAD BEANS

THE JUNE DROP
Many apple and pear trees shed fruitlets in late June or early July. This 'June drop' may alarm first-time fruit growers, but it is the tree's way of ditching unhealthy fruit and leaving a smaller crop that is easier for it to carry. Do your own thinning after the June drop for a crop of large, healthy fruit, especially on young trees that need to make plenty of strong growth too.

BEAN TOPS
Young shoots at the top of broad bean plants are a magnet for blackfly. Infestation can be pre-empted by pinching out the soft tips of these shoots between your fingers when the plants are in full flower. This also helps direct the plant's energy into swelling the beans rather than producing more leaves.

See COMMON PESTS pages 236–239

GROWING FEATURE

Effective irrigation

Gardeners look for rapid growth and copious flowering and fruiting from their crops. Plants can achieve this only if they have a consistent supply of moisture at their roots. In all but the lightest of soils or drought conditions, most outdoor plants do well with moderate watering, but those under cover need more attention.

When to water

Apart from container-grown or greenhouse crops, the plants that require the most careful watering are those that are newly planted or transplanted. Until their roots have become established, they are highly vulnerable to drying out. Watch your young plants for the earliest hints of wilting and leaf-yellowing, and water them promptly if danger signs appear.

Water is often in short supply, especially in summer, so use it efficiently. Don't water in the middle of the day, when the sun is at its most intense, because the water can scorch leaves, and any moisture in the soil evaporates quickly. It's better to water in the cool of early morning or evening, when the water can penetrate deep into the soil and reach the roots of your plants. A layer of mulch on the soil surface helps to prevent evaporation. Make sure that the soil is damp before you add a thick layer of organic material, such as well-rotted compost or manure, or a film that can be planted through, such as black plastic.

(left to right) **Half plastic bottles** make excellent funnels, channelling water directly to plant roots, where it's most needed. **Mulching** shields the soil around the plant from the sun, keeping it cool and preventing moisture from evaporating so readily.

WATER AT THE BASE
Concentrate your efforts at a plant's base when watering, as the water will then soak down directly to the roots. Be careful that water pressure from a hose doesn't erode the soil.

SEEP HOSE
This is a long perforated pipe that leaks water along its length. Seep hoses can be buried in beds or laid on the surface, and are particularly useful for watering under cloches or tunnels.

WATERING KITS
Greenhouse watering kits are irrigation systems that connect to a mains water tap or water butt. A timer controls the supply of water through narrow pipes to drip-feeders placed near the plants.

WATERING PROBLEMS

Inadequate watering leaves plants more susceptible to disease, as well as harmful disorders caused by a lack of essential nutrients.

Blossom end rot on tomatoes (p.240) is caused by calcium deficiency, resulting from inadequate watering.

Mildew on plants is commonly caused because they are kept too dry, leading to white fungal growth on the foliage.

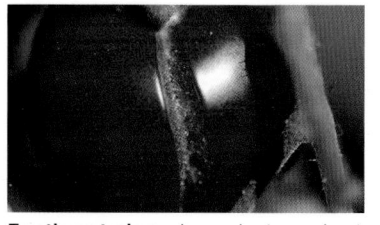

Erratic watering, where plants are kept too dry before watering, often results in fruit with split or corky skin.

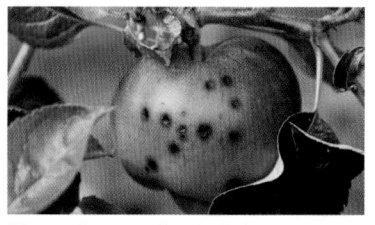

Bitter pit on apples (p.240) is caused by calcium deficiency, resulting from inadequate watering. It is easily cured.

Give the soil a good soaking when you water. A light sprinkling is wasteful, as the water will go no further than the soil surface and cannot reach the plant roots, where it is needed most.

Space efficiency

However large your plot, you'll want to make the most of the space. This could be as simple as finding gaps in the flower border for fruit and vegetables, but by planting fast-growing crops, you can squeeze extra harvests out of the vegetable plot as well. Sow them in empty soil that is waiting for the next crop to be planted (catch-cropping), or grow them between slow-maturing plants (inter-cropping).

Catch-cropping

Even with meticulous planning it's inevitable that sometimes you will be left with bare soil during the growing season – after one long-term crop is harvested and before the next is ready to plant. This gives you an opportunity to sow a fast-growing crop that will use the space in the meantime, and will finish in plenty of time to prepare the ground in readiness for the crop to follow.

Catch-cropping is particularly useful to fill the gap between winter brassicas, the last of which are often picked in early spring, and tender summer crops that

(left to right) **The last early potatoes** are lifted in summer, leaving the bed temporarily empty. **Sow radish next**, to harvest in 6–8 weeks, just in time to make way for new spring cabbage seedlings, transplanted from their bed.

can't usually be planted outdoors until towards the end of May. Another lull may come between lifting early potatoes and planting spring cabbages in late summer. Keep a stock of seeds handy of quick-growing crops that are ready to harvest in 6–8 weeks, such as radishes, beetroot, and pak choi, right through the growing season and your plot will always be full.

Inter-cropping

Effective inter-cropping takes advantage of the fact that some crops are quicker growing than others, and that they can be grown closely together without competing. Slow-growing crops, such as Brussels sprouts and parsnips, take months to mature, locking up your beds for long periods. In contrast, turnips and beetroots are ready to harvest in just 8–10 weeks, so it's a good idea to make use of their speedy growth. To achieve multiple crops from the same bed, water and feed the plants regularly, and try not to disturb your maincrop plants.

1 MAINCROP FIRST
Plant out maincrop vegetables, such as sweet corn, into their final positions. Firm them in and water well. Insert any stakes at this stage to avoid damaging the intercrops later.

2 SOW INTERCROPS
Make seed drills in between the young maincrop vegetables, and sow intercrops directly. Sow later crops around the developing maincrop to prevent them from being shaded.

TRY THESE

Inter-cropping and catch-cropping requires fruit and vegetables that mature quickly, to avoid interrupting the cycle of maincrop harvests.

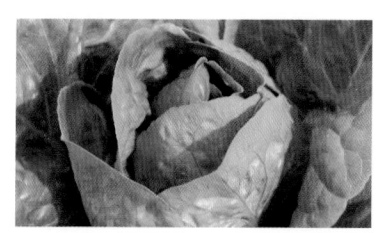

Lettuce can be harvested as leaves in a matter of weeks. If time allows between crops, let them form heads.

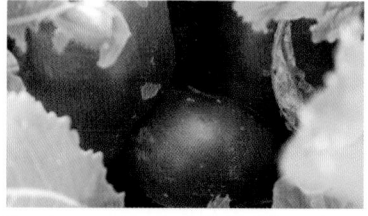

Turnips can be ready in just 6 weeks, making them ideal for inter-cropping between onions, shallots, and beans.

Pak choi matures quickly and can also be cut as baby leaves, allowing you to sow new crops until the last minute.

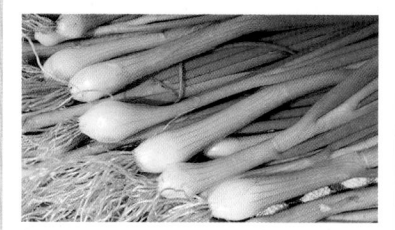

Spring onions are ideal as an extra crop between maincrop onions and shallots, as well as rows of carrots.

Don't let space go to waste in the vegetable plot. In the scheme shown here, courgettes and various fast-growing salad crops have been planted around bean wigwams.

June: what to harvest

TASTE OF SUMMER
June is the peak month for strawberries, when early varieties, like 'Honeoye', bear fruit. Pick berries with their hulls attached, when fully ripe and entirely red. Fruit will ripen every day or two, so keep picking them at their best. Eat fresh, or use in jams (pp.128–129) or cordials (pp.144–145).

CUT ARTICHOKES
Globe artichokes are ready to cut now. Cut them young if you like them tightly closed and tender, or let them mature more if you prefer a fuller flavour. Don't leave them too long or they become hard and inedible. Planted in April, fully mature specimens will often produce a second flush of flowerheads in late summer.

HARVEST

STRAWBERRIES

GLOBE ARTICHOKE

PEAS

FLORENCE FENNEL

PEAS OFFERING
Peas are at their best for a short time, and should be picked often and eaten soon, before their sweetness fades. Pluck the pods of shelling peas when they look full, but not solid, and are still bright green. Mangetout varieties snap cleanly in half at their prime, but might still need strings removing from pods. When the harvest is over, cut the plants down, leaving the nitrogen-rich roots in the soil.

FIRST FENNEL
Harvest Florence fennel once the bulbs reach a useful size. Either cut them with a knife as close to soil level as possible, or cut 2.5cm (1in) above the soil, leaving the stump. Crops sown in April may give a second flush of flavoursome shoots. Don't forget, the ferny leaves pack a delicious aniseed punch, too.

VEGETABLE FEAST

Pull kohl rabi and turnips, sown in spring, once they reach the size of a golf ball. Maincrop turnips are good to eat when much larger, but early varieties can become woody. Pak choi is often ready just 6 weeks after sowing, when it can be uprooted or cut about 2.5cm (1in) from the base and left to grow back. Calabrese and the first summer cauliflowers are also ready to harvest now, and mature rapidly. Cut the heads while the buds are tightly closed. Split surplus heads into florets for freezing (pp.148–149).

EARLY GARLIC

Planted in autumn, garlic is usually dug in August, but uproot some now for juicy bulbs, milder than any in the shops, and use immediately. Garlic bulbs can grow deep in the soil, so lift them with a fork. Overwintered onion varieties, planted last year (p.167), will also be ready to harvest now. Loosen the soil at their roots and lift as required.

BRASSICAS

GARLIC & ONIONS

NEW POTATOES

TASTY NEW POTATOES

Harvest new potatoes (pp.48–49) when the plants flower, loosening the soil with a fork. Lift all the tubers – any left may sprout and encourage disease.

'FOREMOST'
Good for salads, boiling and baking, this first-year variety is white-skinned, and has an excellent waxy texture.

'RED DUKE OF YORK'
A good all-rounder in the kitchen, this variety has a red skin, yellow flesh, and a dry texture. It also has a wonderfully strong flavour.

'INTERNATIONAL KIDNEY'
This is the variety widely sold in supermarkets as 'Jersey Royal'. Best boiled, it has a waxy texture and delicious, yellow flesh.

DON'T FORGET

Check your new potatoes are ready to harvest by scraping away soil from the base of the plants to reveal the tubers. If they look small, cover them again and give them longer to grow.

Try MAKING SOUP
pages 226–227

Making simple fruit jam

Easy to make and convenient to keep, homemade jams are one of the best ways to preserve soft fruit crops. All you need are surplus fruit and plenty of sugar to make delectable preserves that will retain the flavour of the fresh fruit much better than any mass-produced equivalents. Stick to single-fruit classics, such as raspberry, blackcurrant, or plum, or mix what you have grown to create something unique.

Raspberry jam

Makes 450g (1lb) of jam (2 small jars)
Takes 25–30 minutes, plus standing time
Keeps 6 months

Ingredients
650g (1½lb) fresh raspberries
Juice of ½ lemon
500g (1lb 2oz) granulated sugar

Equipment
Large, deep, wide-based saucepan or preserving pan
Wooden spoon
Jars with lids
Waxed paper covers
Labels

1 **Wash the fruit**, leave it to drain thoroughly and pick through it, removing any damaged berries. Place the berries in a large saucepan or preserving pan. Add the lemon juice and about 150ml (5fl oz) of water.

2 **Simmer the fruit** for 3–5 minutes until it has softened and the juice starts to run. Add the sugar to the pan, and stir over a low heat until it dissolves completely. Take care not to let the sugar burn.

Jo's tips

Jam sets because of the interaction of sugar and fruit acids with a substance called pectin, a setting agent which occurs naturally in plant cells. Some fruits, such as apples and plums, contain a lot of pectin, so jam made with these will set more easily than jam made with berries.

To sterilize your preserving jars, wash them in hot soapy water, place them on a rack in a moderate oven, and leave them there to dry thoroughly.

3 **Turn up the heat** and boil the mixture for 8–10 minutes. To test the setting point, put a little jam on a cold saucer. If it develops a jelly-like skin it is ready, you can turn off the heat; if not, boil for a few more minutes.

4 **Allow the jam to stand in the pan** for 15 minutes and remove any scum with a spoon. Ladle the mixture into sterilized jars while they are still warm (see Jo's Tips, left), top with the waxed discs, and screw on the lids.

Once you have opened the jam, it will keep in a refrigerator for about 1 month.

TRY THESE

Use this jam-making recipe with other fruit. The amount of sugar added varies according to the fruit used, but the ratio is always around 50:50 sugar to fruit.

Blackcurrant – This jam has a rich, dark colour and lovely sharpness. It's also one of the easiest to make.

Strawberry – The essential topping for scones can be tricky to set, so add lemon juice or use preserving sugar.

Gooseberry – Its natural tang counters the sugar perfectly, giving a delicious jam that's an unexpected pink colour.

Plum – Use a glut of fruit to produce plenty of firm-textured jam, but remember to remove the stones first.

MAKING SIMPLE FRUIT JAM

July: ready to eat

Revel in the bonanza of berries and currants and remember to preserve plenty for leaner months ahead. Tasty tomatoes, peppers, and cucumbers will be ready to harvest, along with crisp French and runner beans.

Kohl rabi are best diced and boiled

Enjoy a cornucopia of **currants**

Globe artichokes make elegant eating

Eat fresh **onions** and **shallots**

Make the most of **calabrese** and **summer cauliflower**

Crop **herbs** often to encourage tasty new shoots

French and **runner beans** are ready to pick, cook, and eat

Eat new season **summer raspberries**

Gooseberries are going over soon, so pick what you can

First **tomatoes** – a summer high

Rhubarb finishes this month – make fools, pies, and crumbles

Steam **spinach** and fresh **summer cabbage**

If you've run out of spinach, use colourful **Swiss chard** instead

Spring onions, cooked or raw, add flavour to many dishes

Strawberries – don't miss a single berry

Don't forget what's underground – tasty roots like **beetroots** and **turnips**

Delicious **new potatoes** are best cooked simply, and eaten often

Eat fresh **pak choi**, and crisp **Chinese cabbage**

Florence fennel adds a sweet aniseed-tang to a variety of summer dishes

The first **blackberries** are a must

Pick your **courgettes** often for a long crop

Salad is the essence of summer and now is peak **lettuce** season

Add **edible flowers** to your salads for extra colour

Cherries and **apricots** don't keep; eat quickly or preserve them now *pages 162–163*

pages 162–163

Cut-and-come-again salads do just that, again and again

Cucumbers right on cue

Fiery **summer radishes** are so easy to grow

Curiously-shaped **summer squash** are delicious roasted

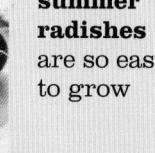

Pick **peas** and **mangetout** when young and tender, and freeze a surplus *pages 148–149*

pages 148–149

New **peppers** are a sweet treat

July: what to sow

STILL TIME TO SOW

Outdoors, sow: radish (p.27), kohl rabi (p.41), turnip, calabrese, (p.54), Florence fennel, endive (p.74), kale, lettuce, cauliflower (p.75), carrots (p.94), chicory, chard (p.95), and Chinese cabbage (p.110). Plant late maincrop potatoes (p.83).

BETTER BEETROOT

HARVEST: AUG–OCT

This is your last chance to sow beetroot outdoors for an autumn crop. Choose round varieties, and sow 2cm (¾in) deep, thinning to 10cm (4in).

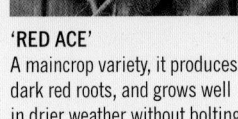
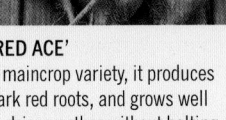
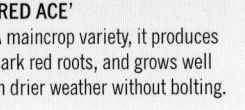
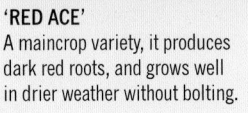

'RED ACE'
A maincrop variety, it produces dark red roots, and grows well in drier weather without bolting.

'CHIOGGIA PINK'
The plump, red and white striped roots fade to pink when cooked, but are sweet and tender to eat.

'PABLO'
This variety is a good all-rounder that can be grown for early baby roots, as well as autumn crops.

SOW

BEETROOT

LATE SEASON PEAS

SPRING CABBAGE & WINTER RADISH

SOW AUTUMN PEAS

HARVEST: SEP–OCT

Act now, and there's still time go grow a fresh crop of peas in time for autumn. Choose dwarf varieties of shelling-types or mangetout, and sow them direct.

1 PREPARE THE SITE
To avoid summer heat, pick a slightly shaded spot and prepare the soil for planting. You can also use large containers, kept shaded.

2 SOW THE SEED
Sow seed 4cm (1½in) deep in drills, spaced 15–20cm (6–8in) apart. Station-sow in pots at the same depths and distances.

3 GROW THEM ON
Cover the seed with soil and insert pea sticks or plastic netting for support. Keep well watered and tie new growth to supports at first.

COLD SEASON CROPS

There always seems to be a cabbage to sow and this month it's spring varieties, like 'Pixie'. These can be sown in a seedbed, but if space is tight, try sowing them in modules outdoors to plant out later, once mature enough. Large winter radishes should also be sown outside now, 1cm (½in) deep, in drills spaced 30cm (12in) apart. Thin to 15cm (6in) spacing for good-sized roots.

HARVEST: VARIOUS

July: what to plant

PLANTING LEEKS OUTSIDE

HARVEST: **DEC–APR**

Late varieties of leek, such as 'Musselburgh' (p.225), sown in late spring into trays or in a seedbed, should be large enough to plant out.

Prepare the site by weeding it thoroughly, and dig in plenty of well-rotted compost to encourage strong, leafy growth.

1 LIFT AND SEPARATE
Carefully lift the young leeks from the seedbed, or tip them from their tray, and separate the roots.

2 PLANT DEEPLY
Leeks need to be planted into holes, 15cm (6in) deep, to give them blanched, white stems. Use a dibber.

3 PROVIDE SPACE
Leave room to grow. Space the plants at 15cm (6in) intervals, in rows 30cm (12in) apart.

4 ALLOW TO SETTLE
Water well but don't firm the soil. Let the holes naturally fill with earth, blanching the stems.

LEEKS

PLANT

STRAWBERRIES

ENDIVE & WINTER CABBAGE

SUMMER BERRIES

Strawberries do well on a free-draining, sunny site, where plenty of well-rotted manure has been added. Avoid beds where strawberries have been grown recently because they're prone to soil-borne diseases. Plant until early autumn for fruit next year, spacing the plants about 45cm (18in) apart, with 75cm (30in) between rows. Position the crown at the base of the leaves level with the soil.

HARVEST: **JUN–SEP**

TASTY LEAVES

Plant out endive and winter cabbage, sown April (p.74) and May (p.95). Both crops like a sunny bed and moist, fertile soil. Space the cabbages 50cm (20in) apart each way, and the endive, 30cm (12in). Cover cabbages with fine net to keep out butterflies. Crop them December – March. Harvest the endive September – March.

HARVEST: **VARIOUS**

Strawberries

Strawberries are the ultimate summer fruit treat and it's possible to grow them in any garden, either in the soil or containers. They are prone to disease, so plants are usually replaced, and beds moved, every 3 years. To extend the fruiting season, grow strawberries under cover, and plant perpetual and day-neutral types.

TAKE YOUR PICK

Summer strawberries

These are the strawberries that are worth waiting for. Warmed by the early summer sun, their syrupy sweet aroma and smooth juicy flesh must be one of the best things it's possible to produce from your own garden.

The trouble with summer-fruiting varieties is that they only fruit for 2–3 weeks and that's your lot. Where there's space, grow a combination of early-, mid- and late-season varieties for a succession of fruit from late May until the middle of July. They can also be moved into the greenhouse or cloched in late winter, which should give berries 3 weeks earlier than unprotected plants.

If you are looking for a crop in the first year, buy cold-stored runners in late spring, plant them straight away, and all being well you should have a harvest in July. Ordinary field-grown plants that are potted up for sale in late summer should crop well the following year if planted before autumn sets in.

Perpetual-fruiting

Also known as 'ever-bearing' and 'remontant' strawberries, these varieties produce sporadic bursts of fruit from late summer until they are stopped by the first autumn frosts. If the weather is not too cold, and you can cover them with cloches, plants may continue fruiting into midwinter, especially container-grown plants moved under cover. Their flavour and texture are rarely considered a match for summer-fruiting strawberries, but modern varieties are starting to come close, and their yields are improving too. Plant them in late summer or early autumn for a crop the following year. Replace plants annually if possible, because they won't produce as many berries in following seasons.

All-season strawberries

Different again are day-neutral strawberries, which have been bred in America to be insensitive to day-length. This means that they can grow and fruit at any time of year, as long as the temperature is kept at a minimum of 10°C (50°F). Their dry, firm flesh means they are no real competition for summer-fruiting varieties, but they are worth planting in pots midsummer and moving into the greenhouse in mid-autumn for flushes of fruit right through winter. Try them indoors on a bright windowsill.

STRAWBERRIES

SUMMER-FRUITING

1 'Honeoye' is a reliable variety that gives a good crop of juicy, bright red fruits in early summer. Disease-resistant, it is a good choice for beginners. Try growing it in containers.

2 'Symphony' is a late-season variety that fruits mid-July, giving a good crop. The firm fruit have a rich flavour, and are delicious fresh or cooked. Grow it with an early variety for a longer harvest.

3 'Pegasus' gives a large crop of sweet, juicy berries, mid-season, June to July. The fruit are firm and last well once picked, but are best eaten fresh. This variety has good disease resistance.

4 'Florence' is a straightforward variety to grow that gives a good crop of large, firm, dark red berries in midsummer. It is resistant to pests and diseases, so is a good choice to grow organically.

5 'Korona' is a reliable, early variety that gives a generous harvest of large, red, sweet-tasting fruit in June and July. It is disease resistant. Plant it with a later variety for a prolonged crop.

PERPETUAL VARIETIES

6 'Mara de Bois' produces sweet, fragrant fruit, with a delicious wild strawberry flavour. It fruits twice, early and late summer, or you can remove the earlier flowers for a stronger late crop.

7 'Flamenco' crops early and late summer, producing occasional fruit in between. The fruits are large, firm, and juicy, with a good flavour. They are very good for freezing (pp.150–151).

ALL-SEASON STRAWBERRIES

8 'Fern' will crop whenever it's warm enough, producing good-sized, bright red fruit. Plants have berries at different stages, making them attractive to grow in pots. Good for freezing.

9 'Selva' gives a good crop of large red berries throughout summer and into autumn. The fruits have a dry texture and a mild flavour, and are best used for making jam (pp.128–129).

July: what to do

EARTH UP BRASSICAS

Lofty winter brassicas, such as purple sprouting broccoli and Brussels sprouts, can be rocked or pulled out of the soil by autumn and winter winds. Now is the time to get them well anchored in the ground, ready for a change in the weather. Draw up soil around the base of their stems and firm it as they grow. In exposed gardens it is worth staking each plant as well.

PINCH OUT

Climbing French and runner beans will keep going upwards for as long as you let them, so pinch out their leading shoots when they reach the top of their supports. This helps divert energy into the production of flowers and beans, and prevents tangled stems.

TEND

BRASSICAS

BEANS

BRASSICA PESTS

TOMATOES

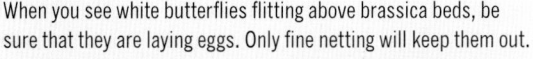

CABBAGE WHITE CAUTION

When you see white butterflies flitting above brassica beds, be sure that they are laying eggs. Only fine netting will keep them out.

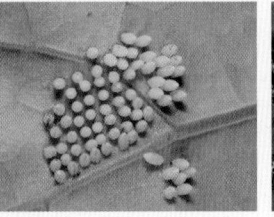
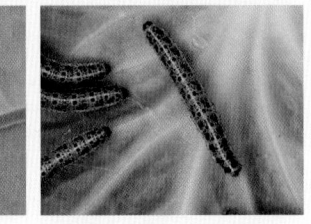

EGGS

Check the undersides of brassica leaves. If you have good eyesight, you will see clusters of the cabbage white butterfly's tiny pale eggs.

CATERPILLARS

Hoards of hungry green or black speckled caterpillars will soon hatch out. Pick them off before they start to devour your crops.

STOP YOUR CORDONS

If you are growing cordon tomatoes (pp.60–61), it's time to "stop" them, so they develop fruit rather than leaves. Pinch out the tops of plants when they reach the top of their canes or the apex of the greenhouse. Stop outdoor plants after they have formed four or five trusses of flowers and fruit. Water your plants regularly to help prevent the fruit splitting (pp.122–123) or developing blossom end rot, right (p.240).

TRIM TRAINED TREES

Apple and pear trees that have been trained into cordons, espaliers, or step-overs, need pruning this month. A trim will maintain the shape of the tree and prevent new growth from taking up space needed by the developing fruit. Use clean, sharp secateurs to cut back new shoots coming from the main stem to three leaves from their base. Also cut back shoots arising from existing fruiting spurs or sideshoots to one leaf.

SUMMER TRIM

Acid cherries fruit mostly on shoots formed the previous year, and established trees must be pruned now to encourage new growth for next year. After harvesting, and into early autumn, cut back a quarter of the shoots that bore fruit to a healthy bud near their base. Also cut damaged or unproductive wood from older acid cherry and plum trees.

APRICOT FAN

PRUNE APPLES & PEARS

ACID CHERRIES & PLUMS

SUMMER FAN PRUNING

Summer pruning of established, fan-trained apricots, plums, and cherries is important, because it helps to form fruiting wood for future years.

1 TIE IN
Choose which new shoots you want to grow on for producing fruit and tie them into the fan where they will fill gaps.

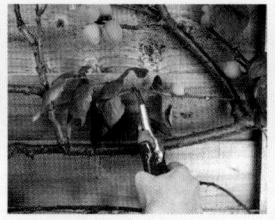

2 SHORTEN
Look for new shoots that you don't need to tie in to form part of the framework and shorten them to six leaves from their base.

3 CUT BACK FURTHER
After the fruit has cropped, the untied shoots that you have already shortened need further pruning. Cut them back to three leaves.

DON'T FORGET

If you are going on holiday, ask friends or neighbours to water your plants. Tell them to reward themselves by picking any fruit or vegetables that ripen during your absence.

July: more to do

PEST WATCH

Treat large infestations of aphids (p.236) on your crops; they can spread cucumber mosaic virus (p.241), causing leaves and fruits of cucumbers and courgettes to become blotchy and distorted. Destroy any plants showing symptoms. Also look out for gooseberry sawfly (p.237), whitefly (p.239), and caterpillars.

TRAIN GRAPE VINES

Vines, grown indoors or out, are commonly trained as cordons, with a single vertical main stem and horizontal laterals that carry flowers and fruit. In summer, pinch out any weak flowers to leave one truss per lateral, then cut each lateral back to two leaves beyond the flower truss. Cut back any lateral without flowers to five leaves, and any sideshoots from the laterals to one leaf. Thin the fruit in each bunch while small.

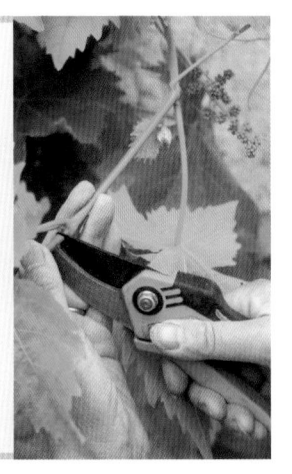

TEND

INSECT PESTS

GREENHOUSE CROPS

CURLY ENDIVE

GRAPES

DAILY CARE

In a hot summer, greenhouse crops need daily attention. Container plants need watering once a day and feeding with a high-potash fertilizer weekly once the first fruit has set. Good ventilation is also vital to cool the greenhouse and create air movement to help stop fungal diseases. Open all vents and doors fully on hot days, but close them at least partially at night to prevent plants being chilled by low temperatures.

BLANCHING

Blanching whitens and sweetens stems and leaves. Blanch endive when it is mature. Cover the centre with a plate, or put a pot over the whole plant, for about 10 days. With trench celery (p.98), either tie the stems loosely with twine and gradually earth them up, or tie a collar around them when the stems are about 30cm (12in) tall.

ENCOURAGE YOUR BEANS
In hot, dry summer weather, runner bean flowers may be less likely to set, which means that no beans will start to form. To help prevent this, give the plants plenty of water at their bases: soak them well at least two or three times a week if the weather is particularly dry. You can also mist the flowers with water using a fine spray. If you have a persistent problem, it's worth experimenting with white-flowered varieties, such as 'White Lady', which seem to set beans more reliably in hot weather.

THIN OUT FRUIT
The natural 'June drop' of fruitlets (p.121) can continue into July. Once this has finished, continue to thin fruit by hand. On apple trees, remove more of the fruitlets to leave one or two apples per cluster. Pears don't require as much thinning as apples. Thin them once the fruit is pointing downwards, to two fruits per cluster.

RUNNER BEANS　　**APPLES & PEARS**

WEEDS

UNWELCOME PLANTS
Weed your vegetable beds regularly to prevent annual weeds seeding into the soil and the perennials establishing large, hard to remove roots. Hoe between crop rows to destroy weeds as soon as they appear, or use a hand fork to tackle stubborn patches.

HAIRY BITTERCRESS
Long seed pods develop when the flowers of this weed die down. Hairy bittercress is fairly easy to pull out when it is still in early growth.

GOOSEGRASS
Also known as cleavers, this plant has sticky leaves covered with tiny clinging hooks. It spreads rapidly and should be dug up by its roots.

GROUNDSEL
The yellow flowers of this plant develop into fluffy white seed heads like those of dandelions. Root it out before the seeds disperse.

BINDWEED
This persistent creeper and climber can quickly smother crops. It is hard to eliminate, as it can regrow from any fragment of overlooked root.

See PRUNING FRUIT IN AUTUMN pages 206–207

Pruning fruit in summer

Where autumn pruning concentrates on the long-term shape and structure of your fruit trees and bushes, the aim of summer pruning is to maintain their immediate size, health, and productivity.

Most pruning tasks now are simple to do, and take just a new minutes, and can make all the difference between having neat, fruitful plants; and a messy garden and a disappointing crop.

Cut down to size

The main focus of summer pruning is to control soft new growth, which not only attracts insect pests, but also restricts airflow at the middle of the plant, encouraging diseases, such as powdery mildew (p.243). It is also an opportunity to cut out weak or diseased growth. This is also a good time to train vines.

When pruning, always cut just above an outward-facing bud, using sharp secateurs, cutting at 45° away from the bud. This drains rainwater away from the bud, preventing disease.

RED- AND WHITECURRANTS
Now is the time to prune all of this year's new growth, except the branch leaders, back to five leaves by midsummer. The main formative pruning is done in the winter (p.206).

GOOSEBERRIES
To help prevent mildew (p.243), prune branches in the middle of the bush to improve air flow. Cut back new growth to five leaves, leaving the leading tips of the branches uncut.

Jo's tips

Gooseberry bushes have a tendency to form droopy branches. To help keep the bush upright, prune to inward- and upward-facing buds, rather than to outward-facing buds, as you normally would with other shrubs and bushes.

Blackcurrants produce their best fruit on last summer's growth, so removing new wood now will affect the following year's crop. Prune these bushes during winter instead (p.206).

SUMMER-FRUITING RASPBERRIES
As soon as each cane has finished cropping, untie it from its support and cut it at ground level to remove it completely. Tie the young canes that will fruit next year into the supports.

FAN-TRAINED FIGS
Pinch back the growing tips of new shoots to five leaves. This will encourage lower buds on the shoot to produce embryonic fruit that will overwinter and ripen next summer.

Grape vine pruning

There are two main techniques used to train and prune grapes. The "single cordon" system involves maintaining a single upright stem, from which multiple fruiting laterals are trained against wires. It is often used for indoor grapes.

The "double guyot" system entails training two new branches horizontally each year, from which upright fruiting shoots develop. This system is widely used for outdoor vines. Whichever method you use, summer pruning is essential for a good crop, and to keep your vines under control.

1 TRAIN SINGLE CORDONS
Tie in the central leader against a cane attached to a framework of horizontal wires. Cut back all lateral stems that have no flowers to five leaves from the central leader.

2 CUT BACK LATERALS
On mature plants, cut back flowering lateral stems to two leaves beyond the last truss, and tie them to the wires. Thin surplus trusses and pinch out sideshoots to one leaf.

1 TRAIN DOUBLE GUYOT GRAPES
Tie in new vertical shoots growing from branches trained horizontally in autumn (p.205). Remove growing tips at the top wire and any sideshoots. Thin trusses to every 30cm (12in).

2 CHOOSE THREE STEMS
Train three sideshoots upwards from the vine's centre to provide next year's fruiting arms. Tie them into the supporting wires, and pinch back any sideshoots to one leaf as they grow.

PRUNING TOOLS

Choosing the right tool for the job makes pruning easier, and also helps prevent accidental damage, such as tears, occurring to your plants.

Secateurs must be clean and sharp. Use them to cut new growth, and woody material up to pencil thickness.

Pruning saws are ideal for thicker stems and branches, although you need good access to saw effectively.

Loppers can be used to cut stems too thick for secateurs, but too thin for a saw. Avoid twisting them as you cut.

Bow saws are only suitable for cutting thick branches. They are liable to tear smaller stems, causing damage.

July: what to harvest

PLENTIFUL BERRIES
Blackberries and summer raspberries will start cropping over the next few weeks, so pick every couple of days. Pick raspberries when they've turned a rich pinky-red, pulling the soft fruit away from the core. Blackberries should be harvested when entirely black and glossy, and often come away with the core still in place. Both fruits keep fresh for only a day or two, so freeze any extra (pp.150–151).

CUCUMBERS NOW
Sown in April (p.74) and grown indoors, the season's first cucumbers will be ready for picking now. Cut the fruit with some stalk, once they are a usable size. Baby fruits are especially delicious. Pick regularly to avoid a glut because cucumbers cannot be stored.

HARVEST

RASPBERRIES

CUCUMBERS

BEANS

CURRANTS

PICK BEANS OFTEN
The secret with French and runner beans is crop often. Pick the pods small and tender for the tastiest crop, which will also help keep the plants productive for longer. French beans that are past their best can be podded for delicious green haricot beans. Whole beans freeze well, if you get overwhelmed, (pp.148–149), but allow some to develop and ripen fully for seed (pp.172–173).

CURRANT CROP
Currants of all colours are cropping this month in abundance. Pick sprigs of red- and whitecurrants whole, as they ripen. Usually, blackcurrants develop over a longer period, so pick the berries individually. Currants don't keep; pick and use them quickly, and freeze any that you can't eat straight away.

PICK COURGETTES AND SUMMER SQUASH

These two crops are closely related and are grown in the same way (p.74 and p.115). They can both be picked when tiny, tender, and at their sweetest, or left to grow larger for stuffing.

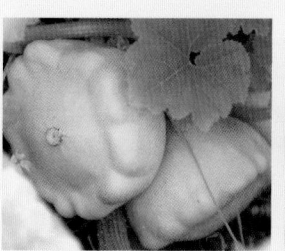

'PATTY PAN'
This variety produces a large crop of saucer-shaped fruit that can be eaten whole when small and young, or allowed to grow on to full-size.

'SUNBURST'
Produces bright yellow fruit that can be harvested as a baby vegetable, or allowed to grow on. They taste delicious when roasted or fried.

'TROMBONCINO'
These elongated fruit can reach up to 1m (3ft) long but are best cut when they reach 30cm (12in). Allow plants to trail or train upwards.

ALSO HARVEST

With lots of fruit and vegetables ready to crop this month, check your broad beans — and don't overlook leafy crops. Harvest pak choi, Chinese cabbage, and red- and sugarloaf chicory until autumn.

TOMATOES

ONIONS & SHALLOTS

COURGETTES & SQUASHES

INDOOR TOMATO TIME

Tomatoes are a sure sign of summer, and the first indoor fruit, sown in spring, are ready to harvest. Pick them as soon as the entire fruit turns red or yellow, depending on variety. Cherry-types should ripen first, followed by salad tomatoes, plum varieties, then the mighty beefsteaks. Pick regularly to encourage a prolonged crop. Best eaten fresh, if you have surplus tomatoes, try oven-drying them (pp.160–161).

FIRST ONIONS

Start lifting onions and shallots now as you need them, as soon as they're big enough to use. At this stage the edible leaves should still be green, and the bulbs juicy, with a slightly milder flavour than later, dried harvests. Lift whole clumps of shallots together, as they will keep well in their fresh state for a week or so.

See MAKING SIMPLE CHUTNEY pages 212–213

Making fruit cordials

What could be better than capturing the essence of home-grown soft fruit in delicious cordials, to enjoy on long, hot summer days? A simple combination of fresh fruit, sugar, and water are all it takes to make these quick and easy syrups. Children love the fruity flavours and bold candy colours; just dilute to taste and serve with a straw. You can also freeze the cordial to make refreshing ice lollies.

Blackcurrant cordial

Makes 500ml (16fl oz) of cordial
Takes 25 minutes
Keeps 1–2 months, refrigerated

Ingredients
450g (1lb) blackcurrants
(or loganberries)
350g (12oz) caster sugar
1 tsp citric acid

Equipment
Large saucepan
Wooden spoon
Fine sieve
Measuring jug
Sterilized glass bottles

Jo's tips

If you make more cordial than you can use up in 1 or 2 months, try freezing some of it, undiluted, in ice-cube trays. It will keep well like that for up to 6 months, and you can use the ice cubes to cool, brighten up, and flavour glasses of water or other drinks.

Don't just dilute your cordial with plain water, try adding some fizz to it with sparkling water or lemonade. For a colourful and fruity 'Kir Royale' cocktail, mix champagne with homemade blackcurrant cordial.

1 Place the fruit in a pan and add just enough water to cover the bottom. Simmer the fruit very gently for the least time necessary to extract the juice, 3–5 minutes only. Pulp the fruit with a wooden spoon as it cooks.

2 Remove from the heat and allow the fruit mixture to cool a little, so it's safe to handle. Pour the fruit through a muslin or fine sieve over a jug, squashing the cooked fruit to extract as much juice as possible.

3 Pour the juice into a measuring jug and add 350g (12oz) of sugar to every 500ml (16fl oz) of liquid. Add the citric acid, and keep stirring until all the sugar is fully dissolved. Spoon off any floating fruit debris.

4 Pour the syrup into sterilized bottles, fasten the caps, and allow it to cool fully before storing it in the refrigerator. Drink the cordial diluted with water, adding plenty of ice cubes. Drink diluted cordial straightaway.

Homemade cordials are an additive-free alternative to those available in shops, and rich in colour and flavour.

TRY THESE

Many different fruits can be used to make delicious summer cordials with the technique shown. Mix fruits and vary the amount of sugar to taste.

Raspberries – A true taste of summer, this cordial is best with lemon juice added to give it a little acidity.

Rhubarb – More of a grown-up treat, rhubarb gives cordial a sharp tang that is wonderfully refreshing.

Strawberries – Cook these delicate fruits very gently to preserve their bright red colour and sweetness.

Redcurrants – Although weakly flavoured, redcurrants add glorious colour to mixed fruit cordials.

MAKING FRUIT CORDIALS

Making relishes and pesto

Relishes are tangy sauces that are easy to make and the perfect way to use up and store a glut of vegetables and fruit from the garden. You can cook or pickle all kinds of produce in this way to provide delicious homemade accompaniments to burgers, cheese, cold meats, and barbecued food. Experiment with textures and flavours: smooth or chunky, sweet or spicy, fiery hot or mellow and fruity.

RECIPE IDEAS

Sweet corn and pepper relish

Makes 1kg (2¼lb) (2 small jars)
Takes 35–40 minutes
Keeps 3 months

Ingredients
4 sweet corn cobs
2 red peppers, deseeded and diced
1 red chilli, deseeded and sliced
2 celery sticks, sliced thinly
1 onion, sliced
450ml (15fl oz) white wine vinegar
225g (8oz) granulated sugar
2 tsp sea salt
2 tsp mustard powder
½ tsp ground turmeric

1 **Holding the corn cobs upright,** strip off the kernels with a sharp knife. Blanch the kernels in a pan of boiling water for 2 minutes and then drain. Place all the ingredients in a large saucepan and bring to the boil.

2 **Stir the mixture** until the sugar dissolves, then lower the heat and simmer for 15–20 minutes, stirring frequently. Let the mixture thicken until a spoon drawn across the base of the pan leaves little liquid behind.

Jo's tips

Cucumbers make an ideal relish base. Cut out the seeds and salt the cucumber for an hour to draw off excess moisture.

If you want your pesto to last for a few months, freeze some of it in ice-cube trays and then bag it up when frozen.

To sterilize your preserving jars, wash them in hot soapy water, place them on a rack in a moderate oven, and leave them there to dry thoroughly.

3 **Check the relish for flavour,** and adjust the seasoning according to taste, before carefully ladling it into warm, sterilized preserving jars (see Jo's Tips, left). The relish should have a wetter consistency than chutney.

4 **Seal the jars** with non-metallic lids and leave them to cool. Label, and store your relish in a cool, dark place for up to 3 months. You can use the relish straight away; once it has been opened keep it in a refrigerator.

Preserve the taste of summer garden produce by making a few jars of relish for your cupboard.

TRY PESTO

Traditional homemade pesto perks up pasta and adds vibrant flavour to many meat and fish dishes. It is made in minutes and needs no cooking.

Makes 200g (7oz) (1 small jar)
Takes 10 minutes
Keeps 2 weeks in refrigerator or 6 months frozen

Ingredients

65g (2½oz) basil
1 garlic clove, lightly crushed
30g (1oz) pine nuts
freshly ground black pepper
30g (1oz) Parmesan cheese, grated
7 tbsp extra virgin olive oil
salt to taste

1 Pull the leaves off the basil and put them in a food processor with the garlic, pine nuts, black pepper, Parmesan, and 2 tablespoons of the olive oil, and blend coarsely.
2 With the blender running, add another 4 tablespoons of olive oil, a little at a time, and blend to a shiny paste. Add salt to taste.
3 Spoon the pesto into a sterilized jar (see Jo's Tips, opposite page) and top with the remaining oil to make the mixture airtight. Put the lid tightly on the jar and store in a fridge. If you use a little at a time, cover the rest with more oil.

MAKING RELISHES AND PESTO

Freezing vegetables

Freezing is a convenient way to store summer gluts. It preserves fruits and vegetables, and their nutrients, for several months. Some freeze well simply cleaned, while some should be blanched – briefly immersed in boiling water – first. Others are only worth freezing once made into soups, sauces, or purées. Get to know what works; there's nothing more satisfying than having a freezer filled for winter.

Freezing vegetables

There are two general methods to use when freezing vegetables, depending on how long you want to store them. For short-term storage (less than 3 months), cut the vegetables into usable-sized pieces and freeze them spread out on a tray. Then bag them up, return them to the freezer, and use them as required.

For longer-term freezing, you need to blanch the vegetables before freezing to destroy natural enzymes that spoil flavour, colour, and texture. Freeze root vegetables only after cooking into soups or stews first or else their texture will be spoiled.

1 **Bring a large pan of water** to a vigorous boil. Immerse smaller vegetables for 2 minutes, and larger ones for 4 minutes only. Drain the vegetables into a large strainer or net, to remove them all at the same time.

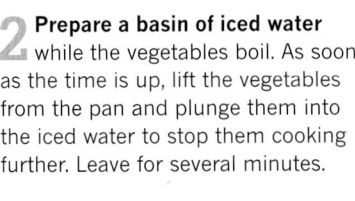

2 **Prepare a basin of iced water** while the vegetables boil. As soon as the time is up, lift the vegetables from the pan and plunge them into the iced water to stop them cooking further. Leave for several minutes.

HARVESTING IDEAS

Jo's tips

Always wrap food securely, and squeeze as much air as possible out of freezer bags before sealing. This helps to prevent freezer burn, which dries out frozen produce and causes it to spoil prematurely.

Label food clearly, including a date, so that you can identify what soup is what in 3 months' time, and also so you can use up older produce first.

3 **Remove the vegetables from** the iced water as soon as they have cooled, and drain them. Allow them to dry in a colander, or spread them out on clean tea cloths or kitchen paper and blot them dry.

4 **When dry, divide the vegetables** into portion-sized quantities, pack them into freezer bags or sealed containers, label and date them, and place in the freezer. They will keep well for up to 6 months.

Freeze vegetables as individual portions and you can then simply defrost what you need.

TRY THESE

This freezing technique is suitable for a wide range of vegetables, including those listed below. Try to use all frozen vegetables within 6 months.

French and runner beans – Best picked young, when they snap between your fingers. Blanch before freezing.

Sprouting broccoli – It's easy to end up with a glut of broccoli, so cut the spears, wash, blanch, and tray freeze.

Asparagus – For asparagus to eat into late summer, blanch thin stems for 2 minutes, thick ones for 4 minutes.

Herbs – Finely crop herbs, such as basil and mint, and freeze them into handy cubes in an ice tray.

FREEZING VEGETABLES

Freezing fruit

When you grow your own, summer gluts of fruits such as berries, currants, and plums are unavoidable. The good thing is that fruit is quick and easy to freeze; you'll be able to make enough delicious pies and desserts to see you right through autumn, winter, and beyond. Freezing retains the original flavour and texture of most fruits and is also the best way to preserve their valuable nutrient content.

HARVESTING IDEAS

Tray freezing

This simple freezing method suits small soft fruits well. All you need to do is spread the berries out in a single layer on a baking tray, quickly freeze them, then bag-up or box the fruit for long-term storage. Putting the fruit on a tray allows it to freeze faster than it would if densely packed into a bag or box. Rapid freezing creates smaller ice crystals than slow freezing, causing less damage to the fruit's cells and preventing everything from collapsing into a juicy mush on thawing. Tray freezing also stops fruit freezing into a solid lump, so you can take what you need, rather than having to defrost the whole batch.

1 **Choose ripe, undamaged** fruit and freeze it as soon after harvesting as possible. Pick through it to remove any leaves and stems. Wipe or wash the fruit if necessary and spread it out in a single layer on a baking tray.

2 **Place the tray** in the coldest part of the freezer and allow the fruit to freeze until it is completely solid. This should take no longer than 2 hours for small soft fruits such as blueberries or currants.

Jo's tips

Cherries and plums both freeze well, but you should remove the stones first, otherwise they will give the fruit a bitter taint.

Strawberries are not well suited to freezing whole, because they have a high water content, which causes them to become soggy once thawed. Try making sorbet, ice cream, or freezing them as a purée instead.

3 **For long-term freezing**, transfer the fruit from the tray into freezer bags or boxes. Package it in single portions or larger quantities, as required. After tray freezing, the fruits shouldn't stick together in the bags.

4 **Once you have filled the bags**, gently squeeze them to remove as much air as possible and then seal them. Label and date each bag. Put them in the freezer, where they will keep for 6 months.

Tray frozen before being
bagged up, blueberries will
keep their shape and texture.

TRY THESE

Tray freezing can be used to preserve a wide range of soft fruits. All of those below will freeze well to give you a taste of summer in the depths of winter.

Gooseberries – Top and tail these sharp, green berries before freezing so they can be used from the bag.

Raspberries – Remove the central plugs prior to freezing and wipe clean any dirty fruit rather than washing it.

Cherries – Remove the stalks and stones before freezing. They are worth the work for their gorgeous flavour.

Currants – All currants are easy to freeze. Just pull them gently from their stems directly onto the tray.

FREEZING FRUIT

August: ready to eat

Keep a close eye on crops to pick them perfectly ripe. Beat the birds
to plums and damsons, and pluck chillies as they turn orange and red.
Garlic, onions, and shallots are delicious now – dry some for storing.

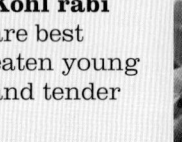

Kohl rabi
are best
eaten young
and tender

It's peak season for
onions and **shallots**
– use them fresh and
leave some for drying

Enjoy plentiful salad crops,
such as **cucumber**, **lettuce**,
radish, and **tomatoes**

Still time for **new potatoes**

Include fresh **calabrese**
and **summer cauliflower**
with your Sunday roasts

Relish new season
aubergines this month

Eat the last **red-**,
white-, and
blackcurrants before
they get past their best

Make the most of
Chinese cabbage,
pak choi, and **summer
cabbage** this month

Eat **globe
artichokes**

Pick
**sweet
peppers**

Keep cropping your
cut-and-come-again
salad leaves

Use the
last of
the **fresh
garlic**

Harvest **herbs** now
and use them fresh
or dry them for later
in the year *page 161*

Broad bean season
is nearly over

New season **chillies** are hot this month

Keep eating your spinach beet and Swiss chard this month

Eat the season's first **melons**

Eat **courgettes** young or allow them to grow on as marrows for a later crop

High summer brings **peaches**, **nectarines**, and **apricots** to the table

Florence fennel doesn't store well so use it now while it's still good to eat

New season **blueberries**

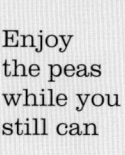

Enjoy the peas while you still can

Raw or cooked, enjoy **raspberries** and **blackberries**

Serve wilted **spinach** with butter and nutmeg – it's lovely

Cut your first new season **celery**

Feast yourself on new season **plums and damsons**

It's a beanfeast, with **French** and **runner beans** ready now

Carrots, **turnips**, and **beetroots** will keep cropping for weeks – plan storing some for winter *pages 210–211*

August can be **fig heaven**

Strawberries are still going strong; eat them fresh and store what you can for later in the year

August: what to sow

STILL TIME TO SOW

The growing season is coming to an end, but at the start of the month, there's still time to sow Swiss chard and leaf beet (p.95) directly, and red and sugarloaf chicory (p.95) into modules.

LATE SEASON CROPS

HARVEST: **AUG–DEC**

Make one more sowing of these quick crops now for a last harvest before the end of autumn, although they may need cloching in cooler areas.

ROCKET
Sow in a slightly shaded bed to prevent bolting, 1cm (½in) deep in drill, thinning to 15cm (6in) apart.

KOHL RABI
Ready to crop in 4–5 weeks, sow in 1cm (½in) deep drills, spaced 25cm (10in). Thin to 10cm (4in).

TURNIP
Sow like kohl rabi, and lift some as baby roots in a few weeks, allowing others to mature fully.

JAPANESE ONIONS

CARROTS

ROCKET, TURNIPS, & KOHL RABI

SPRING BULBS
Certain types of onion, often described as Japanese varieties, can be sown towards the end of late summer, and overwintered for an early crop of bulbs in late spring. Try sowing a variety such as 'Buffalo' or 'Senshyu', in rows 30cm (12in) apart and thin to 5–10cm (2–4in) apart. This should give you sturdy young plants that will see out the winter and shoot away quickly in spring.

HARVEST: **MAY–JUN**

LAST CARROTS
To make a last outdoor sowing of carrots, use a faster maturing early-variety, like 'Early Nantes', and cloche the crop at the onset of autumn. Sow thinly in drills with 15cm (6in) between them, and thin seedlings to 5cm (2in) apart. A real advantage of sowing carrots this late is that they shouldn't have any problems with carrot fly.

HARVEST: **AUG–DEC**

August: what to plant

HARDY WINTER CROPS

HARVEST: **VARIOUS**

Spring cauliflowers and winter sprouting broccoli, sown in early summer, will now be ready to transplant into their winter beds. Space them 60cm (2ft) apart each way, firm the soil around plants to stop them rocking in windy weather, and net to keep off hungry pigeons.

'CLARET'
A sprouting broccoli, this is a late maturing variety that crops well into early spring. Good for cooler regions.

'RUDOLPH'
This early sprouting broccoli produces flavour-rich, dark florets in midwinter. Freeze surpluses.

'WINTER AALSMEER'
For well-formed, smaller curds, try this hardy variety. It ripens over a longer period than most hybrids.

'WALCHEREN WINTER PILGRIM'
Very winter hardy, this robust cauliflower gives a good spring crop of large white heads.

WINTER CAULIFLOWER

BABY LEAF SALAD

CHICORY

PLANT

SALAD LEAVES 24/7

HARVEST: **SEP–FEB**

If you've been sowing salad crops all summer, transplant some seedlings now and bring them under cover for fresh leaves in the lean winter months.

1 PICK YOUR PLANTS
Choose a selection of baby leaf plants, picking the largest, heathiest specimens. Lift them with as much root as possible.

2 POT THEM UP
Fill a large container with compost and plant the baby leaf plants, leaving enough space around each one to grow a little.

3 GROW AND HARVEST
Water well and grow the plants on under cover. Harvest regularly, giving the plants time to re-grow, especially in cold periods.

WINTER CHICORY

Outdoor chicory crops are prone to rotting in wet winter conditions. To enjoy a reliable harvest of leaves during the coldest months, plant module-raised seedlings, sown at the beginning of this month, under cover in a greenhouse or cold frame. Choose red or sugarloaf varieties and plant out them as soon as they're large enough, spacing the plants 20–25cm (8–10in) apart. Water in well.

HARVEST: **OCT–MAR**

August: what to do

LET IN LIGHT

Tomatoes, winter squashes, and pumpkins all need plenty of sunlight to ripen, but the fruit is often shaded by foliage. By late summer, with growth slowing, it's safe to remove some of their overshadowing leaves. Take off the lower leaves of tomato plants so that the more mature fruit trusses near the base ripen first. Any leaves that are shading squashes and pumpkins can be removed.

POTATO BLIGHT

A fungal disease called potato blight commonly occurs in warm, wet summers. The infection causes brown patches on the edges of leaves. Remove affected plant tops as soon as they start to die down. Don't compost them; ideally burn them.

TEND

SWEET CORN

TOMATOES & SQUASHES

RASPBERRIES

POTATOES

READY TO EAT?

Sweet corn tastes good only when perfectly ripe. Wait until the tassels at the top of the cob turn dark brown before checking.

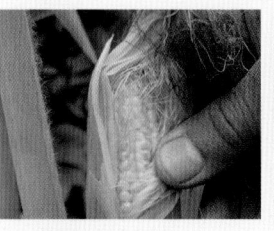

1 CHECK THE COB
Carefully pull back some of the leaves covering a cob. The kernels are ripe when they are a buttery shade of pale yellow.

2 HARVEST LATER
Test several cobs, wrapping each one up again if it is not ripe. It's better to wait until next month (p.175) than pick too soon.

CUTTING CANES

As soon as the last berry is picked from summer-fruiting raspberries, cut the fruited canes right down to ground level. The new canes that came up this year will be the ones that bear next year's crop. These need to be spread evenly along the supporting wires and tied in with twine. Cut out any new canes that look weak and spindly, leaving only strong, healthy stems coming from each plant.

BEAT THE SLUGS
In some gardens, small soil-dwelling slugs can cause considerable damage by burrowing into potato crops. The spoiled parts can just be cut out if the potatoes are being eaten straight away, but if you plan to store your crop into the winter (pp.210–211), slug damage will allow rot to set in. If you see signs of slug attack on crops destined for storage, lift unmarked tubers as soon as possible to minimize the problem. Make sure the potatoes are dry before storing them in paper sacks somewhere cool and dark.

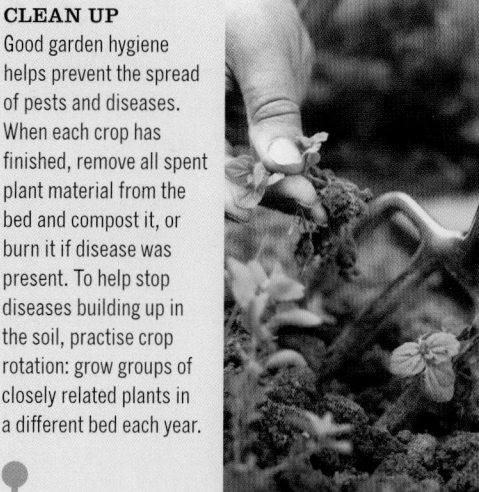

CLEAN UP
Good garden hygiene helps prevent the spread of pests and diseases. When each crop has finished, remove all spent plant material from the bed and compost it, or burn it if disease was present. To help stop diseases building up in the soil, practise crop rotation: grow groups of closely related plants in a different bed each year.

POTATOES

GARDEN HYGIENE

DISEASES

HEALTH CHECK
Hot, dry conditions in summer cause plants stress and leave them vulnerable to disease (pp.240–245). Feed and water them, and watch for danger signs.

MAGNESIUM DEFICIENCY
Look out for yellowing leaves. Plants affected include fruit trees, potatoes, and tomatoes. Feed magnesium as a foliar spray.

BROWN ROT
This fungus spreads rapidly among tree fruits, causing rot. Cut off all infected fruits, together with their branch tips, and burn them.

BOTRYTIS (GREY MOULD)
Many plants can be infected by this airborne fungus. Keeping your garden cleared of debris and dead plants is the best defence.

DON'T FORGET
To encourage your cobnuts to produce more fruit buds and to reduce vigour, snap without breaking off lateral shoots over 30cm (12in) long. This practice is called "brutting".

See STARTING A COMPOST HEAP pages 190–191

August: what to harvest

SUMMER MELONS

If your melons were sown in April (p.74) and planted in the greenhouse in May (p.101), you'll know when they're ripening because of the rich melon scent that fills the air. Melons are ready to pick when, in addition to their sweet aroma, they're slightly softer at the stalk end, and they come away from the stalk when lifted. Pick when fully ripe and eat immediately. Melons don't store well.

READY OR NOT

It can be tricky to tell when aubergines are ripe because not all varieties develop the tell-tale, smooth, shiny skin. Swelling around the middle of the fruit indicates the seeds are forming, and time to harvest. Cut and cook as soon as possible.

HARVEST

MELONS

AUBERGINE

PEPPERS & CHILLIES

CELERY

PICK YOUR PEPPERS

Both these crops need lots of heat to ripen fully, and during poor summers in cooler regions, even under glass, they may stay green.

1 PICK GREEN
Cut the first full-sized fruits of peppers and chillies while still green, to encourage further fruit to develop on the plants.

2 LEAVE TO RIPEN
Allow later fruit to mature to yellow, orange, or red for a richer, sweeter flavour. Green fruits have a slightly bitter taste.

STEM CELERY

Self-blanching celery will start to become ready over the next few weeks. You can either cut individual stems at the base to use as you need them, or lift the whole plant in one go with a fork. Sown in spring, celery is best eaten as soon as the stems are crisp and juicy. If you can't eat them all, freeze the surplus (pp.148–149), or leave plants in the ground until the first frosts. Don't wait too long, as it may become dry and pithy.

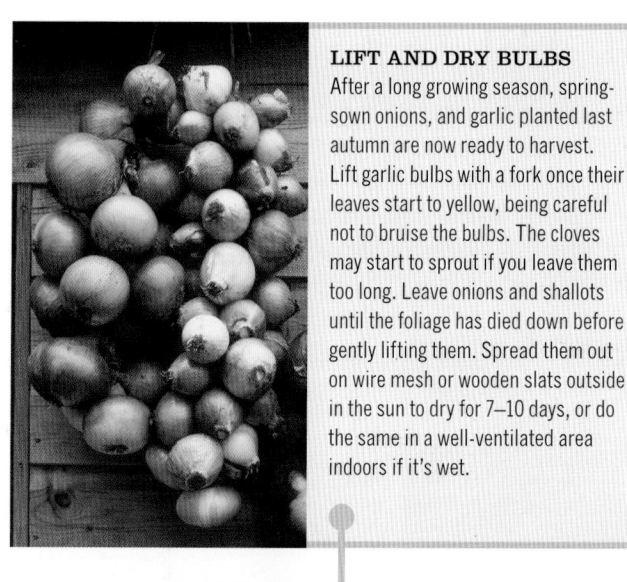

LIFT AND DRY BULBS

After a long growing season, spring-sown onions, and garlic planted last autumn are now ready to harvest. Lift garlic bulbs with a fork once their leaves start to yellow, being careful not to bruise the bulbs. The cloves may start to sprout if you leave them too long. Leave onions and shallots until the foliage has died down before gently lifting them. Spread them out on wire mesh or wooden slats outside in the sun to dry for 7–10 days, or do the same in a well-ventilated area indoors if it's wet.

RIPE TO EAT

Now is peak season for cherry, plum, damson, apricot, and peach trees, but exact ripening times depend on variety and weather. Even on a single tree, the fruit will ripen at different times, so check often. To pick, pull plums and damsons from their stalks, cut cherries with their stems, and lift and twist apricots and peaches in your palm.

ONIONS, GARLIC, & SHALLOTS

TREE FRUIT

BLUEBERRIES

BEAUTIFUL BLUEBERRIES

Blueberries, planted in autumn (p.198), crop over a few weeks. Pick and eat them as soon as possible. If dry, they will store in the fridge for a few days.

'BLUETTA'
A free-fruiting variety that bears deep blue berries, roughly 1cm (½in) across. It flowers later than many, so is good for cooler regions.

'SPARTAN'
Early-cropping variety with light blue fruit that have a sweet, tangy flavour. Like all blueberries, the taste is more intense when cooked.

'EARLIBLUE'
This variety also crops early, producing a high yield of pale blue fruit, held in conveniently large clusters. Eat fresh or freeze.

HANDY HINT

To help your chillies develop their distinctive fieriness, water them only sparingly as the fruit grows. If you prefer milder chillies, water the plants more.

Try WINE MAKING pages 180–181

Drying fruit and vegetables

Drying is a simple, effective method of preserving fruit and vegetables, for a few weeks, to several months. The key to success is ensuring the produce is totally dehydrated as any moisture allows mould to develop. In cooler regions, oven-drying is the most reliable way to dry crops with a high water content, like apples. Those with a low water content, like chillies and herbs, can be easily air-dried indoors.

HARVESTING IDEAS

Oven-drying fruit

An ordinary oven is all you need to dry gluts of fruit, such as apples, plums, and tomatoes. Wash and dry the fruit well, and halve or slice larger ones to speed up the drying process. Set the oven at a low temperature and place your produce on wire racks on the lower shelves. How long they take to dry depends on the fruit and how moist it is – the juicier it is the longer it'll be. Leave them at least 2 hours, then check them every 30 minutes. Larger fruit may take some hours.

1 **Wash the fruit well.** Leave berries whole, but cut plums and tomatoes in half. Strawberries and apples need to be sliced to dry well. Core apples, stone plums, and dip into lemon juice to prevent them browning.

2 **Lay the fruit out evenly** on a wire rack, so it doesn't overlap, and so there is plenty of room for air to circulate. If the pieces are too small to sit on a rack, arrange them on a lightly oiled baking tray instead.

Jo's tips

As an alternative way to eat dried fruit, make 'fruit leather'. Purée fruit and remove the seeds by hand or by sieving. Spread it 5mm (¼in) thick on a well-oiled baking tray. Place in the oven on a low heat for several hours until the purée is dehydrated and leathery. Break into pieces and enjoy as a snack, or add it to cereals.

If you don't have a place to hang crops, you can buy or build a wooden drying box with ventilation holes. This offers an effective way to dry home-grown produce.

3 **Switch your oven** to the lowest setting and put the fruit inside. The idea is for the food to dehydrate, not cook it. To prevent the temperature getting too high, open the oven door periodically. Check the fruit regularly.

4 **After several hours,** when the fruit feels light and dry to the touch, remove it from the oven. Allow it to cool completely before tipping it into airtight jars, sealing, and storing in a cool dark place for 2–4 weeks.

Dried apple rings will keep for a few weeks, but chillies and herbs last for months if kept dry.

Air-drying

One of the best ways to preserve crops that have a low moisture content is to air-dry them. This is a slower process than oven-drying, and is particularly well suited to chillies, bunches of herbs, and de-podded beans, which will all keep for months if properly dried and stored. All you need for this technique is somewhere indoors that is warm and well-ventilated, such as a spare room, or even a shed or garage. Avoid kitchens due to the steam caused by cooking, which prevents effective drying.

Chillies and beans – The easiest way to dry chillies and beans is to lay them out on a wire rack and place them in a dry, airy place for a few weeks. Chillies can also be threaded onto a string and hung in bunches to dry.

Herbs – Cut sprigs of woody-stemmed herbs, such as sage, sweet bay, and marjoram, and hang them in bunches somewhere dry and well ventilated. Soft-leaved herbs, such as basil and coriander, don't dry well – instead freeze them into ice cubes.

Bottling fruit in syrup

There's an air of luxury to bottled fruit that sets it apart from even the finest jams and frozen berries. Flawless, home-grown fruits, suspended in clear, richly coloured syrup, look impressive but are easy to achieve. You don't even have to cook the peaches used in this recipe. The trick to bottling is to catch your fruit at perfect ripeness; under-ripe, it'll be hard and lack flavour, over-ripe and it will disintegrate.

Bottled peaches

Makes 450ml (15fl oz) (2 small jars)
Takes about 15 minutes
Keeps 1 year

Ingredients
4–5 firm, ripe peaches
115g (4oz) granulated sugar
600ml (1 pint) water

Equipment
Large saucepan
Sharp kitchen knife
2 x preserving jars with lids

1 Remove skins from the peaches. If they are difficult to peel, dip the fruit in boiling water for about 30 seconds; the skins should then slip off easily. Cut the peaches in half and carefully remove the stones.

2 Place the sugar and water in a large pan, bring to the boil, and continue to boil for about 2 minutes, or until the sugar has dissolved. The quantities given here make a medium-sweet sugar syrup. Add more to taste.

Jo's tips

As well as peaches, other softer fruits such as berries, cherries, and plums can also be packed into jars raw and covered with sugar syrup to preserve them. Larger, firmer fruits such as apples and pears are usually cooked for a few minutes before bottling.

To sterilize your jars, wash them in hot soapy water, place them on a rack in a moderate oven, and leave them to dry thoroughly.

3 Stand your sterilized jars in a roasting tray while they are still warm (see Jo's Tips, left). Fill the jars with fruit, leaving a space of about 1cm (½in) below the rim. Ladle in the hot sugar syrup until the jars are full.

4 Seal the jars with their lids while they are still hot. Allow them to cool, add labels, and store in a dark, cool place. It takes time for the fruit and syrup to fully infuse, so leave for at least 6 weeks before opening.

Bottled fruit looks attractive on display but store it in the dark to preserve its colour.

TRY THESE

Tree fruits often crop heavily, so there are usually plenty for bottling. It's a good way of using a glut of fruit that doesn't keep, such as plums and cherries.

Figs – Leave the fruit whole, don't cut off ends and stems, and cook in a light sugar syrup for just a few minutes.

Cherries – Bottled cherries are ideal for festive desserts. Pit fruits and bottle in syrup with a splash of kirsch.

Pears – Peel the fruit, cut in half lengthways, and core before boiling in syrup for about 5 minutes.

Plums – These soft fruits can simmer in spiced syrup, or be packed into jars raw. Remove the stones first.

BOTTLING FRUIT IN SYRUP

September: ready to eat

Autumn is in the air, with early apples ready for harvest, ripe sweet corn, and pumpkins and winter squashes hardening their skins in the sunshine. Parsnips and early leeks are coming round again, too.

New season cobs of **sweet corn** are plump and ripe for picking

Cauliflowers planted out in early summer should have tight-packed curds now

Enjoy **summer peas** and **beans** while they last

Collect **seeds** for storing *pages 172–173* from herbs such as fennel, dill, and coriander

Pick a head of crunchy fresh **celery**

Use some **turnips** now, let others grow larger for storage *pages 210–211*

Eat luscious **blackberries**

Pick **spinach** sown in early summer

Globe artichokes are at the very end of their season

The **strawberry** crop will come to an end this month

It may be autumn, but **summer salad crops** continue – cucumber, lettuce, tomatoes, and radish can still be harvested

You may have a final **melon** in the greenhouse

Figs are ripe and heavy on the tree, so pick and eat them quickly

The **maincrop carrot** harvest should be keeping you well supplied

This month sees the last of the **peaches**

Let new season **pumpkins** and **winter squashes** harden off for storing

Pick **courgettes** while young, and eat the male flowers, too

Dry **onions** and **shallots** for a week or two before using

Grill some **aubergines** — on the BBQ if the weather is mild

Autumn **raspberries** are perfect for special treats

Time to harvest the first **maincrop potatoes**

Beetroots sown in the summer are ready for harvesting – pull them while they're small

Eat early **grapes,** if they're sweet enough, or try making wine *pages 180–181*

Use the last **blueberries** to make healthy fruit shakes

Steam or stir-fry versatile **Chinese cabbage**

Early apples are crisp and full of juice

New **leeks** are ready – don't hesitate to try them

Mild-flavoured **calabrese** goes well with chicken or pasta dishes

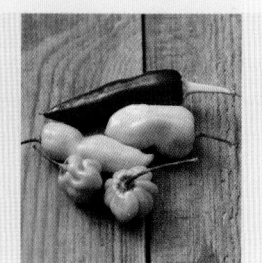

Use **chillies** fresh, or dry or freeze them *pages 148–149* for later

Harvest **Florence fennel** bulbs for cooking and use the leaves for salads

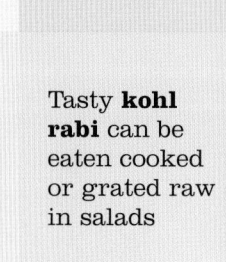

Tasty **kohl rabi** can be eaten cooked or grated raw in salads

September: what to sow

GROW YOUR OWN SOIL IMPROVERS

Sow green manure crops now to protect and improve empty beds during winter. Dig in the young plants 4 weeks before next year's crops are planted, to improve the soil with nutrients and organic matter.

ALFALFA
This plant has a long taproot that penetrates into heavy soil to help break it up and aid drainage.

RED CLOVER
A legume, this plant absorbs nitrogen from the atmosphere and locks it into the soil for plants.

GRAZING RYE
This dense grass helps to suppress weeds, while its fine roots improve soil structure. Good on light soil.

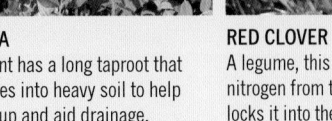

GREEN MANURES

SOW

SPINACH & WINTER LETTUCE

SPRING ONIONS & RADISH

LATE LEAVES
Now is your last chance to sow spinach and winter lettuce to grow on under cover for winter crops. Choose fast-growing spinach varieties, such as 'Triathlon', and winter varieties of butterhead and crisphead lettuce, like 'Valdor' and 'Winter Density'. All will crop through the coldest months. Sow 1cm (½in) deep, and plant out in a cold frame or greenhouse before the end of autumn.

HARVEST: **NOV–MAR**

SOW ONIONS
Make a last sowing of spring onions and radish now. Use a hardy spring onion variety, like 'White Lisbon', for a winter crop, sowing thinly, 1cm (½in) deep, in rows 15cm (6in) apart. In cold areas, cloche spring onions in winter. Also sow summer radishes thinly in drills 1cm (½in) deep, thinning to 2cm (¾in), to crop in autumn.

HARVEST: **OCT–DEC**

September: what to plant

FEELING PEACHY

HARVEST: **AUG–SEPT**

Container-grown trees can be planted at any time, but wait until winter to plant bare-root specimens. Dig in plenty of compost, especially at the base of walls, and plant to the same depth as the soil mark on the trunk. Water well and stake, or fix fan-trained trees with wires.

PEACH 'DUKE OF YORK'
Grown against a warm wall, this variety will produce a good crop of large, yellow-fleshed fruit.

PEACH 'PEREGRINE'
This is a heavy-cropping variety, with sweet, red-flushed fruit. Give it a warm, sunny, sheltered site.

NECTARINE 'FANTASIA'
This hardy variety produces large, juicy, yellow-fleshed fruit that ripen throughout July. Suitable for pots.

NECTARINE 'LORD NAPIER'
Late-ripening, this variety has thin-skinned, very juicy fruit that mature red. A reliable cropper.

JAPANESE ONIONS

SPRING CABBAGE

PEACHES & NECTARINES

PLANT

ONION SETS

HARVEST: **MAY–JUN**

For the earliest onions to harvest next year, plant out sets of Japanese over-wintering varieties, such as 'Buffalo', outdoors.

1 PLANT THE SETS
In a sunny, weed-free bed, push each set into the soil so that just the tip is showing.

2 FIRM THEM IN
Space the sets 5–10cm (2–4in) apart, and allow about 30cm (12in) between rows.

PLANT OUT CABBAGES

Between now and mid-autumn, transplant spring cabbages, sown in modules or seedbeds (p.132), into their final positions for overwintering. Find a sunny spot, with fertile soil that has not recently been dug over or manured. This will avoid the plants producing soft leafy growth that can be damaged by frosts. Space plants 30cm (12in) apart each way to encourage good-sized heads.

HARVEST: **APR–JUN**

See CHOOSING AND PLANTING TREES pages 202–203

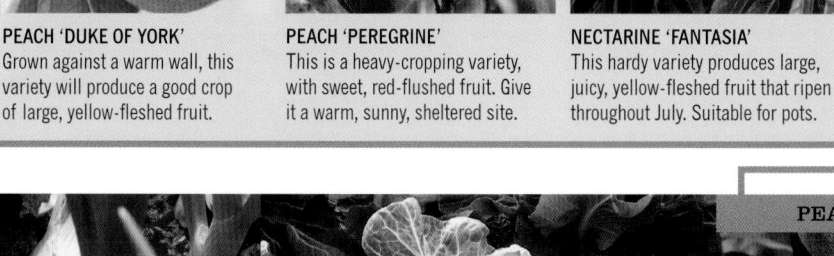

September: what to do

CUT DOWN ASPARAGUS
The tall feathery fronds of asparagus will have turned yellow now and may be starting to topple over. Cut them down with a pair of sharp secateurs, clipping off the stems as close to the soil as possible. The foliage is prickly, so be careful how you handle it. Once you have cleared the asparagus bed, spread a well-rotted organic mulch over it to help keep the soil in good condition for next year.

FEED LEEKS
A bed of large, healthy leeks should see you through winter. These tough plants rarely require watering, but they do benefit from an occasional feed with a balanced liquid fertilizer, so give them a boost before the end of the growing season.

TEND

PROTECT   ASPARAGUS   CELERIAC   LEEKS

FROST PROTECTION
Early autumn is often mild, but if you live in a cool area where night frosts are likely, then consider covering your late crops.

FLEECE TUNNEL
Make a protective tunnel cloche by securing horticultural fleece over wire hoops. You can easily remove the fleece in the daytime.

PVC CLOCHE
This type of cloche can be left open during the day for ventilation. For frost protection, close off the ends at night with plastic sheeting.

CELERIAC CARE
To encourage the stems of celeriac to bulk out for a good winter crop, regularly remove any damaged or older leaves. Just pull them away with a firm tug near the base of the plant. The tops of the swollen stems will soon start to appear above the soil. Celeriac plants will benefit from plenty of water during dry weather. The regular application of a balanced liquid fertilizer will also help to keep them growing strongly.

EMPTY THE BINS

Autumn may see a glut of compostable waste as plants die back and you tidy up for the winter. Make room for this by using up what is already in your compost bin (see pp.190–191). Apply a mulch of home-produced compost around crops that are going to overwinter or add it to recently cleared beds. With your bin empty, you can start again. Plants that have finished cropping mix well with autumn garden prunings, grass clippings, and fallen leaves to produce more compost for the following year.

RIPEN INDOORS

If frost threatens, take action to salvage the remainder of your outdoor tomatoes. Cut down cordon varieties, and either hang them up or lay them out flat, somewhere light to let the fruit finish ripening, in either a greenhouse, garage, or conservatory. Container-grown bush varieties can simply be moved under cover and grown on.

COMPOST

TOMATOES

PERENNIAL HERBS

LIFT AND DIVIDE HERBS

This is the ideal time to lift and divide perennial herbs, such as mint, either to plant in the garden or to pot-up and bring them indoors for a winter crop.

1 LIFT THE PLANT
Large clumps of herbs need splitting. Use a fork or spade to lift the entire plant from the soil. Tip out established pot-grown plants.

2 SPLIT OFF CLUMPS
For larger divisions, use your hands or a hand fork to break off clumps from the original rootball, which you can then replant.

3 TAKE CUTTINGS
Propagate from the spreading stems, or runners, of mint by taking cuttings of small rooted sections and potting up.

DON'T FORGET

As you do your autumn tidying, clear up as you go along. Don't leave piles of clippings and other debris lying around to rot and harbour pests. Compost or burn them as soon as possible.

Getting ready for winter

Winter still seems a long way off but around now, nights turn cooler and the days shorten, signalling the timely end of summer and that it's time to get ready for the season to come. With so much to harvest right now, it's hard to think ahead, but take advantage of September's golden weather to get a few jobs done.

Healthy balance

Tidying up your growing spaces is important to help prevent pests and diseases from lingering in plant waste, ready to attack new growth in spring, and to stop mats of fallen leaves from smothering over-wintering plants, such as perennial herbs. Weeds will still be growing now, so don't allow them to take hold at this late stage, either.

However, it's important to strike a balance. Wildlife relies on food and shelter to survive the cold winter months in the garden. A pile of leaves left in a corner or under a hedge, or a small log pile, is enough to make a winter home for hedgehogs and beneficial insects. Birds will flock to fallen fruit during a cold snap, and to any plants you allow to run to seed. Leave your plot tidy, but not bare during winter.

Jo's tips

If you have large trees in or near your garden, and you have the space, construct a post and chicken wire cage for making leaf mould (p.205). Tree leaves compost more slowly than many other types of garden waste, so it's a good idea to keep them out of the usual heap.

MULCH BARE SOIL
Bare soil and winter weather are not a good combination. Heavy rain leaches nutrients from the soil and ruins its structure. Apply thick mulch to large gaps between plants, and to beds after you have removed spent crops.

GENERAL TIDY UP
Clear away weeds, finished crops, and general plant debris from your beds and containers to prevent pests and diseases overwintering among them. Also rake up fallen leaves to stop them smothering your winter crops.

FIT GREASE BANDS
To help protect your fruit trees from insect damage, tie grease bands to the trunks, 60cm (2ft) above the ground. This will trap pests making their way the trunk to lay their eggs.

SUNDRY ROUND UP
Round up pots, labels, wire, watering cans, and other odds and ends that have become scattered during the growing season. Clean and dry them before storing them tidily.

CLEAN UP

Many essential autumn tasks are quick to do but are easily forgotten. Tidy your shed and clean your equipment to keep it in good working condition.

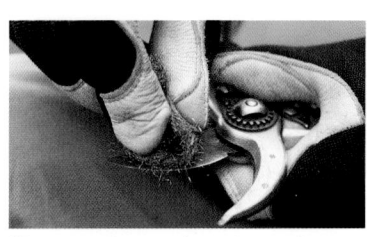

Clean secateurs using wire wool to remove sticky sap and other debris that has adhered to the blades.

Wipe off canes and plant supports used during summer. Tie them in bundles and store under cover.

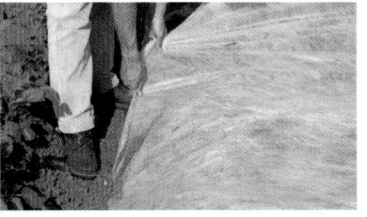

Before the first hard frost, check you have enough fleece to protect crops and insulation for your greenhouse.

Remove greenhouse shading now – any remaining crops will need all the heat they can get from the sun.

Collect fallen leaves periodically to make leaf mould (see Jo's Tips, opposite) before they pile up, smothering over-wintering crops, and harbouring pests and diseases.

GETTING READY FOR WINTER

Saving your own seeds

As well as growing crops to eat, it's easy harvest your own seeds to sow the next year. This not only saves money, it also allows you to select and grow on your favourites, and to produce fresh seed organically. Saving seed also gives you a good excuse to let vegetables bloom, and enjoy flowers you wouldn't normally see.

Saving seed

Collecting home-grown seed is doubly satisfying, as it gives two crops in one. Since you can choose the actual plants you save seed from, you can select those that tasted best or gave the biggest yield. Repeat this process over successive years and you can even develop your own unique strains, just as plant breeders do.

A drawback of saving seeds is that plants must flower, which means leaving them in the ground without harvesting them. This may not be feasible if you have a small crop, or little space to allow the plants to grow on. Also, unless you can isolate the plants, natural cross-pollination between varieties means the seed won't be exactly the same as the parents. This means there's little point saving seed from expensive F1 hybrids, as they won't be true to type.

FLOWERS FIRST
To collect seeds, you must first allow the vegetable plants to bloom. Most leaf and root crops are normally harvested before they flower, so to save your own seeds, you need to leave a few plants unharvested.

STORE DRY SEED
Many plants, such as rocket, produce seed in capsules or pods. To harvest these, wait for the pods to turn brown but collect the seeds before they fall to the ground. Empty the seeds out and leave them to dry before storing them.

Jo's tips

Whatever type of seed you save, make sure it is completely dry before storing it in paper bags or small envelopes. Label the packages with the name of the plant and the date the seed was collected. Always store seed in a cool, dry place, protected from mice.

SEED FROM PODS
Unless the summer is wet, leave fruiting pods, such as beans, on the plants to turn dry and papery. If wet, pick the pods, spread them out to dry indoors, then empty out the seeds.

SEED FROM WET FRUITS
When collecting seeds from moist fruit, such as tomatoes, let the fruit ripen on the plant, pick it, cut it open, and remove the seeds. Spread them on tissue paper to dry, then store.

TRY THESE

The best seeds to collect are those that are expensive to buy, or from crops you plan to grow a lot of next year. You can also share seeds with your friends.

Herbs – Many herbs, such as fennel, caraway, and dill, are grown for their seeds as well as their leaves.

Peas – Leave only the last few pods to mature and dry fully; this will allow the plants to flower and fruit for longer.

Beans – Collect the same way as peas. Dried beans can be used for cooking or sowing. Store them in labelled jars.

Squash and pumpkin – These large fruits are packed with seeds. Collect only those from the best fruits.

Salad vegetables such as lettuce run readily to seed. Leave them in the ground and allow them to flower, and collect seeds from the strongest plants.

September: what to harvest

PICK APPLES AND PEARS NOW

As the main season for harvesting apples and pears begins, it's now time to start checking the fruit on your trees for ripeness. To do this, lift apples gently in your hand, and if they come away easily with their stalk intact, they're ready to eat. Pears are trickier. Early-autumn ripening varieties should be picked when slightly underripe or they will become brown-centred and mealy. Test pears regularly, and if they come away with a lift and a gentle twist, then pick them and leave in a cool place for several days to ripen fully.

CUT CABBAGE, LIFT LEEKS

Red and summer cabbages, sown in March and planted out in May, can be cut as soon as the heads are a usable size. They should crop well into autumn, but they won't survive very cold weather. Once mature, some varieties stand in the ground longer than others, but watch out for signs of bolting, which spoils them. The first leeks, sown in spring, are ready for lifting. Harvest later-sown crops through winter into spring.

HARVEST

APPLES & PEARS

CABBAGE & LEEKS

RASPBERRIES

AUTUMN TREATS

Autumn raspberries, planted in October (p.185), bear ample fruit from now until the first frosts. Less favoured by birds than earlier varieties, they shouldn't require netting, although the tough cores mean they're more fiddly to prepare. They are best eaten as fresh.

'AUTUMN BLISS'
This variety is shorter than most and can be grown without support. It fruits freely, producing tasty red-pink berries, well into autumn.

'JOAN J'
Spine-free and self-supporting, this compact, sweet-tasting variety is suitable for containers. Keep it well watered and fed if pot grown.

'POLKA'
This variety bears especially large fruit that are produced in abundance until November. The berries are noted for their taste and sweetness.

'ALL GOLD'
Similar to 'Autumn Bliss', it's fruit matures yellow and doesn't stain clothes or fingers, so is ideal for gardeners with young children.

GOLDEN SWEET CORN

Sweet corn tells you it's ready to pick when the silk tassels at the top of the cobs turn brown. To be completely sure it's ripe, pull back the leaves that surround the cob and look for pale, butter-yellow kernels. Sweet corn sown inside in April (p.75), and planted in June (p.115), should be ready now. To pick it, twist the cobs from the stems, snapping them at the base. Their sweetness rapidly fades, so use them quickly, otherwise blanch and freeze them (pp.148–149). Sweet corn doesn't keep well in the fridge.

LIFT POTATOES

Cut potato plants off to just above ground level in early autumn, leaving the tubers in the soil to mature for 2 weeks before lifting with a fork. Lift those for storage on a dry, sunny day, and leave them on the soil surface for up to 2 hours to dry without going green. Store undamaged tubers in large paper sacks, in a dark, frost-free place.

SWEET CORN

SQUASH & PUMPKINS

FIGS

POTATOES

BUMPER CROPS

Squashes and pumpkins sown in April (p.74) should be cut fresh when required. To store, pick mature fruit with plenty of stem, when they're well coloured and the stem has cracked. Before the frosts come, cure the fruit for 10 days in the sun outdoors, or in a greenhouse or indoors in poor weather, to harden the skin so that they keep. Store in a cool, frost-free place.

SWEET FIGS

Figs don't ripen further once picked, so wait until they're hanging heavy from the tree and feel soft. If sap appears at the base of the fruit, it's a good indication of ripeness. Pick the fruit carefully without bruising it and eat quickly. Figs keep fresh for a week or so in a cool place, but are also excellent cooked.

See STORING VEGETABLES pages 210–211

Making cold pickles

Cold pickles can be made using either single crops or a medley of fruit and vegetables for a colourful combination. The method is straightforward and there is no cooking involved. One thing cold pickles need is a good crunch when you bite into them. The best way to ensure a crisp finish is to salt your vegetables for some hours to draw out excess moisture before they are pickled raw in vinegar.

Pickled gherkins

Makes 1kg (2¼lb) (2 small jars)
Takes about 20 minutes, plus salting time
Keeps 6 months or longer

Ingredients
500g (1lb 2oz) small pickling cucumbers
125g (4½oz) sea salt
3–4 shallots, peeled
1–2 garlic cloves, peeled (optional)
2–3 dried chillies (optional)
2–3 cloves (optional)
½ tsp coriander seeds, peppercorns, or dill seeds, or 1 crumbled bay leaf
2 sprigs tarragon, dill, or thyme
1 vine leaf (optional)
750ml (1¼ pints) white wine vinegar

Jo's tips

Pickle chillies or slices of sweet pepper raw in sweetened white vinegar to eat with cheese or meat, or to use chopped in salsas. Shred red cabbage finely with onions, soak in brine for 6 hours, rinse, and pack in jars with sweetened, spiced vinegar.

To sterilize preserving jars, wash them in hot soapy water, place them on a rack in a moderate oven, and leave them there to dry.

1 Wash and dry the cucumbers, rubbing each with a cloth to remove the fine down. Snip off the stalks and any dried blossom. Either leave whole or cut into quarters lengthways, or into 3mm (⅛in) slices.

2 Put a layer of salt in a bowl, then a layer of cucumbers. Repeat until the cucumbers are used up, ending with a layer of salt. Stand at room temperature for 24 hours, then rinse the cucumbers to remove the salt.

3 Pack the cucumbers into sterilized jars (see Jo's Tips, left), leaving about 1cm (½in) at the top. Add the shallots, garlic, spices, and herbs, and a vine leaf to keep the pickle crisp. Cover the cucumbers with vinegar.

4 Seal the jars with non-metallic lids, because metal will react with the vinegar and spoil the pickle. Label, and store your pickles in a cool, dark place for at least 3–4 weeks to let the flavours develop before eating.

Sharp and crisp, pickled gherkins are excellent with cheese, cold meats, and sandwiches.

TRY THESE

Choose the firmest fruits and vegetables for making cold pickles. Those shown here all have distinctive flavours that blend well with spices.

Shallots – Pickle these small onions whole, either on their own or mixed with other vegetables.

Garlic – Pickle garlic by itself with some spice, or use it to add extra flavour to mixed vegetable pickles.

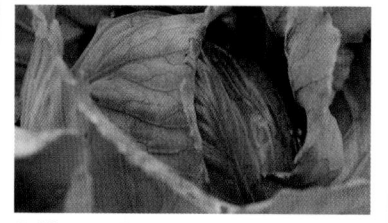

Cabbage – Firm red or white cabbage, finely sliced, is delicious pickled. Try adding caraway or cumin seeds.

Cauliflower – Break red or white heads into bite-sized florets. Pickle on its own or mixed with other vegetables.

MAKING COLD PICKLES

Making hot pickles

This time-honoured method of preserving fruits and vegetables using vinegar is an effective and delicious way of keeping produce for many months without it spoiling. Hot pickling enables you to create a whole range of new flavours by using different vinegars and spices or combining crops. Fruit pickles are all made following the same basic steps, as illustrated in the recipe below.

RECIPE IDEAS

Spiced pear pickle

Makes 900ml (1½ pints) (2 medium jars)
Takes 40 minutes
Keeps 9 months

Ingredients
1kg (2¼lb) firm pears, peeled, cored, and quartered

To make the syrup
350g (12oz) granulated sugar
175ml (6fl oz) cider vinegar
Zest of ½ lemon
2.5cm (1in) piece fresh root ginger, chopped
Seeds from 6 cardamom pods

Jo's tips

The hot pickling method produces soft-textured condiments. If you enjoy eating something with a crunch, try the cold pickling technique (see pages 176–177).

Once you have opened a jar of pickles, make sure the remaining contents stay covered by their liquid and keep them refrigerated.

To sterilize your preserving jars, wash them in hot soapy water, place them on a rack in a moderate oven, and leave them there to dry thoroughly.

1 Put all the syrup ingredients into a large preserving pan or heavy-based, stainless steel saucepan and bring to the boil, stirring until the sugar dissolves. Simmer for 5 minutes then remove from the heat.

2 Put the pear quarters into the syrup, making sure they are covered. Poach for 5–10 minutes, until just soft. Test each piece with a skewer and remove it from the pan as soon as it reaches the right consistency.

3 Pack the cooked pears into warm, sterilized preserving jars (see Jo's Tips, left). Return the syrup to the heat, bring back to the boil and cook for a further 5 minutes, or until the liquid has reduced by about a third.

4 Carefully pour the boiling syrup over the pears, completely covering them. Top with waxed paper discs and seal the jars with non-metallic lids. Label, and store in a cool, dark place for 1 month before using.

Spicy fruit pickles keep well in a store cupboard. They are especially good with rice dishes.

TRY PICCALILLI

This is a classic hot pickle that combines summer vegetables with spices. Try varying the vegetables you use according to the crops you've grown.

Makes 2.25kg (5lb) (3 medium jars)
Takes 35 minutes
Keeps 6 months

Ingredients

60g (2oz) sea salt
1 large cauliflower
2 large onions, diced
900g (2lb) mixed vegetables
2 tbsp plain flour
225g (8oz) granulated sugar
1 tbsp turmeric
60g (2oz) English mustard powder
900ml (1½ pints) pickling vinegar

1 Dissolve the salt in 1.2 litres (2 pints) of water and soak the vegetables thoroughly for 24 hours. Drain, rinse, and blanch in hot water.
2 Mix the dry ingredients in a bowl with a little vinegar to make a paste. Put in a saucepan, add the rest of the vinegar, bring to the boil, then simmer, stirring, for 15 minutes.
3 Add vegetables, coat well with sauce, then spoon into sterilized jars, leaving no air pockets. Cover with vinegar-proof lids. Store in the dark; start using after 1 month.

Making wine

You don't need a vineyard to make your own wine, in fact you don't need grapes at all. With the right technique, many different fruits and vegetables can be turned into a delicious alcoholic tipple.

Plum (and greengage) trees fruit heavily in late summer, and with basic equipment you can turn this bounty into glorious homemade wine. Once you feel confident, you can go on to more complicated wines.

Plum wine

Makes 4.5 litres (1 gallon)
Takes 2 hours, plus time to freeze the fruit, ferment, and stabilize

Ingredients
2kg (4½lb) plums or greengages, washed
Juice of 1 lemon
1 tsp pectolase
1 tsp wine yeast
1.5kg (3lb 3oz) unrefined cane sugar

Equipment
Large fermentation bucket with lid
Potato masher
Demijohn with cork and airlock
Plastic funnel and sieve
Plastic measuring jug
Plastic tubing for siphoning

1 Stone the fruit, freeze, thaw, and mash it, and add the lemon juice. Put in a bucket with 3.5 litres (6 pints) of boiling water. Let cool, and add the pectolase. Leave at room temperature for 24 hours, add yeast, and cover.

2 After 4–5 days, strain the pulped fruit into a sterilized container to remove any large solids. Dissolve the sugar fully in about 1 litre (1¾ pints) hot water and add this to the mashed fruit. Stir the mixture thoroughly.

Jo's tips

Plums, gages, and certain other fruits such as apples, are naturally high in pectin, which can cause your wine to become cloudy. Adding the enzyme pectolase breaks down the pectin, but as a further precaution, freeze and thaw the fruit before mashing. This also helps destroy the pectin.

Always use sterilized equipment for wine-making, or you run the risk of producing vinegar.

3 Using a sterilized funnel, carefully pour the liquid into a sterilized demijohn. The liquid still contains fruit solids at this stage, which are essential to fermentation. These will settle and can be filtered out later.

4 Fit and fill the airlock and leave the liquid to ferment at room temperature for 2 months. When no more bubbles appear in the airlock, siphon the wine into bottles, seal, and store them in the dark for 6 months.

Homemade wines are ready to drink after 6 months and keep well for about 2 years.

TRY THESE

Variations on this basic technique can be used to make wine from many different fruits and vegetables. Look for a specific recipe before you start.

Parsnip – These, and most other root vegetables, are high in natural sugars, and make excellent, potent wine.

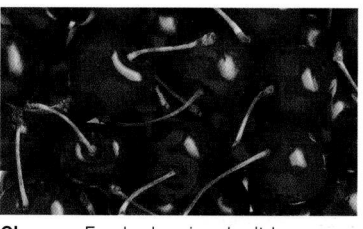

Cherry – Fresh cherries don't keep well, so if you have plenty of them, the fruits make a gloriously dark-red wine.

Rhubarb – An established rhubarb plant can provide a mountain of stems, so use spare ones for wine-making.

Blackberry – All summer berries can be used for wine. Mix the last of your crops together for a mixed berry wine.

October: ready to eat

Before the first frosts, lift potatoes, carrots, and beetroots for storage. To replace them, new autumn crops, including celeriac and swedes, are coming in; their rich, earthy flavours suit the season perfectly.

Fresh greens are guaranteed with cut-and-come-again **rocket**

Spinach beet and **Swiss chard** are useful, whatever the season

End-of-season **main crop potatoes** should see you through the month

Enjoy the last of the **summer cauliflower** and **calabrese**

Leeks are still new, tender, and full of flavour

Roast the last of the **sweet corn** and serve with melted butter

Pears are best picked while still slightly hard

Taste **grapes** for ripeness before cutting a whole bunch

Gather the last **aubergines, peppers, courgettes,** and **tomatoes** to make a tasty ratatouille that will freeze well

Cut the last sprigs from summer **annual herbs**

It's the end of the summer **onions**, unless you plan to dry some for winter use

Have a sweet feast with the last **cane fruits**

Keep some **beetroot** for storage *pages 210–211*

Late **plums** make great pies and crumbles

Harvest **cobnuts** – unless the squirrels have beaten you to it

Steam **pak choi** as a delicious and healthy side dish

Winter squashes make delicious, filling soups

Pick the remaining **sweet peppers**

Use the last fresh **chillies** and dry any surplus

Lift your **turnips** before they grow too large – the little ones have the best flavour and texture

Florence fennel won't be around during the winter – so make the most of it now

Lift new season **trench celery** – it's deliciously crisp and tasty

Say goodbye to summer with the final harvest of **peas** and **runner** and **French beans**

Even windfall **apples** taste good

Not too late in the year for a summer salad of **lettuce, tomato,** and **cucumber**

Sugarloaf chicory adds a distinctive tang to salads and soups

Celeriac comes in this month to replace some of your summer favourites

Summer and **winter radishes** are both available this month

The new **swede** crop is ready for lifting and eating as mash or soup

New season **kale** tastes wonderful

Monster **pumpkins** are better for ornament than eating

October: what to sow

SOW CAULIFLOWER
For an extra early crop of summer cauliflowers, sow them now under cover into modules or drills 1cm (½in) deep. Thin drill-sown seedlings as they grow to 10cm (4in) apart, ready for transplanting in spring (p.62). Keep the seedlings protected but not heated until then. Water as required, and protect them against slugs.

HARVEST: **MAY–JUN**

EXTRA EARLY BEANS
HARVEST: **APR–JUN**

If you have a well-drained soil, and want extra-early broad beans, sow hardy varieties now, 5cm (2in) deep, and protect the plants with cloches.

'STEREO'
This variety is like mangetout in that you can eat the entire pods. They can also be eaten skinned.

'SUPER AQUADULCE'
This is one of the hardiest bean varieties, and is suitable for growing in colder areas.

'THE SUTTON'
A dwarf variety, suitable for smaller gardens, it produces large pods with five beans apiece.

SOW

GARLIC

SUMMER CAULIFLOWER

PEAS

BROAD BEANS

GROW GARLIC
HARVEST: **JUN–AUG**

Garlic needs a long growing season, and on well-drained soil it can be planted outside now. If you have a heavy soil, plant in small pots under cover for now.

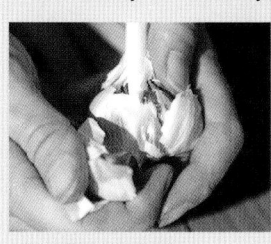

1 BREAK UP BULB
Buy certified disease-free garlic bulbs and break them into individual cloves, removing most of the outer papery layers of the bulb.

2 PREPARE SITE
Choose fertile soil that has not been recently manured, dig it over lightly, and rake it to remove any large clods and stones.

3 PLANT OUT
Push cloves into the soil, 2cm (¾in) deep, 20cm (8in) apart each way. Plant flat-end down. Use a dibber to make holes if it helps.

SUPER EARLY PEAS
Even tough pea seeds will rot in wet winter soils, but if yours is well-drained, or you have a raised bed that drains freely (p.33), you can sow now for an extra early crop. Choose early varieties, like 'Feltham First', and sow thinly, 4cm (1½in) deep in drills, about 15cm (6in) wide. Insert pea sticks or taut plastic netting for support, and tie in the young plants as they grow. Cover plants in extreme weather.

HARVEST: **MAY–JUN**

October: what to plant

BLACKBERRIES, RASPBERRIES, & FAMILY

HARVEST: JUL–OCT

Bare-rooted blackberries, raspberries, and their hybrids (below), should be planted now. Plant raspberries 45cm (18in) apart, 8–10cm (3–4in) deep, with 1.5m (5ft) between rows. Plant blackberries and hybrids 2m (6ft) apart. Cut canes to a bud 25cm (10in) above the soil.

BOYSENBERRY
A cross between a blackberry, loganberry, and raspberry, its dark red fruit have a rich bramble taste.

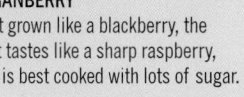

LOGANBERRY
Best grown like a blackberry, the fruit tastes like a sharp raspberry, and is best cooked with lots of sugar.

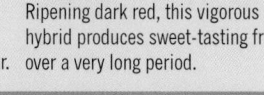

TAYBERRY
Ripening dark red, this vigorous hybrid produces sweet-tasting fruit over a very long period.

JAPANESE WINEBERRY
This distinct species has small, soft, orange-red berries with an unusual wine-like flavour.

SUMMER BERRIES

PLANT

GOOSEBERRIES & CURRANTS

WITLOOF CHICORY

PLANT BARE ROOTED

Plant bare-root gooseberries and currants now in a sunny, sheltered site, in fertile, well-drained soil. Soak first, setting gooseberries, red- and whitecurrants 1.5m (5ft) apart, and blackcurrants 1.8m (6ft) apart. Plant to the same depth as the soil mark on the stems, then prune (pp.206–207). Choose blackcurrant plants that are certified free of blackcurrant reversion virus (p.240).

HARVEST: **VARIOUS**

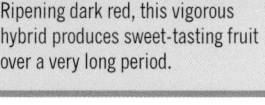

FORCED CHICORY

If you want Witloof chicory roots to force indoors for winter, lift plants sown in May, from now until early winter. Leave the roots in a shed for a week, cut off all the leaves 2cm (¾in) above the root, and store them flat in sand-filled boxes. These can then be potted up in December, ready for forcing for a New Year crop (p.216).

HARVEST: **JAN–MAR**

See PRUNING FRUIT IN AUTUMN pages 206–207

Raspberries

Summer raspberries are one of the season's great joys, and given support and protection from birds, they are easy to grow. Also try autumn varieties (p.174).

1 'Glen Fyne' produces a heavy crop of rich red berries with an excellent flavour, mid-June to mid-August. Spine-free, it is a rewarding and easy variety to grow; good for beginners.

2 'Malling Jewel' is a traditional, compact, virus-resistant variety, that is good for smaller gardens. It gives a reasonable crop of flavoursome berries from early July to mid-August.

3 'Glen Prosen' is a spine-free variety that produces a large, crop of tasty berries, mid-July to mid-August. The berries are particularly firm, making them ideal for freezing (pp.150–151).

4 'Cascade Delight' is a heavy-cropping raspberry that tolerates wet conditions better than many varieties, making it ideal for cool, damp regions. The rich-tasting fruit is large and firm.

5 'Tulameen' is a very hardy variety that gives an excellent crop of large, tasty fruit, mid-July to mid-August. The canes are tall, 2m (6ft), but have few spines. Don't cut back after planting.

Other varieties to try:
'Glen Ample'
'Glencoe'
'Glen Moy'
'Malling Admiral'
'Octavia'

Blackberries

Most gardens only have room for one or two of these large, free-fruiting plants, which require only simple pruning and training for a bumper crop (p.118).

1 'Waldo' is a compact variety that gives a good-sized crop in midsummer, but takes up little space. It is also thornless, making it easier to pick from, and safer to grow near children.

2 'Black Butte' produces exceptionally large fruit, twice the normal size at 5cm (2in) long, which are good for cooking and eating raw. It is also an early variety, ready for picking in mid-July.

3 'Loch Ness' is a bushy, compact variety, and a good choice for where space is limited. Thornless and free-fruiting, it can also be grown in containers. It crops late summer.

4 'Silvan' is a thorned variety that produces a heavy, early crop of large, richly flavoured berries. It is a full-sized variety, and requires about 4m (12ft) of wall or fence space.

5 'Oregon Thornless' is a vigorous variety that fruits into autumn. It has attractive, dissected foliage, and can also be grown as an ornamental, making it easy to accommodate in smaller plots.

Other varieties to try:
'Apache'
'Fantasia'
'Helen'
'Karaka Black'
'Veronique'

RASPBERRIES AND BLACKBERRIES

October: what to do

STORE IN THE SOIL

As the foliage on tall Jerusalem artichoke stems dies back, its goodness is taken up by the underground tubers. Once the leaves are brown, cut the stems down to 8–10cm (3–4in) above the soil, and chop them into small pieces for composting. Leave the tubers where they are, because they keep best in the soil.

GREENHOUSEKEEPING

Keep your greenhouse free from pests and diseases and insulated from the winter cold. Mid-autumn is a good time for these maintenance jobs.

1 CLEAN
Clear plant debris, wipe away shading paint with a dry cloth, and clean the glass inside and out.

2 DISINFECT
Scrub glazing bars, hard paths, and shelves or staging with a diluted disinfectant solution.

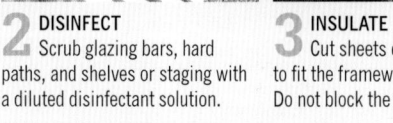

3 INSULATE
Cut sheets of bubble wrap to fit the framework of the glazing. Do not block the vents.

TEND

ARTICHOKES

CELERIAC

CONTAINER-GROWN FRUIT

GREENHOUSES

WARM BEDDING

With the right preparation, both parsnips and celeriac can be left in the soil during the winter. To protect their roots from extremely cold weather, or to prevent soil freezing and enable lifting during winter, mulch them with a thick layer of straw. Celeriac keeps its leaves throughout the winter, so tuck the straw under the leaves to make sure that the roots have maximum protection from frosts.

REPOT FRUIT

For good yields you must repot fruit trees and bushes every year until they are full sized. Knock the plant out of its pot in mid- to late autumn and tease the roots out of the edge of the rootball. Repot into a container about 10cm (4in) wider at the top than the last. Use John Innes No. 2 compost for soft fruit and John Innes No. 3 for trees.

PROTECT SALAD CROPS
Many leafy vegetable crops, such as winter lettuce, chard, and spinach, are resistant to cold and can be kept going well into the winter. However, they need some protection because their foliage can quickly be ruined by harsh and wet weather. Cloching your crops at this stage in the season will protect the plants from the worst of the weather, allowing them to keep producing fresh leaves for longer. If you take precautions now, you will have top-quality leaves available for picking into winter.

BRING INDOORS
Citrus trees in containers that have enjoyed a sheltered, sunny spot outside all summer should now be brought back indoors. Find them a well-ventilated place, with plenty of light and a minimum temperature of 7°C (45°F). Keep them away from radiators and cold draughts. They will not need further feeding until spring.

SALAD CROPS

CITRUS

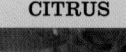

ROOT CROPS

LIFTING AND STORING ROOTS
Root crops, such as Jerusalem artichoke, can be left in the ground during winter and actually store better in the soil. However, if your soil is heavy or you live in a cold area, it's worth being cautious and lifting what you can now to store under cover (pp.210–211).

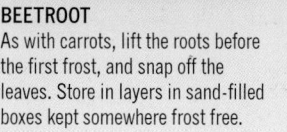

CARROTS
Dig up before the frosts and cut off the foliage to within 1cm (½in) of the root. Store in layers in soil or sand-filled boxes. Keep frost free.

POTATOES
Lift potatoes on a dry day and leave them on the soil surface to dry for a few hours. Store in paper sacks or in a clamp if you have a large crop.

BEETROOT
As with carrots, lift the roots before the first frost, and snap off the leaves. Store in layers in sand-filled boxes kept somewhere frost free.

TURNIPS
These can be harvested until winter, but if the weather allows, lift them now and store the roots in boxes of dry soil or sand. Keep frost free.

See CITRUS pages 222–223

Starting a compost heap

Every garden, however small, should have at least one compost heap to provide free and fabulous soil improver. The process could not be simpler – in goes green and twiggy garden debris, and kitchen peelings that would otherwise go in the waste bin, and in 6–12 months, out comes amazing, crumbly garden compost.

GROWING FEATURE

Making compost

To make good compost, mix waste material together as you build the heap, to allow moisture and air to penetrate into the centre. This creates ideal conditions for the correct bacteria, fungi, and insects to flourish, and quickly break down the waste, without any nasty smells. A good mix of about half carbon-rich woody material and half nitrogen-rich green material helps to keep composting organisms working well.

Check your heap regularly, and if it is wet and slimy and smells bad, then too much nitrogen-rich waste, such as vegetable peelings, has been added. To remedy this, mix in small or shredded woody material. Similarly, a dry heap won't break down quickly, so mix in moist green waste, add water, and turn the heap if the edges dry out (p.47).

MIX IT UP
Avoid adding material in thick layers, which will prevent air and moisture circulating. When adding lots of one type, mix it into the heap using a fork.

To achieve finished compost, stop adding fresh waste material when your bin is full, and cover the top with old carpet or the lid. Wait for the level in the bin to stop going down and turn the contents to

TURN REGULARLY
You need to turn your heap at least once to make good compost. The easiest way is to have another, empty heap, and swap material across.

make sure all material is fully broken down. The compost should then be ready in a month or two, so have a second bin to fill in the meantime. Once the first bin is finished, empty it and start again.

Types of compost bins

Choose to make or buy a bin that suits your garden. Site it in sun or part shade, directly on the soil, rather than on paving, to help attract beneficial organisms. Work out how much waste you will have to put on the heap, and try to match this to the size of your bin. Also consider access, and pick a design you can reach into easily when filling or emptying the bin.

(left to right) **Build your own bin** to look attractive or blend into the background, with sliding slats at the front for hassle-free turning. **Plastic bins** are compact and cheap, and offer a quick way to get started, but aren't always easy to turn. **Builder's bags** are large and often free, and are a good option for allotments or large gardens.

TRY THESE

Compost heaps need a mixture of moist and dry material. Avoid adding in perennial weeds, cooked food, diseased growth, and thick branches.

Vegetable peelings contain nitrogen and moisture; collect them along with tea bags and coffee grounds.

Shredded paper and card are great for adding carbon to wet, nitrogen-rich compost. Avoid plastic-coated paper.

Prunings and annual weeds make up the bulk of a compost heap. Avoid composting any diseased material.

Thin woody prunings, less than a pencil thickness, help to aerate larger compost heaps, and also add bulk.

Compost heaps can be just that, a straightforward heap. If you have space, and somewhere to keep it out of sight, simply pile up your garden waste into a heap and it will slowly compost.

STARTING A COMPOST HEAP

October: what to harvest

LAST SUMMER HARVEST
For a final taste of fresh summer vegetables, go out picking now while the weather allows, and harvest the last of your peas, sweetcorn, marrows, courgettes, carrots, cucumbers, and Florence fennel, before they're spoiled by the frost. Many of these plants will already be winding down for winter, so harvest and enjoy what is there, then remove and compost any remaining plant material.

CELERY STICKS
Don't delay in lifting the last of your self-blanching celery, sown in February (p.40), because it won't survive in the soil through frost. Stems deteriorate in quality anyway through autumn. The small, inner stems keep well if stored in a plastic bag in a cool place after harvest.

HARVEST

NUTS

LATE SUMMER CROPS

APPLES & PEARS

CELERY

HARVEST NUTS NOW
Nuts are a real mid-autumn treat that should not be overlooked. Pick cobnuts from among the branches when their shells have hardened and turned brown. If you're lucky enough to have a walnut tree, gather the nuts from the ground as soon as they have fallen, remove their husks straight away, and scrub the shells to remove husk fibres before drying. Both types of nut can be eaten fresh now, or spread out in a warm place and allowed to dry for storage in a cool, airy place. They will keep well for weeks; check occasionally for pest damage.

LATE APPLES AND PEARS
Late varieties of apples and pears should be left on the tree to ripen for as long as possible. Even then, most pears will stay hard and need a period of storage to bring them to perfection (pp.194–195). The trick is to leave the fruit on the tree for as long as you can, hoping that it won't be knocked off and damaged by autumn weather, making it useless for storing. Of course, any windfall apples and pears will still be delicious, although they cannot be stored because of their impact bruises. If you have a glut, juice them or make them into wine (pp.180–181).

PICK YOUR OWN GRAPES

Grapes require patience, because even though they may look ripe, they need time on the vine to allow the fruit sugars to develop.

Mid-autumn grapes need 4 weeks, late varieties want 10 weeks. When picking, use secateurs to avoid spoiling the fruits' white bloom.

'BOSKOOP GLORY'
This is a good dessert variety for cooler areas, and gives a reliable harvest of delicious dark grapes that can be eaten straight from the vine.

'REGENT'
A vigorous variety, it bears large, sweet blue-black fruit. Its foliage also develops rich colouring, so it doubles as an ornamental climber.

'SIEGERREBE'
Dessert grape, its sweet, juicy fruit ripen with a rich brown tint, and can be eaten fresh or used to make wine. It is suitable for cooler regions.

'MÜLLER-THURGAU'
This variety is widely grown for wine-making, and is a good choice for cooler areas. The grapes are also sweet enough to eat fresh.

GRAPES

BEANS

TOMATOES, PEPPERS, & CHILLIES

LAST BEANS

Now brings the last crops of French and runner beans that have been growing all summer. Pick bright and tender pods whole. If your French bean pods are swollen and stringy, leave them to mature, then bring them indoors to dry fully. The white beans inside are actually haricot beans, and can be stored dry. Runner beans are not as palatable dried in this way.

RIPEN INDOORS

If your last harvested tomatoes are refusing to ripen, put them in a paper bag or fruit bowl with some bananas, which give off natural fruit-ripening vapours. Peppers and chillies won't ripen further once picked. Green peppers don't keep well, but freeze your chillies whole and use them when needed.

Try DRYING FRUIT & VEGETABLES pages 160–161

HARVESTING IDEAS

Storing apples and pears

Old-fashioned methods are often the best, and if you are lucky enough to get a good crop of apples and pears every year, the easiest way to keep them is the traditional method of tucking them up in a store.

Some late varieties need storage of this kind to ripen properly, and it's a pleasure to have fruit stored in its natural state, to take out and use throughout the winter, as and when you please.

How to store fruit

Finding a place with suitable conditions is vital for the success of this storage method. The temperature needs to be fairly stable, below 10°C (50°F), but frost-free. There should be good air circulation to reduce the risk of rotting, and measures must be taken to exclude pests such as mice and birds. A cool attic, cellar, or insulated shed can all work well, but anywhere in a centrally heated house generally won't. Also ensure that fruit is kept away from chemicals such as pesticides, paint, and wood preservative.

1 Pick your fruit carefully (see Jo's Tips, left) and the majority should be suitable for storing. Discard or use immediately any with damage and signs of disease. Dry off wet fruit to help prevent decay during storage.

2 Wrap up apples individually to stop them shrivelling during storage. Use waxed paper, such as baking paper. Cooking apples can be wrapped in old newspaper. Leave stored pears unwrapped.

Jo's tips

The stage at which fruit is picked makes a big difference to how it tastes after storage. Pick all but the latest apples when they're ripe and come away with their stalks when lifted. Pick pears before they're fully ripe, when they still require a twist and tug to pull them away with their stalk. Organize your store so that different fruits and their varieties are stored separately. Never store bruised or damaged fruit, because rot will set in.

3 To arrange your fruit, wrapped apples can be stored touching and piled up in layers. Leave small spaces between unwrapped pears, and keep them in a single layer to allow air circulation and to prevent bruising.

4 Stack boxes or trays of fruit, or leave them on shelves, making sure there is ventilation between them. Check stores regularly to catch fruit at the peak of ripeness. Check for signs of deterioration.

Unwrapped apples are easier to inspect, although are more at risk of drying out.

TRY THESE

Some varieties suit storage better than others. Culinary types are often successful, but meltingly ripe dessert fruit is always a winter highlight.

Apple 'Egremont Russet' – This mid-season variety retains its nutty flavour when picked in mid-autumn.

Apple 'Idared' – One of the best keepers, picked mid-autumn, this late variety holds on to its sweet flavour.

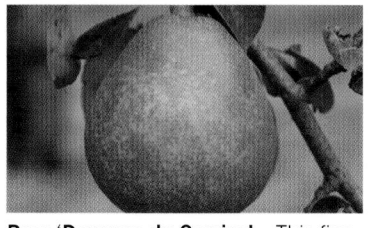

Pear 'Doyenne du Comice' – This fine dessert pear is picked and stored mid-autumn and eaten to early winter.

Pear 'Concorde' – A reliable, heavy cropper, this mid-season dessert variety keeps well through winter.

STORING APPLES AND PEARS

November: ready to eat

Add late apple and pear varieties to your stores and harvest hardy celeriac roots and winter cabbages as you need them. Salad leaves grown undercover, such as chicory, lettuce, and rocket, are a fresh touch of green.

Stir-fry late-season **pak choi**

Start using stored **apples** and **pears**

Cut-and-come-again salads give a fresh taste of summer all year long

Harvest new season **Brussels sprouts**

If they're too sour to eat, use the last **indoor grapes** to make your own **homemade wine**
pages 180–181

Enjoy super tasty swede

Slice fresh **spring onions** directly into your dishes

Eat the last of this year's lettuce crop, grown under cover

Leaf chicory has a rich, bitter taste that goes well with bread and cheese

Use late root veg as a base for rich and spicy chutneys

Serve new season **kale**, lightly steamed, with your Sunday roast

Use dried bunches of **herbs** and **chillies** – they don't last long
page 161

Use fresh, crisp **Swiss chard** as an alternative to spinach in your pasta dishes

Harvest the last crisp Chinese cabbage

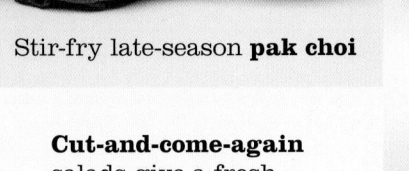

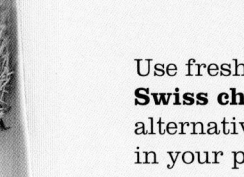

Eat late fresh **apples** and **pears**

Make a spicy curry with the last of your **autumn cauliflower**

Pick the last of the **kohl rabi**

Use oven-dried **tomatoes** to add Mediterranean flavour *page 160*

Cut the last of the **autumn cabbage**, with its strong, rich taste

Give a mild onion flavour to your soups and stews with fresh **leeks** *pages 226–227*

Relish the last of your **summer radishes**, and the first of the **winter varieties**

Slice and fry delicious **mushrooms** grown indoors

Defrost frozen **pesto** made in summer *page 147*

Crop the last of your **spinach**

Fresh **parsnips** and **celeriac** are the route to a good meal

Savour the nutty flavour of new season **salsify**

Roast freshly-pulled **turnips** and **carrots**

Mash new season **Jerusalem artichokes** for a culinary treat

Add tasty, vitamin-rich **sprouting seeds** to your sandwiches, salads, and stir-fries

Pick evergreen herbs, including **rosemary**, **thyme**, **sage**, and **bay**

November: what to plant

THRIVING VINES

Vines thrive in sunshine and a well-drained, enriched soil. Before planting, put up horizontal wires, spaced 30cm (12in) apart. Plant the vines 1.2–1.5m (4–5ft) apart. Between now and early spring, prune the stems down to two buds above the soil or graft union.

HARVEST: **AUG–NOV**

TIME FOR TREES

Plant fruit trees while the soil is warm and the plants are dormant. Choose a well-drained, sunny site away from frost pockets. Allow each tree ample space, dig in compost, and drive in a stake for free-standing trees or put up horizontal wires for wall-trained trees. Dig a hole, spread out the roots, backfill and firm the soil gently. Keep the trunk 5cm (2in) from the stake.

HARVEST: **VARIOUS**

PLANT

BLUEBERRIES

RHUBARB

GRAPE VINES

FRUIT TREES

POT BLUEBERRIES

Blueberries are easy to grow if you can get the soil right. They need a moist, acid soil with a pH of 4–5.5, so unless your garden naturally has these conditions grow them in pots filled with ericaceous compost. Knock plants from their pots and plant 1.5m (5ft) apart in the soil, or in containers a little larger than their rootball. Firm the soil lightly and water thoroughly. Keep moist until established.

HARVEST: **AUG–SEPT**

RHUBARB SETS

Well-fed rhubarb plants will crop prolifically for many years. Choose an unshaded patch and improve the soil with a generous amount of well-rotted manure before planting. Space the sets (young plants) at least 90cm (36in) apart and plant them with their crowns just above soil level to stop rot setting into the new buds during winter.

HARVEST: **MAR–JUL**

HARDY HERBS

Many tough perennial herbs, such as mint and fennel, are happy to be planted out in late autumn. Unless they are in a sheltered position, Mediterranean herbs, such sage, thyme, and rosemary, may struggle through cold winters when newly planted. Protect them with fleece.

BAY
This tolerant shrubby herb will grow in full sun or partial shade, in moist or dry soil. It is best in milder areas.

CHIVES
Plant this bulb-forming herb in full sun and well-drained soil. It will tolerate shade but becomes leggy.

LEMON BALM
This is a hardy, highly aromatic herb that grows best in a sunny site with free-draining soil. Good in pots.

ROSEMARY
Grow this woody herb in a sheltered, sunny site, with well-drained soil. It is best in milder regions.

PERENNIAL HERBS

FIGS

PATIO FRUIT

MAKE A FIG PIT

HARVEST: **AUG–SEP**

Figs are vigorous plants that are often planted in a restricted area to stop them growing too large.

1 DIG THE PIT
Dig a hole 60cm (24in) square and deep. Line the sides with paving slabs and put in a layer of rubble, allowing good drainage.

2 PLANT AND SUPPORT
Fill the hole with good topsoil, attach strong horizontal supporting wires to the wall, 30cm (12in) apart, then plant and tie in the fig.

PATIO FRUIT

The full range of fruit trees will flourish in containers, which restrict the size that trees can grow to. This is the ideal way to grow fruit in small gardens. Choose a pot a little bigger than the root system and layer the base with crocks. Plant the tree in the soil at the same level as the original soil mark on the stem. Back fill firmly with John Innes No. 3 compost. Water in well and keep the tree moist.

HARVEST: **VARIOUS**

See DRYING FRUIT AND VEGETABLES pages 160–161

Apples

Select the right varieties and you be could harvesting apples from early autumn onwards, and still enjoying stored fruit throughout the long winter months.

1 'James Grieve' is a versatile, soft-fleshed variety that ripens in September. It can be enjoyed as a dessert apple although, because of its sharp flavour, some prefer to use it as a cooking variety.

2 'Egremont Russet' is a long-established and popular variety of dessert apple with a crisp flesh. Pick these sweet, nutty-tasting russets in October.

3 'Greensleeves' has sweet-tasting, golden-yellow flesh. This dessert apple produces heavy crops that are ready to harvest in October. It is probably best eaten freshly picked rather than stored.

4 'Ashmead's Kernel' is a firm-fleshed dessert apple with an outstanding flavour, both sharp and sweet. It is ready for picking in mid-October and develops its full flavour in storage.

5 'Falstaff' has been highly praised for its excellent flavour and resistance to disease. The crisp-fleshed fruits of this dessert variety are bright red when fully ripened in October.

6 'Golden Noble' is regarded as one of the best cooking apples. It has a tangy, but not acid, flavour. This variety, which is well suited to cooler areas, is ready for harvest in early October.

Other varieties to try:
'Bramley's Seedling' – cooking
'Discovery' – dessert
'Ellison's Orange' – dessert
'Scrumptious' – dessert

Pears

Beautiful blossom and aromatic fruit make a pear tree welcome in any garden. If a large tree isn't an option, train an espalier or a cordon on a sunny fence.

1 'Doyenne du Comice' is regarded as an outstanding dessert variety for flavour and texture. This pear needs plenty of warmth and should be placed in a sheltered spot. The fruit is ripe for picking around mid-October.

2 'Packham's Triumph' produces good crops of sweet, juicy fruit that ripens in mid-October. This dessert pear keeps well and if the fruit is stored with care it should last until the end of the year.

3 'Concorde' is a late-ripening dessert variety that is ready for picking around late October. The fruit has juicy flesh with a delicate flavour, and will store well until after Christmas.

4 'Beurre Superfin' is a large pear with a well-rounded shape and fine-textured, juicy flesh. It is an excellent dessert and cooking variety. Start picking the fruit in late September or early October.

5 'Williams' bon Chrétien' is one of the best-known varieties of pear in the world, and has been popular for over two centuries. It has fine, white flesh that is suitable for both eating raw and cooking. This pear ripens in September. Use it straight from the tree as this fruit does not store well.

Other varieties to try:
'Beth' – dessert
'Black Worcester' – cooking
'Conference' – dessert/cooking
Glou Morceau' – dessert
'Onward' – dessert

Choosing and planting fruit trees

Fruit trees will be with you for years to come, so consider your choices carefully, and if planting more than one, select early, mid- and late varieties for a longer harvest. Some fruit trees need a pollinator to grow alongside, while others are self-fertile and can be planted singly. Many trees are also grafted to control their size. Seek advice from a fruit nursery to help decide what best suits you and your plot.

PLANTING IDEAS

Choosing a tree

Once you have decided which fruit to grow there are still other considerations, too. For instance, would you prefer sweet dessert fruit or a culinary variety suited to cooking and preserving?

Fruit trees are grafted onto a rootstock, which determines their final size. Dwarfing rootstocks are ideal for smaller gardens, but need good soil to thrive, whereas semi-dwarfing rootstocks tolerate a wider range of conditions.

Many trees need a partner with an overlapping flowering period for pollination to occur and fruit to set. Varieties that flower at the same time are classed in the same pollination group, and for a good crop, plant two from the same group. If you lack space for two trees, look for possible pollinators growing in neighbouring plots.

Planting in pots

Growing fruit trees in pots limits their size, which is ideal for smaller plots. Select a container 8cm (3in) wider than the root system, ensure it has drainage holes, and add crocks to improve drainage further. Using soil-based compost (p.84), fill around the roots to the soil mark on the stem. Stake, firm in, and water the new tree well.

CONTAINER GROWN
Container-grown trees are available year-round. They can be planted at any time of year, but preferably not during hot summer weather. They can be expensive to buy.

BARE-ROOT
Field-grown, bare-root trees are lifted and sold dormant, mainly by specialist nurseries, in autumn and winter. Plant immediately, soaking the roots. Only buy well-rooted, undamaged plants.

PLANTING IN POTS
The best fruit trees to grow in containers are compact varieties grafted onto semi-dwarfing rootstocks. Ask your fruit supplier to recommend suitable varieties.

Planting new trees

The basic approach to planting container-grown and bare-root trees is similar, although there are important differences.

When planting container-grown trees, tease some of the outer roots away from the rootball first, to help them establish properly in the surrounding soil. A good bare-root tree has plenty of spreading roots, which should be soaked before planting if they look dry. Trim any that are damaged.

Always stake new trees to steady them in the wind, and to allow new roots to establish into the soil without being broken.

1 DIG A HOLE
Choose a sunny site, sheltered from wind and any frost pockets. Dig a hole large enough for the roots. If planting bare-root trees, mound the soil in the centre. Hammer in a stake.

2 POSITION THE TREE
Place the tree in the hole, level with the soil mark on the stem. Spread out the roots and ease soil around them, firming well. Attach the tree to the stake using a cushioned tie.

3 WATER AND FIRM IN WELL
Firm the tree in, ensuring the trunk is upright. Water it in well and apply a thick mulch of organic matter to help conserve moisture and gradually nourish the establishing tree.

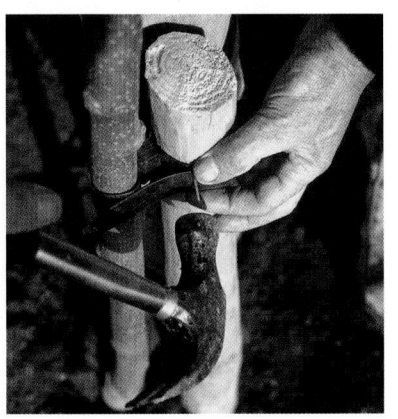

4 STAKING AND AFTERCARE
Attach the tree tie to the stake using a nail. Check a few weeks later to ensure the tie is still in place, and is not rubbing against the tree. Adjust if necessary. Keep the tree watered.

Trained trees

Espaliers and cordons take up little space trained against a wall or fence, making them ideal for smaller gardens. Cordons are single stems, usually trained at a 45° angle, with lots of short, fruiting sideshoots; while espaliers have long arms branching from a central stem, so need more room. These tree forms are controlled by summer pruning (p.137). Buy ready-trained trees from specialist nurseries to avoid much of the formative, autumn pruning of young trees (pp.206–207).

Espalier – The orderly tiers of a well-trained espalier look magnificent, but need plenty of space to spread; allow 3m (10ft) for trees grafted on dwarfing rootstocks. Espalier trees are usually limited to two or three tiers.

Cordons – This single-stemmed form suits apples and pears. It requires only 75cm (30in) between each tree, which means several varieties can be trained along an average-sized garden fence. Avoid tip-bearing varieties, which won't fruit well when pruned in this way.

November: what to do

MARK PARSNIPS

These hardy roots will happily sit in the soil over winter, so if you are short of storage space, they can stay in the ground until you need them. But finding them once their leaves have died down, or if there is snow on the ground, can involve a bit of guesswork. Take a moment to mark the rows with canes that are easy to spot, to make it easier to earth up your parsnip crop later on.

WORK SOIL

Late autumn is the ideal time to cultivate heavy, clay soils, working in organic matter to improve the structure. Digging sticky soils is hard work but allows frosts to help break the clods into crumbs by repeated freezing and thawing. Light, sandy soils are best protected with mulch now and dug over in early spring.

TEND

WINTER POTS

PARSNIPS

DIG BEDS

PREPARING POTS FOR WINTER

Planted or empty, pots and pot-grown plants can be damaged in winter, particularly by frosts (above). Take time now to protect them.

Smaller pots, and those made from terracotta and thin materials are most at risk. Heavy concrete pots are usually winter-proof.

CLEAN EMPTY POTS
Pots made of porous materials may become stained by algae or lime scale. Although harmless, take the opportunity to clean your pots now.

LINE CLAY POTS
In colder areas, line pots with bubble plastic before planting trees in them, to help protect the roots from hard frosts. Don't block drainage holes.

RAISE POTS OFF GROUND
To help keep terracotta pots dry in winter, and protect them against frost damage, raise them off the ground to ensure they drain freely.

WRAP TENDER POTS
In colder areas, protect your pots, and any plant roots inside, from hard frost by wrapping them in bubble plastic, fleece, or hessian sacking.

PROTECT TALL POTS

Safeguard larger container-grown plants, such as fruit trees and bushes, and shrubby herbs, from winter damage, by moving them to a sheltered spot. Strong winds can blow plants over and break containers. Pot-grown plants are also at risk of frosted roots, so move tender plants nearer to the house for warmth.

PRUNE OUTDOOR VINES

Now is the time to prune outdoor vines trained using the double guyot system (p.141), where two arms are tied horizontally to bear vertical, fruiting shoots.

 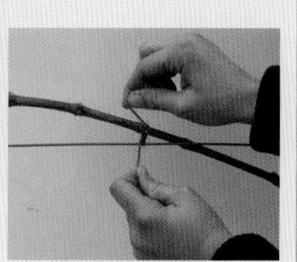

1 REMOVE SPENT STEMS
Using sharp secateurs or loppers, cut out the two horizontal arms that fruited last summer. Cut them close to the main stem.

2 PLAN AHEAD
Cut back the middle shoot to three healthy buds. This will grow and bear the three new shoots to train the following season (p.141).

3 TRAIN NEW SHOOTS
Tie down the two outer shoots, trained in summer (p.141), onto the wire; one to the left, one to the right. These will sprout fruiting stems.

TALL POT PLANTS

GRAPES

WINTER PROTECTION

FALLEN LEAVES

COLD COMFORT

Most crops that grow through winter are fully hardy but can still be damaged by harsh winter winds and rain. If you live in an exposed area, it's well worth providing extra support for taller crops, such as Brussels sprouts and kale, by staking them. Short wooden stakes are best, hammered in close to each plant. If you have a small bed of crops, consider screening right around it with windbreak fabric.

LEAF MOULD

Rather than burning fallen leaves, pile them into their own composting bay to slowly break down into leaf mould. Construct a simple bin using posts and wire mesh, fill with leaves, and in a year or two you'll have crumbly compost for potting and mulching. If space is limited, and you have few leaves, compost them in damp plastic bags.

See PRUNING FRUIT IN AUTUMN pages 206–207

Pruning fruit in autumn

Until late winter, fruit trees and bushes are dormant, making this the best time to prune them. Removing old, unproductive growth will encourage a good supply of new shoots to bear bumper future crops.

The pruning methods used for each type of fruit are straightforward, made easier by the leafless branches that allow you to clearly see the shape of the plant, and to identify diseased or weak growth.

Pruning fruit bushes

As well as established plants, you should also prune newly planted fruit bushes now (p.31).

To prune, make the cuts just above the buds at a 45° angle sloping away from the shoot, so rainwater drains off the wound. Use clean, sharp tools, and remember to clean the blades between one plant and the next, to prevent the spread of disease.

When pruning in autumn, make use of currant and gooseberry prunings for hardwood cuttings. Insert them into the soil, 15cm (6in) deep, buds pointing upwards, and they will soon take root.

REDCURRANTS
These fruit at the base of one-year-old shoots and on older wood, so leave a permanent framework of branches. Cut branch leaders by half and side-shoots pruned in summer to one bud.

GOOSEBERRIES
Remove stems crowding the centre, and any dead or diseased wood. Cut back sideshoots pruned in summer to two buds, and prune half of this year's growth from leading shoots.

SINGLE CORDON GRAPES
Prune established vines trained under glass. Cut back the top growing point so about 2.5cm (1in) of new growth remains, and prune this summer's sideshoots back to a single bud.

BLACKBERRIES AND HYBRIDS
Now that the old canes have finished fruiting, untie them from the supports and cut them at the base. Train the new canes that will fruit next year onto the wires and tie them in securely.

BLACKCURRANTS
These fruit best on new wood from the previous summer. Prune a third of the oldest shoots to the base to encourage plenty of strong new growth that will bear fruit next year.

Pruning fruit trees

Tackling a large, established tree can be daunting, but only moderate pruning is required to keep an open shape, letting in light and air, and to encourage new growth to fruit next year. Over-pruning causes vigorous, vertical, unfruitful growth, while under-pruning leaves trees congested and prone to disease, so try to get the balance right. Fruit trees are either spur-bearers (producing fruit along their shoots on short, dumpy stems) or tip-bearers, which fruit at the shoot tips. Check your variety and prune accordingly.

PRUNING SPUR-BEARERS
Cut back long sideshoots to about six buds to encourage new fruiting-spur formation. Prune back branch leaders by a third of last season's growth. Thin out congested or shaded spurs.

PRUNING TIP-BEARERS
Prune lightly, removing older shoots that have already fruited to their base. This should give rise to new, young wood that will fruit next year at the tips. Always prune the weakest growth.

REMOVE POOR GROWTH
Cut back to healthy growth any branches that show signs of disease, such as canker (p.241) and coral spot (shown). Remove thick material with a pruning saw and burn infected growth.

IMPROVE THE SHAPE
Look at the overall tree, and thin out any branches that crowd the middle of the framework, plus any that cross over each other, or rub together. Cut to outward-facing shoots.

CUTTING BRANCHES

When pruning large branches from fruit trees, first reduce their length and weight to prevent causing unnecessary damage and ripped bark.

1 Part undercut the branch midway along, then saw through from the top, slightly further from the trunk.

2 Remove the short stump, sawing it off just beyond the crease where the branch and trunk meet.

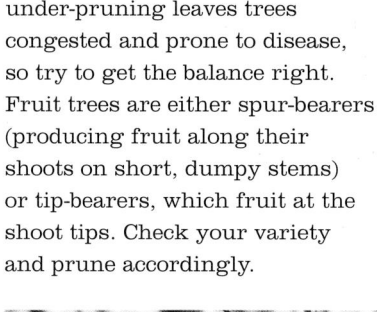

3 Allow wound to heal naturally, don't apply pruning paint. It will eventually form a weather-tight scar.

4 Clean the saw after use with detergent to reduce the spread of diseases, then apply oil to prevent rust.

PRUNING FRUIT IN AUTUMN

November: what to harvest

ROOT THEM OUT
Having grown all summer, Jerusalem artichokes have now died back until spring, so you can start lifting the strange-looking, knobbly tubers, with their delicious, nutty flavour. Dig them out using a fork only when needed in the kitchen, as they soon dry out and spoil. The roots keep very well in the soil and can be dug up all through winter, providing the ground isn't frozen. When lifting the tubers, be sure to get even the tiniest ones, because they will re-grow and spread next year if left behind. This perennial crop can be invasive.

FROSTED FIRST
From a spring sowing, parsnips can be lifted now, although they develop the sweetest flavour after a few frosts, so leave some to lift through winter. In light soils the roots can reach a good length. Loosen the earth around them with a fork, and lift them carefully to avoid damage. They're best harvested as required because they keep better in the ground. If you must store them to make space outside, see pages 210–211.

HARVEST

KOHL RABI

JERUSALEM ARTICHOKES

PARSNIPS

KOHL SHORTAGE
Late-growing kohl rabi (p.154) plants endure cold weather, but will be spoiled by frost. Either pull them up and use the swollen stems before winter arrives, cloche the remaining plants, or lift them, remove the outer leaves and store in boxes of sand in a cool, frost-free place.

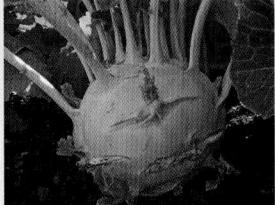

'PURPLE DANUBE'
Dark on the outside, its tasty flesh is pure white, and most tender when harvested young. Older, larger plants can become slightly bitter tasting.

'KOLIBRI'
Best eaten golf-ball sized, and ready in as little as 8 weeks, this variety is good in smaller gardens where it will give several crops during summer.

'LANRO'
Harvest when the swollen green stems reach 5cm (2in) across. They can be eaten diced and boiled, but are delicious grated in salads.

'SUPERSCHMELZ'
Gradually reaching 25cm (10in) across, this is a larger variety that can also be harvested small. It has a mild, sweet, turnip-like flavour.

HARVEST SALSIFY ROOTS

Salsify, sown directly outside in May (p.94), is ready to harvest, allowing you the chance to enjoy the unusual, nutty-tasting roots that have become a 'must have' among top chefs. Dig deeply with a fork to lift the roots as required, from now until spring. Roots left in the soil have a superior flavour to those lifted and stored in sand-filled boxes (pp.210–211), but storing is useful in areas with cold winters, where the ground may freeze. The skins must be removed; smaller roots are easier to peel after cooking.

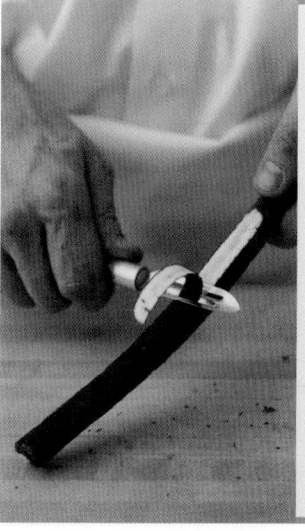

SWEDE SUCCESS

Hearty swedes, sown in May (p.94), will be full of flavour. Harvest them as needed until midwinter. If the weather allows, dig them up and store them in dry boxes, covered with sand. If the weather is poor, wait until spring, although the roots will be woody and tougher to eat by then.

CELERIAC | **SALSIFY** | **WINTER SALAD** | **SWEDE**

WINTER CELERIAC

Celeriac can be harvested this month, right through until spring, making it a really useful crop. The roots are tough enough to be left in the ground all winter in most places, and lifted as required. If you live in a very cold area, where the ground may freeze, lift the entire crop now, trim off the outer leaves, and store the roots in boxes of dry sand, (pp.210–211).

TAKE A LEAF

Winter salad leaves, grown under cover since late summer, are ready to crop. Mizuna, mibuna, oriental mustard, salad rocket, lettuce, perpetual spinach, and corn salad are all plants to take baby leaves from throughout winter. Even under cover, growth will be slow at this time, so these cut-and-come-again crops will take time to re-sprout.

Try MAKING SOUPS pages 226–228

Storing vegetables

By using traditional storage techniques, you can look forward to home-grown vegetables throughout winter, anything from stacks of potatoes to a few prized squash. Some root crops can be left in the soil in mild areas, but most other vegetables should be harvested and stored. The important point is to keep them fresh, and to protect them from frosts, weather damage, and hungry insects and animals.

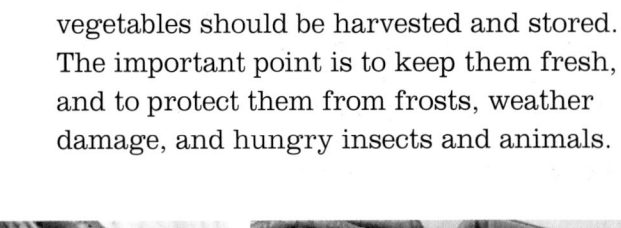

Roots in boxes

If you have space available in a cool, frost-free place, such as a shed, cellar, or garage, then try storing smaller root vegetables in boxes filled with light soil or sand. The method is simple and it keeps roots firm and fresh right through winter. Carrots, beetroot, turnips, celeriac, and parsnips can all be stored like this. You can fit several layers into a single box, which is ideal if you have only limited space indoors.

Whichever roots you store, lift them carefully, if possible when the soil is reasonably dry. If the roots are wet, lay them out on newspaper to dry fully and then brush off loose soil. Check each one, and store only crops that are disease-free and undamaged.

HARVESTING IDEAS

1 REMOVE LEAVES
Remove all foliage before storing. Cut off carrot leaves 1cm (½in) above the roots and twist off the leaves of other vegetables with your hands, leaving a short tuft of stems at the top.

2 PREPARE YOUR BOX
Find a cardboard or wooden box that is wide and fairly shallow. Line it with newspaper if there are any gaps. Cover the base with a layer of light soil or sand about 2.5cm (1in) thick.

3 ARRANGE THE ROOTS
Place the first layer of roots with care to make maximum use of the space without one root touching another. Contact between them could allow rot to spread through the box.

4 LAYER THEM UP
Once the first layer is complete, cover it with at least 2.5cm (1in) of light soil or sand. Repeat the whole process until the box is full. Store in a dry, frost- and rodent-free place.

Jo's tips

The larger the root, the longer it will keep, so when storing in sand-filled boxes, pack the biggest specimens in the bottom layers and the smallest ones at the top.

Not all root crops keep well when lifted. Jerusalem artichokes and salsify lose their flavour and dry out once harvested.

Clamping

This traditional method is ideal for storing large quantities of root crops, and involves piling them in a heap and insulating them with layers of straw. Providing the clamp can be kept dry, crops can be stored this way indoors or out. Stored vegetables must be dry, clean and undamaged, so check them thoroughly first. Outdoor clamps are prone to rodent attack, so watch for signs of disturbance, and set traps if need be. When emptying the clamp, take roots from one end only and carefully replace the layers once you have removed what you need.

1 LAY THE BASE
Spread a 20cm (8in) deep bed of straw on the soil in a sheltered spot, ideally against a wall. Arrange the roots on top to make a tapering heap that is a maximum 60cm (2ft) high.

2 PROVIDE INSULATION
Pack the same thickness of dry straw over the entire heap. If your clamp is indoors you can just cover it with hessian sacking or horticultural fleece weighed down at the edges.

3 ALL-WEATHER PROTECTION
Cover your outdoor clamp with a further layer of soil, about 15cm (6in) thick, to provide extra protection against cold and wet. Pack soil onto the straw from the base upwards.

4 ENSURE GOOD DRAINAGE
Soggy soil will rot stored roots from the base, so improve drainage by digging a shallow ditch around the edge of the clamp, using the soil to finish covering the top of the heap.

TRY THESE

Traditional methods can be used to store a wide range of crops, keeping them fresh to use without taking up space in your refrigerator or freezer.

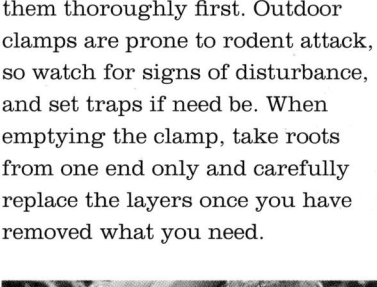

Potatoes – Store maincrop varieties somewhere dry and frost-free in paper sacks, folded over to exclude light.

Bulbs – When dried (p.159), hang onions, shallots, and garlic in bunches somewhere cool, dry, and frost-free.

Squash – Once cured (p.175) store squash and pumpkins under cover, on straw or shredded paper.

Beans – When the pods are dry and brittle, store the beans in screw-top jars indoors. Check them occasionally.

STORING VEGETABLES

Making simple chutney

Chutneys are a gift to gardeners reluctant to waste the mountain of leftover fruit and vegetables as summer turns to autumn. The joy of these preserves, apart from the fact that they are child's play to make, is that you can create your own recipe with almost any produce. The only rules are that a chutney should contain good quality vinegar to prevent spoiling, and sugar and spices for a rich, punchy flavour.

RECIPE IDEAS

Spicy plum and apple chutney

Makes approx 1.35kg (3lb) (3 large jars)

Takes 2 hours

Keeps 1 year

Ingredients

350g (12oz) cooking apples

1kg (2¼lb) plums

2 onions

75g (3oz) fresh root ginger

125g (4½oz) raisins

300g (10oz) light soft brown sugar

1 tsp salt

1 tsp allspice

1 tsp ground cloves

1 tsp ground cinnamon

600ml (1 pint) cider vinegar

Jo's tips

Chutneys should have a thick consistency, so they spread well in sandwiches and sit in appetizing mounds on plates of cold meat. If a watery layer develops on chutney in the jar, it needs more cooking, so pour it back into a pan and simmer until thickened.

To sterilize jars, wash them in hot soapy water, place them on a rack in a moderate oven, and leave them there to dry thoroughly.

1 Start by peeling, coring, and cutting up the apples. Wash the plums and chop them roughly, taking care to remove all the stones. Take the skins off the onions before slicing them, and grate the ginger.

2 Put all the fresh ingredients into a preserving pan or large saucepan, and add the raisins, sugar, salt, spices, and cider vinegar. Bring to the boil slowly, stirring regularly until the sugar has dissolved.

3 Reduce the heat and simmer gently for about 1½ hours, until the mixture is thick, excess liquid has evaporated, and some of the fruit and vegetables have cooked to a pulp. Stir frequently to avoid sticking.

4 Pour or ladle the chutney into sterilized jars while they are still warm (see Jo's Tips, left). Seal the jars while the chutney is hot. Use non-metallic lids as the vinegar will react with metal and taint the chutney.

Chutney improves with keeping, so leave it unopened for at least 4 weeks before eating.

TRY THESE

This technique for making chutney can be used with an array of vegetables, fruit, and spices, such as those suggested below. There are others to try.

Gooseberry and ginger – Deliciously fruity and spicy, this combination makes the perfect partner for cheese.

Beetroot – Rich red, sweet, and flavoured with cloves and allspice, what could be better with cold meats?

Courgette – Beef up the flavour with onions, garlic, and tomatoes, and maybe add some fire with a chilli.

Runner beans – This chutney has a chunky texture. Add tomatoes, turmeric, and mustard for flavour.

December: ready to eat

It's time for fresh Brussels sprouts, kale, and cabbage, along with sweet roasted root vegetables. Bring out the homemade chutney as a tangy accompaniment, and enjoy desserts made from stored summer fruit.

Eat **winter radishes**, pulled fresh from the soil and grated into salads

Keep harvesting fresh cut-and-come-again leaves

New season **winter cabbages** are a high point this month

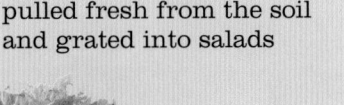

Harvest the last of your **trench celery**

Add the last newly dug **turnips** to stews and hotpots

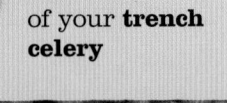

Add **endive**, grown under cover, to give your salads a bitter twist

Enjoy fresh **sprouting seeds** every few days
pages 36–37

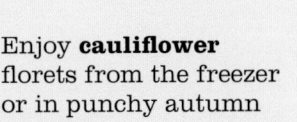

Use up stored **cobnuts**

Try mashed **swede**, using newly dug or stored roots

Enjoy **cauliflower** florets from the freezer or in punchy autumn pickles

Pull fresh **parsnips** or use them from your stores

Eat under cover crops of **Swiss chard** and **spinach beet**

Tasty **kale** will crop for months; try it shredded and stir-fried

Bake stored **winter squash** – eat with a knob of butter

Continue to eat fresh **salsify** – it tastes much better than it looks!

Carry on using your frozen **beans** and **peas**
pages 148–149

'Tis the season... to enjoy your homemade wine
pages 180–181

Use dried, **home-grown herbs**
page 161 in seasonal stuffing

Use leftover **Brussels sprouts** to make the best bubble and squeak

Leeks, lightly fried in butter, have a wonderfully sweet, onion flavour

Use **dried chillies**
page 161 to give your meals some bite

Put a bowl of homemade **chutney** on the table
pages 212–213

Celeriac – looks weird, tastes terrific

Roast stored **potatoes** and root vegetables

Make tastier winter salads using **leaf chicory**, grown under cover

Jerusalem artichokes are costly to buy, so dig your own, fresh, nutty tubers

Make hot puddings from stored **apples** and **pears**
pages 194–195

Homemade **pickles** will keep you going
pages 176–177

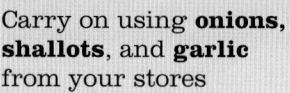

Carry on using **onions, shallots**, and **garlic** from your stores

Eat the last freshly dug **carrots**

December: what to sow

FORCING CHICORY

HARVEST: **JAN–MAR**

Having lifted and stored your Witloof chicory roots (see p.185), they're now ready for the next stage of the forcing process. Act now, and in less than a month, you can be enjoying a leafy luxury that's normally expensive to buy. You might even get a second harvest.

1 POT UP THE ROOTS
Plant several stored roots into a large pot, leaving the trimmed tops above the surface of the soil.

2 BLOCK OUT THE LIGHT
Cover the pot with another the same size, but block the drainage holes to exclude light from the roots.

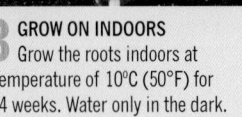

3 GROW ON INDOORS
Grow the roots indoors at a temperature of 10°C (50°F) for 3–4 weeks. Water only in the dark.

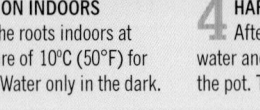

4 HARVEST
After harvesting the leaves, water and re-cover the roots with the pot. They may crop again.

SOW

PEAS

WINTER SALAD CROP

WITLOOF CHICORY

NEW YEAR PEAS

HARVEST: **MAY–JUN**

If you live in a mild area, hardy peas can still be sown directly outside (p.184). In colder regions, sow them under cover for planting out in spring.

'DOUCE PROVENCE'
This is a high yield, dwarf variety that produces masses of sweet tasting peas. It only requires support in exposed sites.

'FELTHAM FIRST'
Very hardy, this dwarf variety gives an early crop of 10cm (4in) long green pods, packed with large peas. It is suitable for containers.

'METEOR'
Dwarf but highly productive, this variety produces abundant small pods, filled with fine-tasting peas. Grows well on exposed sites.

WINTER SALAD

If you have space in an unheated greenhouse or beneath a cold frame, you still have time to sow hardy oriental salad leaves, such as mizuna and mustard, for an early cut-and-come-again crop. Sow 1cm (½in) deep, in trenches 10–15cm (4–6in) wide, directly in the soil. You can also sow into large pots and bring them under cover. Harvest the young plants after a few weeks, although they may take some time to re-grow.

HARVEST: **ALL YEAR**

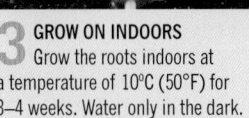

December: what to plant

PICK GARDEN NUTS

HARVEST: **SEP–OCT**

If you have space in your garden for a small apple tree, you could plant a cobnut instead. Depending on variety, you may need two for pollination.

'COSFORD'
This variety produces a heavy crop of thin-shelled, sweet-tasting nuts that are easy to crack open.

'KENTISH COB'
A self-fertile variety, so you only need one plant. It bears delicious, large nuts in late summer.

'RED FILBERT'
This red-leaved variety produces masses of tasty, red-shelled nuts. It is an attractive garden shrub.

COBNUTS

CARE FOR TOOLS

APRICOTS

PLANT

TIMELY TOOL CARE

Finding time to maintain your gardening tools is difficult in the growing season, so make use of the relative lull now to lavish some care on them. Use a wire brush to remove mud from metal tools, and rub them with an oily cloth to prevent rust. Clean the blades of cutting tools, such as secateurs and loppers, with wire wool and sharpen them. Replace any blades that are damaged.

TREE PLANTING

Despite seeming tender, apricots can be planted from now until March, if the soil isn't frozen. To help protect the early blossom from frost and to ripen the fruit, pick a warm position against a south-facing wall. Add compost to the soil, and plant the tree to the same depth as it was in the nursery. Firm the soil and water-in well.

HARVEST: **JUL–AUG**

See CHOOSING & PLANTING FRUIT TREES pages 202–203

Plums

Plums are easy to grow and often crop heavily. They are vigorous, so for smaller plots choose a tree on a dwarfing rootstock or train it as a fan against a wall.

1 'Early Laxton' is one of the first plums to ripen in summer, although not one of the tastiest. It is partially self-fertile, but gives a better crop with a suitable pollination partner nearby.

2 'Opal' is an early variety that gives a heavy crop of tasty red fruit in early August. It is self-fertile, so you'll only need one tree for a crop, making it a good choice for smaller gardens.

3 'Victoria' gives an excellent crop of dark red fruit during late summer, which are deliciously sweet when eaten raw or cooked. Use surplus fruit for jam (pp.128–129) or wine (pp.180–181).

4 'Shiro' is a golden-fruited variety, with pale yellow skin and transparent flesh. It flowers in early spring, and its blossoms can be damaged by frost, so it's best suited to milder regions.

5 'Giant Prune' gives a heavy crop of large dark red fruit in late summer that are particularly good for storing. It is self-fertile, hardy, and disease-resistant, making it a good choice for beginners.

Other varieties to try:
'Blue Tit'
'Czar'
'Majorie's Seedling'
'Methley'
'Warwickshire Drooper'

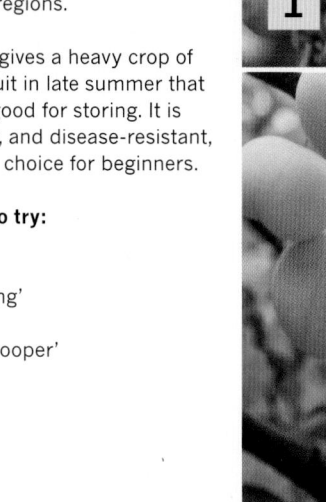

Damsons and gages

Small and dark, with a sharp taste, damsons are best used for cooking and preserving. Gages are sweeter, and delicious in desserts, jams, and cordials.

1 'Merryweather Damson' is a heavy-cropping variety that produces large, blue-black fruit with yellow flesh, which can be eaten raw or cooked. Self-fertile, it sets fruit without a pollinator variety.

2 'Prune Damson' is a traditional variety that bears small, dark, rich-tasting fruit in late summer, which are excellent cooked. The harvest isn't large, but it grows well in cold regions.

3 'Cambridge Gage' is a reliable, free-fruiting variety that gives an ample harvest of sweet, green fruit that are good to eat cooked or raw. Partially self-fertile; it is best with a pollinator.

4 'Old Green Gage' is an old variety that produces rich, sweet-tasting, yellow-green fruit in early autumn. Self-sterile, it must be grown with a pollinating variety for a good crop.

5 'Oullins Golden Gage' produces large, sweet, yellow fruit, with clear flesh. It is self-fertile and a reliable cropper, giving a reasonable harvest in late summer. Eat the fruit raw or cooked.

Other varieties to try:
'Bradley's King Damson'
'Denniston's Superb' – gage
'Farleigh Damson'
'Laxton's Gage'

PLUMS, DAMSONS AND GAGES

TAKE YOUR PICK

Cherries

Choose dwarfing rootstock for cherry trees that are suitable for any size garden. Eat sweet cherries straight from the tree; acid varieties are better cooked.

1 'Stella' produces abundant crops of sweet, dark-red fruit that are ready to harvest from around mid-July to August. This self-fertile variety is easy to grow.

2 'Lapins' has very large, almost black fruit with a superb flavour. These sweet cherries are ready to pick in late June. The self-fertile tree needs little pruning.

3 'May Duke' is a long-established variety used mainly for cooking. This cherry has a tangy flavour midway between sweet and acid. The bright red fruits are ripe for picking in mid-July.

4 'Morello' is an acid cooking cherry, with large juicy fruits that are excellent for pies and jam-making. It crops abundantly and the first cherries are ready for picking in late August.

5 'Sweetheart' has a long picking season, as the sweet, dark red fruit ripens in stages over an extended period. The first crop can be picked from late August onwards.

Other varieties to try:
'Celeste' – sweet
'Nabella' – acid
'Summer Sun' – sweet
'Vega' – sweet

1

2

3

4

5

Currants

Draped in their heavy crops of berries, these bushes look beautiful and will fruit for years in a bed, large patio pots, or trained as space-saving cordons on a fence.

1 'Ben Sarek' is a compact bush that makes a good choice for the smaller garden. This variety is resistant to mildew. The abundant fruit, which freezes well, is ready for picking from around mid-July.

2 'Ben Connan' produces large fruit with an exceptional flavour. Once a bush is well established, you should expect heavy crops in mid-July. This variety is good eaten as a dessert fruit and can also be used for jams and jellies.

3 'White Versailles' has delicate, creamy white fruit that hangs heavily in long trusses. These currants have a sweet flavour and can be eaten fresh or used for cooking. The crop ripens from midsummer onwards.

4 'Blanca' ripens slightly later than most currants. Its large, yellowish-white berries are not fully ripe until the end of July. Pick and eat the fruit fresh from the bush or use it for making preserves.

5 'Red Lake' is a popular redcurrant often recommended for its abundant crops. The fruit, sweet and well flavoured, ripens by mid-July.

6 'Jonkheer van Tets' has plump, juicy, glowing red fruits. This hardy variety is easy to grow and ripens early, usually producing a heavy crop that is ready to pick in early July.

Other varieties to try:
'Ben Lomond' – blackcurrant
'Ebony' –blackcurrant
'Stanza' – redcurrant

CHERRIES AND CURRANTS

TAKE YOUR PICK

Citrus

Citrus trees are handsome evergreen plants that produce gloriously scented white flowers, usually in spring but also sporadically throughout the year. They look attractive in containers and can be grown singly; being self-fertile, they don't need a partner for pollination. Consistent warmth is the secret of success.

The right climate

These exotic plants have been grown in temperate regions for centuries, although almost always sheltered under glass during winter. To successfully produce fruit, citrus trees need periods of several months where the temperature doesn't fall below 15°C (59°F). Where frosts are mild and summers hot, citrus trees can be a permanent outdoor feature. However, most gardeners prefer to grow them in containers in a cool, bright indoor room, conservatory, or heated greenhouse during winter and move them outside to grace a sunny patio in summer.

Winter indoors

Although most citrus trees can survive temperatures around freezing point for short periods, it is best not to test them too severely. Move your container-grown trees under cover as soon as nights become cool at the beginning of autumn.

Citrus trees need high humidity and centrally heated houses tend to have a dry atmosphere, so stand the pot on a tray of wet gravel to keep the air moist. Don't place the container near radiators or in cold draughts. Water the tree sparingly during winter and watch for pests. Indoor citrus plants are prone to attack by aphids, mealy bugs, red spider mites, and scale insects. Squash any pests as soon as you spot them and treat infestations with insecticidal soap or suitable biological controls.

In early spring, repot into a slightly larger container, ideally using a soil-based compost, such as John Innes No. 2. Spring is also a good time for a light pruning to remove crossing or dead branches.

Summer outdoors

Once the last frosts have passed, move citrus trees outside to a warm, sheltered spot for the summer. Do this gradually, hardening them off over a few weeks, and be prepared to protect them with fleece if temperatures drop unexpectedly.

Plants in containers need feeding every 2 weeks during the growing season with a special citrus fertilizer. Citrus trees are sensitive to waterlogging, so make sure that pots are well drained. Small trees can produce only a few fruits without becoming stressed, so limit the crop to about four fruits on the tree at any given time. These will take 6 months or more to ripen, so be patient.

1

4

7

2

5

3

6

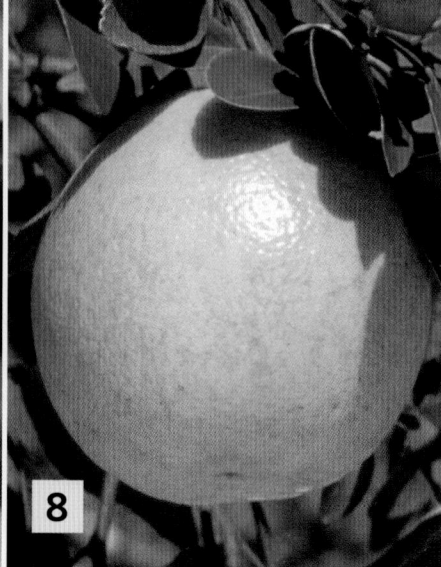

8

1 Kumquat – Although a close relative of other citrus fruits, the kumquat is not a member of the *Citrus* genus. It can tolerate temperatures down to -5ºC (23ºF). Eat the small oval fruit whole.

2 Lime – One of the tenderest citrus fruits, limes will fruit under cover if given adequate heat. The variety 'Bears' is more tolerant of cold than most.

3 Makrut – This citrus, sometimes known as kaffir lime, is grown for its aromatic, double-lobed leaves, which are well known as a key ingredient in Thai cuisine. The knobbly fruit is inedible.

4 Lemon – A fast-growing plant that can flower and fruit throughout the year, this is a good choice for beginners. 'Meyer' and 'Eureka' are excellent varieties.

5 Sweet orange – Attractive trees with beautiful flowers, sweet oranges need reliably high temperatures if the fruit is to ripen. Try 'Valencia' or the seedless 'Navelate' variety.

6 Mandarin – Easy for beginners, the mandarin is more resilient to cold than most other citrus. The thin-skinned, flattened fruits are easy to peel.

7 Calamondin – Popular as an indoor ornamental, this dwarf citrus produces small round fruits. The flesh is sweet but acidic when fully ripe. It is mostly used for making drinks or marmalades.

8 Grapefruit – Only a large tree can carry the heavy fruits, which take many months to ripen fully. Grapefruit needs high temperatures and presents a challenge for any grower.

Other varieties to try:
Blood orange –sweet pink or red flesh
Clementine – mandarin/orange hybrid
Limequat – lime/kumquat hybrid
Satsuma – mandarin/orange hybrid
Sour orange – for marmalades

CITRUS

December: what to harvest

WINTER KALE
Kale is a useful ally among winter vegetables, and can be relied upon to tough-out almost any winter weather. It's a particularly good crop for smaller gardens because, although the plants are quite large and grow all summer, the leaves can be picked a few at a time, all the way through winter. If the weather turns really bad, such as heavy snowfall, harvest the best leaves and freeze them until needed (pp.148–149). Even if your plants are damaged, leave them to recover and they may produce new leaves and shoots.

LAST OF THE CELERY
Able to withstand light frosts, trench celery is hardier than self-blanching types, and can be harvested through winter. As an extra precaution, give it a protective mulch of straw to keep it at its best. Lift earthed-up plants with a fork, or cut those blanched using collars right at the base, as required. Cut stems can be kept somewhere cool, stored in plastic bags, but whole plants are best left growing in the ground until needed.

HARVEST

KALE

TRENCH CELERY

POTATOES

PAK CHOI

LATE POTATOES
If you planted maincrop potatoes in midsummer (p.132), either in the ground or containers, you could well have tubers still to harvest. If the weather is cold, protect the remaining crop from frost by mulching with a thick layer of straw, or by moving containers under cover. Simply unearth the potatoes with a fork as required, and enjoy new potatoes at Christmas.

PAK CHOI NOW
Any late-summer sown pak choi, that were cloched or transplanted under cover in early autumn, should now be ready to harvest. Their fresh, mild leaves make a welcome contrast to the strong-flavoured, hardy winter brassicas. Pull up the plants whole or cut them off just above the soil, and they may well re-sprout.

SWEET WINTER GREENS

The first winter cabbages and endive, planted out in July (p.133), are ready to cut. If you have other vegetables to pick as well, leave a few cabbages growing for later. After a few hard frosts, their leaves become deliciously sweet, and are a real highlight of the season. To harvest, pull up the whole plant, and cut away the stem and any damaged outer foliage, to leave the firm green heart. While growing, these cabbages make handsome garden features, especially when they're dusted with crisp winter frost.

TASTY SPROUTS

Love or hate them, there's no denying that Brussels sprouts give a good winter crop. If you began sowing a succession of sprout varieties in February (p.41), then you'll be picking them from now until spring. Harvest the lower sprouts first, twisting them with your fingers, and work your way up the stem. Don't miss the leafy tops.

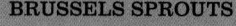

LEEKS

WINTER CABBAGE & ENDIVE

BRUSSELS SPROUTS

LIFT YOUR LEEKS

Mid- and late-season leeks, sown in spring, are ready to lift. Unearth them using a fork to prevent damaging the stems; the small roots grip fast.

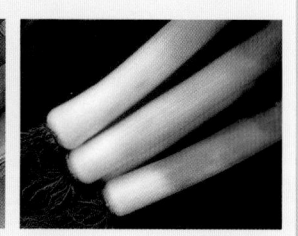

'KING RICHARD'
Although this is an early variety, it stands until December in milder areas. It doesn't need earthing-up and is suitable for growing in pots.

'MUSSELBURGH'
This is a reliable, tasty variety that produces a heavy crop of strong, thick stems. It tolerates cold very well, and is good for exposed sites.

'TOLEDO'
A very hardy, late-season variety, it produces long tasty stems and resists bolting. The harvested leeks also store well if heeled in.

DON'T FORGET

If a spell of very cold weather is forecast, mulch any root crops still in the ground with thick straw. This stops the soil freezing, so they can still be dug up.

Try FREEZING VEGETABLES
pages 148–149

Making soups

Everyone who grows vegetables needs a collection of favourite soup recipes to use throughout the year. Chunky or smooth, rustic and hearty, sophisticated and light, there is a soup for all tastes.

You can make soups with in-season crops or use vegetables from your freezer or winter stores. Soups are also a good way of using gluts, because it's easy to cook large quantities and freeze the surplus.

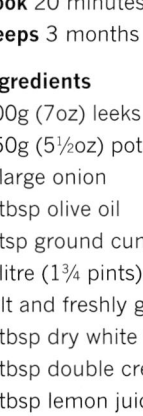

RECIPE IDEAS

Leek and potato soup

Serves 4
Preparation 15 minutes
Cook 20 minutes
Keeps 3 months in freezer

Ingredients
200g (7oz) leeks
150g (5½oz) potatoes
1 large onion
1 tbsp olive oil
1 tsp ground cumin
1 litre (1¾ pints) hot chicken stock
salt and freshly ground black pepper
2 tbsp dry white wine
2 tbsp double cream
1 tbsp lemon juice
chives, to garnish

1 Wash the leeks thoroughly, taking care to remove all grit between the leaves. Using a sharp knife, slice them lengthways and then into 2.5cm (1in) lengths. Dice the potatoes and thinly slice the onions.

2 Heat the olive oil in a heavy saucepan. Add the leeks, onions, potatoes, cumin, stock, salt, and freshly ground pepper. Cover with a lid and bring to the boil, then lower the heat and allow to simmer.

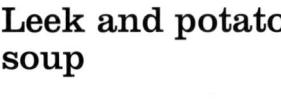

Jo's tips

For great soup, make your own stock or buy the best you can find. Vegetable or chicken stocks let the produce dominate, but sometimes only heavier stock, such as beef in French onion soup, will do.

For richer, sweeter soups, roast vegetables, such as squashes, tomatoes, and parsnips, in the oven for about 40 minutes, before adding to the other ingredients.

3 Simmer the soup gently for approximately 10 minutes, stirring occasionally, then check that the vegetables are tender. It's important not to let the potatoes overcook, as they will disintegrate into the soup.

4 Transfer the soup to a blender, add the wine and whiz until smooth. Stir in the cream and lemon juice, then check the seasoning and adjust to taste. Serve the soup in bowls with snipped chives to garnish.

Satisfyingly thick and tasty, leek and potato soup makes good use of your winter crops.

TRY THESE

Whatever the season, there is likely to be something in your vegetable garden that you can use to make delicious soup for a quick and healthy meal.

Onions – The useful onion finds its way into many soups, but it is outstanding in piping hot French onion soup.

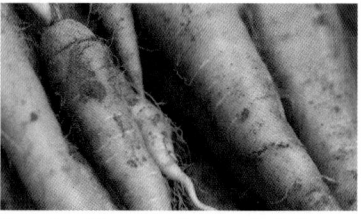

Carrots – These add a wonderfully vibrant colour to soup. Tangy carrot and orange soup is a popular recipe.

Parsnips – Nothing is more filling and warming on a cold winter day than a bowl of curried parsnip soup.

Broccoli – Try melting a blue cheese, such as Stilton, into creamy broccoli soup for a rich blend of flavours.

MAKING SOUPS

At-a-glance advice

In this section you will find quick-reference planners to remind you of the key timings for each crop. There is also a troubleshooting guide to pests, diseases, and nutritional deficiencies, to help you identify whatever is causing unsavoury spots on your apples, or chewing holes in your cabbages.

Fruit: crop planner

Use this table to check when to sow, plant, prune, and harvest your fruit. Timings will vary for different climates so adjust them for your own site and weather conditions. Planting times refer to bare-root plants; container-grown shrubs and trees can be planted year-round.

CROPS		J	F	M	A	M	J	J	A	S	O	N	D
APPLES	SOW												
	PLANT	■	■									■	■
	HARVEST								■	■		■	
	PRUNE	■						■	■				
APRICOTS	SOW												
	PLANT	■	■									■	■
	HARVEST							■	■	■			
	PRUNE			■	■	■	■	■					
BLACKBERRIES & HYBRIDS	SOW												
	PLANT										■	■	
	HARVEST							■	■	■	■		
	PRUNE											■	■
BLUEBERRIES	SOW												
	PLANT	■	■									■	■
	HARVEST							■	■	■			
	PRUNE	■	■									■	■
COBNUTS	SOW												
	PLANT	■	■									■	■
	HARVEST									■	■		
	PRUNE						■	■					
CHERRIES	SOW												
	PLANT	■	■									■	■
	HARVEST						■	■	■				
	PRUNE			■	■			■					
CURRANTS – BLACK	SOW												
	PLANT	■	■								■	■	
	HARVEST							■	■	■			
	PRUNE											■	■
CURRANTS – RED & WHITE	SOW												
	PLANT	■	■								■	■	■
	HARVEST							■	■	■			
	PRUNE						■	■					
FIGS	SOW												
	PLANT	■	■									■	■
	HARVEST								■	■	■		
	PRUNE		■	■			■	■					
GOOSEBERRIES	SOW												
	PLANT	■	■								■	■	
	HARVEST					■	■						
	PRUNE	■					■	■				■	■

KEY

▒▒▒▒▒	SOWN, PLANTED, HARVESTED UNDER COVER
▬▬▬▬	SOWN, PLANTED, HARVESTED OUTDOORS

CROPS		J	F	M	A	M	J	J	A	S	O	N	D
GRAPES – OUTDOOR	SOW												
	PLANT	▬	▬	▬								▬	▬
	HARVEST									▬	▬		
	PRUNE				▬	▬	▬	▬	▬	▬	▬	▬	▬
MELONS	SOW				░	▬	▬						
	PLANT					▬	▬						
	HARVEST								▬	▬			
	PRUNE												
NECTARINES & PEACHES	SOW												
	PLANT	▬	▬									▬	▬
	HARVEST								▬	▬			
	PRUNE					▬	▬	▬					
PEARS	SOW												
	PLANT	▬	▬									▬	▬
	HARVEST									▬	▬		
	PRUNE	▬	▬										
PLUMS, DAMSONS, & GAGES	SOW												
	PLANT	▬	▬									▬	▬
	HARVEST								▬	▬			
	PRUNE					▬	▬						
RASPBERRIES – SUMMER	SOW												
	PLANT	▬	▬								▬	▬	▬
	HARVEST							▬	▬				
	PRUNE		▬			▬				▬	▬		
RASPBERRIES – AUTUMN	SOW												
	PLANT	▬	▬								▬	▬	▬
	HARVEST								▬	▬	▬		
	PRUNE		▬										
RHUBARB	SOW												
	PLANT	▬	▬	▬								▬	▬
	HARVEST			▬	▬	▬	▬	▬					
	PRUNE												
STRAWBERRIES – SUMMER	SOW												
	PLANT							▬	▬	▬			
	HARVEST				░	▬	▬	▬					
	PRUNE												
STRAWBERRIES – PERPETUAL	SOW												
	PLANT			▬	▬	▬	▬						
	HARVEST								▬	▬	▬	░	░
	PRUNE												

Vegetable: crop planner

Use this table to check when to sow, plant, prune, and harvest your vegetables. Timings will vary for different climates, so adjust them for your own site and weather conditions. For continuity, replace crops harvested in spring and summer with plants sown later.

CROPS		J	F	M	A	M	J	J	A	S	O	N	D
ASPARAGUS	SOW												
	PLANT			●									
	HARVEST					●	●						
AUBERGINES	SOW			●									
	PLANT					●	●						
	HARVEST								●	●	●		
BEANS – BROAD	SOW	●	●									●	●
	PLANT			●									
	HARVEST					●	●						
BEANS – FRENCH	SOW					●	●						
	PLANT						●						
	HARVEST							●	●	●			
BEANS – RUNNER	SOW					●							
	PLANT						●						
	HARVEST							●	●	●	●		
BEETROOT	SOW			●	●	●	●	●					
	PLANT												
	HARVEST					●	●	●	●	●	●		
BROCCOLI – PURPLE SPROUTING	SOW				●	●							
	PLANT					●	●	●					
	HARVEST	●	●										
BROCCOLI – CALABRESE	SOW				●	●	●						
	PLANT												
	HARVEST								●	●			
BRUSSEL SPROUTS	SOW			●									
	PLANT					●							
	HARVEST	●								●	●	●	●
CABBAGE – CHINESE	SOW					●	●	●					
	PLANT												
	HARVEST								●	●	●		
CABBAGE – WINTER	SOW					●							
	PLANT							●					
	HARVEST	●	●	●	●								●
CABBAGE – SPRING	SOW				●								
	PLANT									●	●		
	HARVEST				●	●							
CABBAGE – SUMMER	SOW		●	●									
	PLANT				●	●							
	HARVEST								●	●			
CARROTS	SOW			●	●	●	●	●	●				
	PLANT												
	HARVEST					●	●	●	●	●	●	●	●

KEY

░░░░░	SOWN, PLANTED, HARVESTED UNDER COVER
█████	SOWN, PLANTED, HARVESTED OUTDOORS

CROPS		J	F	M	A	M	J	J	A	S	O	N	D
CAULIFLOWER – WINTER	SOW					█							
	PLANT							█	█				
	HARVEST			█	█	█							
CAULIFLOWER – SUMMER	SOW			█	█						█		
	PLANT												
	HARVEST							█	█	█	█		
CELERIAC	SOW		░	░									
	PLANT					█							
	HARVEST	█									█	█	█
CELERY – SELF BLANCHING	SOW		░	░									
	PLANT					█							
	HARVEST								█	█			
CELERY – TRENCH	SOW		░	░									
	PLANT					█							
	HARVEST	█									█	█	█
CHICORY – RED	SOW					█	█	█					
	PLANT							█	█				
	HARVEST	█	█	█	█	█	█	█	█	█	█	█	█
CHICORY – WITLOOF	SOW					█	█	█					
	PLANT							█	█				
	HARVEST	█	█	█								█	█
COURGETTES	SOW				░	░	█						
	PLANT					█	█						
	HARVEST						█	█	█	█			
CUCUMBER	SOW				░	░							
	PLANT					░							
	HARVEST							█	█	█			
ENDIVE	SOW				░	█	█	█					
	PLANT					█	█	█		░			
	HARVEST							█	█	█	█	█	█
FLORENCE FENNEL	SOW				░	█	█						
	PLANT					█							
	HARVEST							█	█	█	█		
GARLIC	SOW												
	PLANT		█	█							█	█	
	HARVEST							█	█				
GLOBE ARTICHOKE	SOW		░	░									
	PLANT				█	█							
	HARVEST	█									█	█	█
JERUSALEM ARTICHOKE	SOW												
	PLANT		█	█	█								
	HARVEST	█	█	█							█	█	█

CROPS		J	F	M	A	M	J	J	A	S	O	N	D
KALE	SOW				■	■	■	■					
	PLANT						■	■					
	HARVEST	■	■	■							■	■	■
KOHL RABI	SOW		▫	■	■	■	■	■					
	PLANT					■	■	■					
	HARVEST						■	■	■	■	■	■	
LEEKS	SOW	▫	▫	■	■								
	PLANT					■	■						
	HARVEST									■	■	■	■
LETTUCE	SOW		▫	■	■	■	■	■	■				
	PLANT				■	■							
	HARVEST				■	■	■	■	■	■	▫	▫	
MUSHROOMS	SOW	▫	▫	▫	▫	▫	▫	▫	▫	▫	▫	▫	▫
	PLANT												
	HARVEST	▫	▫	▫	▫	▫	▫	▫	▫	▫	▫	▫	▫
ONION – OVERWINTERING	SOW								■				
	PLANT									■	■		
	HARVEST						■						
ONION – SUMMER	SOW		▫	■	■								
	PLANT		■	■	■								
	HARVEST							■	■	■	■		
PAK CHOI	SOW						■	■	■				
	PLANT												
	HARVEST							■	■	■	■	■	
PARSNIPS	SOW		▫	■	■								
	PLANT												
	HARVEST	■									■	■	■
PEAS	SOW	▫		■	■	■	■				▫		
	PLANT			■	■								
	HARVEST					■	■	■	■	■	■		
PEPPERS – CHILLI	SOW		▫	▫									
	PLANT					▫							
	HARVEST							▫	■	■	■		
PEPPERS – SWEET	SOW			▫	▫								
	PLANT					▫	■						
	HARVEST							▫	■	■	■		
POTATOES – EARLIES	SOW												
	PLANT			■	■								
	HARVEST						■	■	■				
POTATOES – MAINCROP	SOW												
	PLANT				■	■							
	HARVEST									■	■		
POTATOES – LATE MAINCROP	SOW												
	PLANT							■					
	HARVEST										■	■	■
PUMPKIN	SOW				▫		■						
	PLANT					▫	■						
	HARVEST									■	■		
RADISH – SUMMER	SOW		▫	■	■	■	■	■	■	■			
	PLANT												
	HARVEST				■	■	■	■	■	■	■	■	

CROPS		J	F	M	A	M	J	J	A	S	O	N	D
RADISH – WINTER	SOW								■				
	PLANT												
	HARVEST	■	■	■							■	■	■
ROCKET	SOW	░	░	■	■	■	■	■	■	■			
	PLANT												
	HARVEST		■	■	■	■	■	■	■	■	■	■	■
SALAD LEAVES	SOW	░	░	■	■	■	■	■	■	■			
	PLANT												
	HARVEST			■	■	■	■	■	■	■			
SALISFY	SOW				■	■							
	PLANT												
	HARVEST	■	■	■	■	■						■	■
SHALLOTS – SETS	SOW												
	PLANT		■	■									
	HARVEST							■	■	■			
SPINACH	SOW		░			■	■	■					
	PLANT			■	■	■							
	HARVEST				■	■	■	■	■	■	■	■	■
SPRING ONIONS	SOW			■	■	■	■	■	■	■			
	PLANT												
	HARVEST	■	■	■	■	■	■	■	■	■	■	■	■
SPROUTING SEEDS	SOW	░	░	░	░	░	░	░	░	░	░	░	░
	PLANT	░	░	░	░	░	░	░	░	░	░	░	░
	HARVEST	░	░	░	░	░	░	░	░	░	░	░	░
SQUASH – SUMMER	SOW				░		■						
	PLANT					░	■						
	HARVEST							■	■	■	■		
SQUASH – WINTER	SOW					░	■						
	PLANT						■						
	HARVEST								■	■	■		
SWEDE	SOW					■	■						
	PLANT												
	HARVEST									■	■	■	■
SWEET CORN	SOW				░		■						
	PLANT						■						
	HARVEST								■	■	■		
SWISS CHARD	SOW						■	■	■				
	PLANT												
	HARVEST	■	■	■	■	■	■	■	■	■	■	■	■
SPINACH CHARD	SOW		░				■	■	■	■			
	PLANT												
	HARVEST	■	■	■	■	■	■	■	■	■	■	■	■
TOMATO	SOW			░									
	PLANT				░	░	■						
	HARVEST							■	■	■	■	■	■
TURNIPS	SOW			■	■	■	■	■	■				
	PLANT												
	HARVEST						■	■	■	■	■	■	

Common pests

Most plants in the kitchen garden are prone to attack by many different insect and animal pests. Healthy crops often cope well with attacks, but stay vigilant and check for pests regularly, as some can multiply quickly, seriously harming plants and reducing harvests.

1 APHIDS
Small sap-suckers, aphids include greenfly and blackfly and are found on young shoots of most plants. They distort new growth and transmit viruses. Squash them, encourage natural predators, or use pyrethrum or fatty acid sprays.

2 ASPARAGUS BEETLE
Adult beetles and their larvae feed on asparagus foliage and bark in late spring and summer, causing foliage to die back. Pick off the pest, spray with pyrethrum, or burn cut stems in autumn.

BIRDS (not illustrated)
Hungry birds feed on seeds, buds, fruit, and foliage. Soft fruit and brassicas are favourite targets. Cover vulnerable beds and bushes with netting, well secured at the base to prevent birds getting in and becoming trapped.

3 CABBAGE CATERPILLARS
Several butterfly and moth species lay eggs on brassicas, which then hatch into leaf-eating caterpillars. Pick off eggs and caterpillars, cover with fine netting, or spray with pyrethrum.

4 CABBAGE ROOT FLY
From spring to autumn these white larvae feed on brassica roots, and do serious damage to seedlings and young plants. Place discs around the bases of young plants to prevent eggs being laid.

5 CAPSID BUGS
These tiny insects suck sap from many plants, including currants and apples, causing brown-edged holes and deformed flowers. Control is usually unnecessary, but apples can be sprayed with lambda cyhalothrin after flowering.

6 CARROT FLY
The thin, creamy maggots of this small fly tunnel into carrots and parsnips. Grow resistant crop varieties and cover your seedlings with fleece.

CATS (not illustrated)
Cats love digging in soft seedbeds and may also tear netting and fleece. Use chicken wire to keep them off.

7 CODLING MOTH
The larvae bore into apples and pears in summer, and re-emerge in winter. Use a biological control in autumn or spray with lambda cyhalothrin in summer.

8 COLORADO BEETLE
A serious pest, the black and yellow striped beetle, about 1cm (½in) long, feeds on the foliage of potatoes, tomatoes, aubergines, and peppers. It is not a resident of the UK, so report any sightings to DEFRA.

9 CUTWORMS
Not, in fact, worms but the caterpillars of a nocturnal moth species, cutworms chew through the topmost roots of young plants or make holes in root vegetables. Handpick the pale brown caterpillars from the soil at night when they feed, or apply a biological control.

FLEA BEETLE (not illustrated)
These tiny black beetles pepper the leaves of brassicas with countless little holes, damaging seedlings and spoiling salad vegetables such as rocket. Grow your brassica crops under fleece or treat affected areas with pyrethrum.

10 GOOSEBERRY SAWFLY
The green, black-spotted larvae of the sawfly defoliate gooseberries and redcurrants in spring and summer, and can cause severe damage. Pick them off by hand, use a biological control, or spray with pyrethrum.

11 LEEK MOTH
The young caterpillars create pale brown patches on onion and leek foliage by mining the leaves, while more mature caterpillars bore into the flesh of the vegetables. Look out for silky, pupae-containing cocoons on the leaves and crush them to control numbers.

MEALYBUGS (not illustrated)
Usually found only on greenhouse and indoor plants, these sap-sucking insects are covered in white, fluffy wax and secrete a sticky honeydew. Squash them, treat with biological controls, or use fatty acid sprays.

12 MEALY CABBAGE APHIDS
A pest on all brassicas, these minute aphids have a whitish-grey, mealy coating. They suck sap on the underside of leaves, which damages new growth, and secrete sticky honeydew. Control by crushing them or using a fatty acid spray.

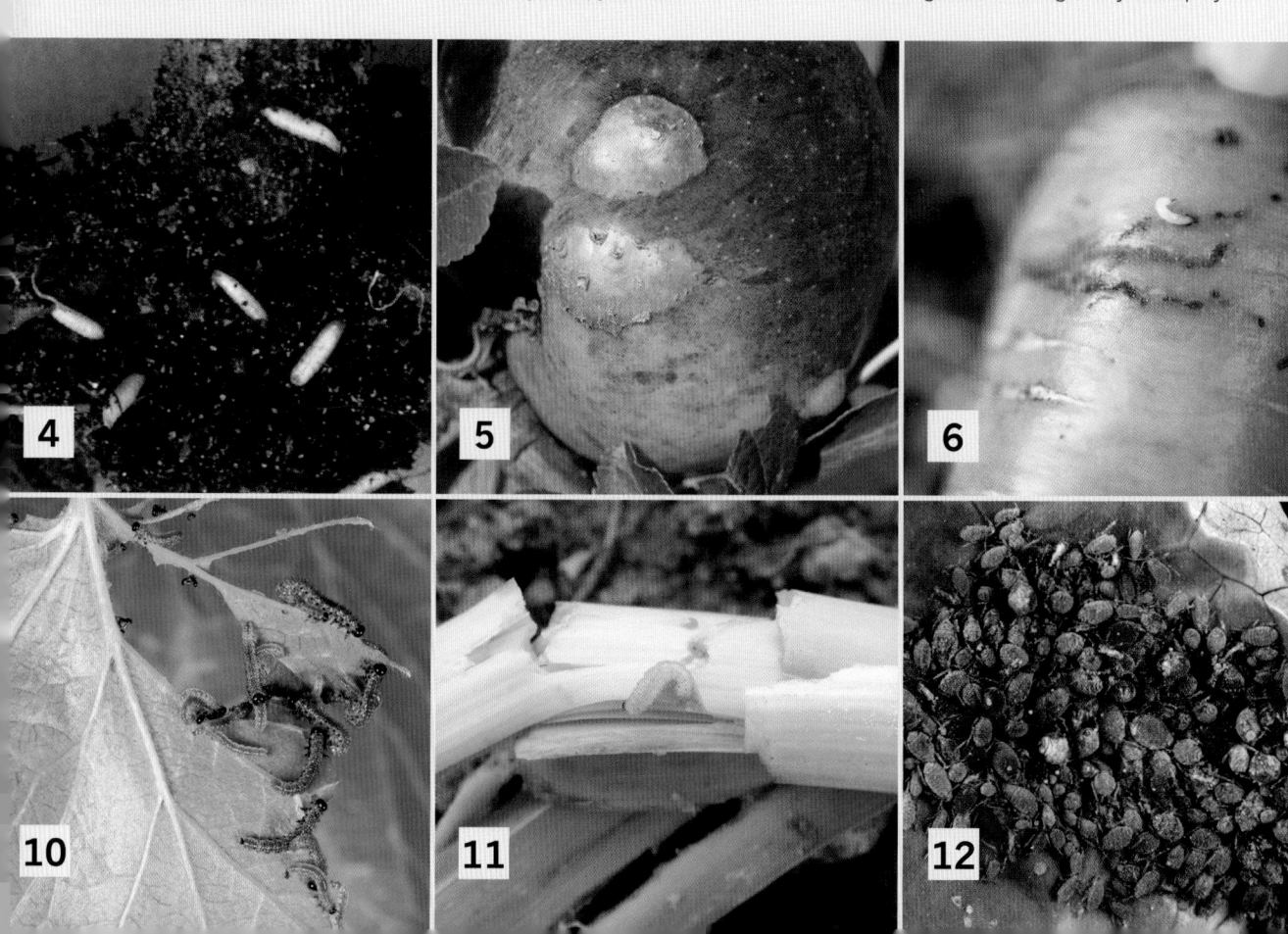

MICE AND RATS (not illustrated)
Pea and bean seeds in the soil, ripe ears of sweetcorn, and stored fruit and vegetables are all irresistible to these destructive rodents. They are difficult to control, but you can set traps where they might be a problem.

13 ONION FLY
The white fly maggots eat the roots of onion and leek seedlings in early summer and tunnel into onions in late summer, causing rotting. Destroy all affected plants and practise crop rotation. It is best to grow onions from sets, which are less vulnerable.

14 PEA AND BEAN WEEVIL
Little grey-brown beetles that nibble notches from leaf edges. The larvae feed among the roots of peas and broad beans. Large plants tolerate damage, but if heavy attacks seem likely, raise young plants in pots.

15 PEA MOTH
Adult moths fly throughout summer, laying their eggs on flowering peas. Caterpillars hatch and grow inside pods, eating the peas. Early and late sowings avoid the egg-laying adults, but summer crops should be netted.

PEAR LEAF BLISTER MITE (not illustrated)
The small pink or yellow blisters caused by this tiny mite appear on pear leaves in spring and darken to black. This damage won't affect the fruit crop. On small trees, pick off affected leaves.

16 PEAR MIDGE
The signs of pear midge are pear fruitlets that turn black at the base, stop growing, and drop by early summer. The maggots hatch from eggs laid in blossom and feed on the fruit. Remove and destroy affected fruitlets to help control pest numbers in the future.

17 PLUM FRUIT MOTH
The pale pink, brown-headed caterpillars feed near the stones of greengages, plums, and damsons, causing significant damage. Hang up pheromone traps in June, to attract and trap adult males and disrupt mating.

POTATO CYST EELWORM (not illustrated)
Potato and tomato plants that turn yellow and die early may have been attacked by these eelworms. The tiny root-feeding worms produce egg-filled cysts that persist in soil for 10 years. Rotate crops and grow resistant varieties.

18 RASPBERRY BEETLE
The grubs of this pest feed on the fruit of raspberries, blackberries, and hybrids. They may be found in the fruit, and they cause dry, grey-brown patches. Control raspberry beetle by spraying pyrethrum or deltamethrin as soon as the first fruits start to turn pink.

19 RED SPIDER MITE

Glasshouse and fruit tree red spider mites both cause dull, mottled leaves on a range of plants. Keep glasshouse humidity high in hot weather and use a biological control. Try fatty acid sprays outdoors.

20 ROOT APHIDS

Crops including carrots, lettuces, and beans attract these white aphids to feed on their roots, affecting growth and causing wilting in hot weather. Rotate your crops annually and water well during summer.

21 SLUGS AND SNAILS

These all-too-familiar slimy pests eat holes in leaves and roots, and can destroy rows of seedlings in a remarkably short time. Limit their numbers by collecting them at night, during winter hibernation, or in traps. Biological control is effective in summer.

22 WASPS

Wasps are good early summer pollinators, but they eat ripe fruit, especially plums, grapes, and apples, as the season progresses. Distract them with honey traps or damaged ripe fruit placed away from trees.

23 WHITEFLY

White-winged, sap-feeding insects that secrete sticky honeydew, whitefly are usually at their worst on greenhouse crops such as tomatoes and cucumbers. Biological control with *Encarsia formosa*, a parasitic wasp, is effective.

24 WIREWORMS

Larvae of the click beetle, these slim, orange-brown worms live in the soil, biting through seedlings and damaging root crops such as potatoes and carrots. Remove any visible larvae and dig up root crops promptly when they are ready to be harvested.

WOOLLY APHID (not illustrated)

A sap-sucking aphid covered in fluffy white wax, the woolly aphid is found on apple trees. Control isn't practical on large trees, but with smaller trees you can brush off the insects or spray with pyrethrum or fatty acids.

For general advice on organic pest control, see pages 104–105.

16

17

18

22

23

24

Common diseases

It can seem like there's an army of bacteria, fungi, and viruses out there to thwart your attempts to grow your own. Fortunately, healthy plants can resist disease, so tend them well, keep the garden tidy, to reduce sources of infection, and rotate crops to prevent disease building up.

1 AMERICAN GOOSEBERRY MILDEW
Powdery white patches on foliage, stems, and fruits of blackcurrants and gooseberries are caused by a fungus that thrives in stagnant air. Grow resistant varieties and prune to improve air flow.

2 BACTERIAL LEAF SPOT
Dead spots on leaves, surrounded by a yellow "halo", indicate bacterial infection, usually spread by water splashes. Brassicas and cucumbers are particularly prone. Remove affected leaves and water plants at the base.

BACTERIAL SOFT ROT (not illustrated)
This causes sunken, rotten areas on the roots and fruits of crops, such as brassicas, potatoes, tomatoes, and courgettes. The infection is spread by insects or dirty tools. Disinfect tools and remove affected plants.

3 BITTER PIT
Dark spots or pits appear on the skin of developing apples, and fruit may taste bitter. The problem is due to drought-induced calcium deficiency, so mulch apple trees and water well in dry weather.

BLACKCURRANT REVERSION VIRUS (not illustrated)
The virus, spread by mites, causes abnormally swollen buds and stunted growth on blackcurrants. Remove and burn infected plants and buy certified disease-free stock.

4 BLOSSOM END ROT
This appears as dark patches at the base of tomatoes, peppers, and other fruit. It is due to calcium deficiency, usually caused by drought conditions. Water consistently to protect developing crops.

BLOSSOM WILT (not illustrated)
A fungal disease associated with brown rot (see below), blossom wilt causes blossom, spurs, and small branches to die back on apples, pears, plums, and cherries. Remove affected flowers, wood, and fruit promptly to prevent spread.

5 BOTRYTIS
This fungus commonly infects plants growing under glass, as well as lettuce, and soft fruit. It causes a fuzzy grey mould, rotting, and die-back. Remove any infected growth quickly and ventilate greenhouses well to reduce humidity.

6 BROWN ROT
A widespread fungus that infects tree fruit by entering through damaged areas, causing rotten patches and creamy pustules. Remove infected fruit promptly, along with branches affected by blossom wilt (see above).

7 CANKER
Many fruit trees are affected by bacterial and fungal cankers, which cause shoots to die back, foliage holes, and sunken bark that may ooze resin. Prune back to healthy growth or treat bacterial infections with copper fungicides.

8 CHOCOLATE SPOT
Dark brown spots appear on foliage, stems, and pods of broad beans, spreading to reduce or destroy the crop. The fungus responsible flourishes in damp conditions, so grow plants widely spaced and on well-drained soil.

9 CLUB ROOT
This fungal infection produces enlarged, distorted roots on brassica plants, causing wilting, purple-tinged foliage, and sometimes die-back. Grow varieties resistant to club root. Reducing the acidity of soil by liming may also help.

10 CUCUMBER MOSAIC VIRUS
The virus is carried by aphids between cucumbers and related crops, such as courgettes. Leaves pucker and yellow, and fruit becomes distorted and inedible. Remove and burn infected plants.

11 DAMPING OFF
The disease causes seedlings, especially those grown under glass, to collapse suddenly. To reduce the risk of damping off, which is caused by fungi, use clean pots and mains water. Sow plants thinly, provide good ventilation, and apply a copper-based fungicide.

12 DOWNY MILDEW
This fungus thrives in humid conditions, causing brown patches on upper leaves, with fluffy growth beneath. Brassicas, lettuces, and many other plants are affected. Destroy diseased leaves and give plants ample space.

FIREBLIGHT (not illustrated)
Apples and pears are infected by this bacterial disease through their flowers. Flowers and shoots rapidly shrivel and die and wood under the bark is stained orange-brown. Cut back and burn all infected material.

FOOT AND ROOT ROTS (not illustrated)
Common in greenhouse-grown melons, cucumbers, and tomatoes, these fungal rots set in at the base of the stem, killing the whole plant. Remove and destroy infected plants, and practise good garden hygiene to prevent further rot.

13 FUNGAL LEAF SPOT
Circular grey or brown spots on leaves, sometimes with tiny black fruiting bodies, are caused by fungi on many types of crops, from strawberries to celery. This is not usually serious, but remove affected leaves to prevent the fungus spreading further.

HALO BLIGHT (not illustrated)
Caused by bacteria, darkening leaf spots with a yellow halo can spread to the pods of dwarf French and runner beans. Pick off affected leaves and avoid overhead watering, which spreads the infection.

14 HONEY FUNGUS
Fruit trees and bushes can be killed by honey fungus, which causes gradual or sudden die-back. Dig up and destroy plants with white fungal growth and a mushroom smell under the bark at the base. If you find honey-coloured toadstools, destroy those, too.

15 ONION NECK ROT
This fungal rot often affects onions, shallots, and garlic in storage, causing softening of the bulb and fuzzy grey mould. Check stores regularly and dispose of any infected bulbs. To prevent infection, don't grow onions, or related crops, in the same bed year after year.

16 ONION WHITE ROT
Yellowing and wilting foliage on onions, leeks, and garlic is a sign that white rot fungus may have attacked the roots and bulb. It is a serious disease that persists in soil for many years, so avoid spreading contamination through soil and plants from infected sites.

17 PARSNIP CANKER
Affected roots have orange-brown damage, particularly near the top. This can usually be cut out to leave the rest of the root still edible. The canker is caused by a fungus that enters through injured roots. To avoid infection, grow resistant varieties on well-drained soil.

18 POTATO BLACK LEG
Yellowing foliage, seen as early as June, and black areas at stem bases are signs of this bacterial disease. Remove and destroy infected plants promptly and rotate crops to prevent infection.

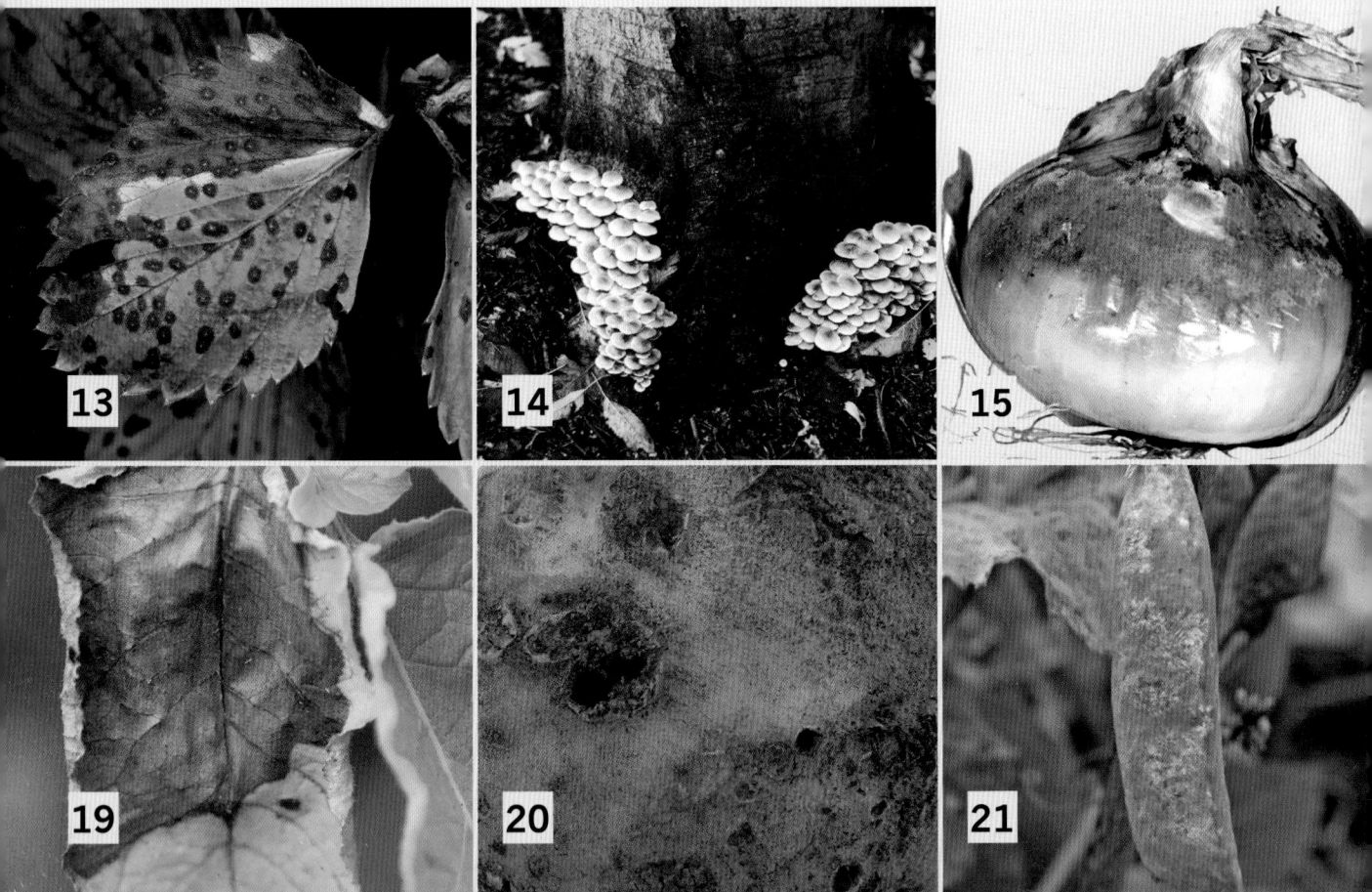

19 POTATO BLIGHT

A problem in warm, wet summers, this fungus affects potatoes and tomatoes (see tomato blight p.244), causing foliage to rot and, later, infecting tubers too. Remove and destroy infected foliage, lift tubers early, and grow resistant varieties.

20 POTATO COMMON SCAB

Potato scab causes unsightly, raised brown, scabby patches on the skins of potatoes. This bacterial infection is worse on dry and alkaline soils, so water well and avoid liming before potatoes crop. Choose resistant varieties.

POTATO POWDERY SCAB

(not illustrated)
A fungal infection causing sunken, spore-filled scabs on potato skins, this disease is more likely to be a problem on wet soils, where it can also infect tomato roots. To avoid, ensure good drainage and opt for resistant varieties.

21 POWDERY MILDEW

Many edible crops, including peas, courgettes, and currants, catch this fungal disease, which causes a white dusty layer on foliage. It is worse in dry conditions, so water well, remove fallen leaves, and use approved fungicides.

22 RASPBERRY CANE BLIGHT

During summer this fungal disease causes leaves to wither and canes to die after becoming split and brittle. Prevent infection by taking care not to damage canes or to plant in infected soil. Cut back and burn affected canes.

RASPBERRY CANE SPOT (not

illustrated)
The white-centred purple spots caused by this fungus appear on canes and leaves of raspberries and hybrid berries, sometimes spreading and killing canes. Cut down and burn affected canes and treat the rest with copper oxychloride.

RASPBERRY VIRUSES (not illustrated)

Yellow mosaic patterns and downward turned edges on the leaves of cane fruits are signs of viruses, some of which are spread by aphids. Such infections reduce crops, so remove and burn all infected plants and avoid replanting cane fruit on the same site.

23 RUST

Beans, leeks, and plums are among various crops infected by fungal rusts. Signs of infection are orange pustules on leaves and stems. Remove and destroy infected material at harvest time or leaf fall, and rotate crops if possible.

24 SCAB

Apples and pears develop small, dark brown patches on their skin, which can spread to leaves and branches. The fungi responsible overwinter on fallen leaves, so tidy up detritus in the autumn. Grow scab-resistant varieties to reduce the risk.

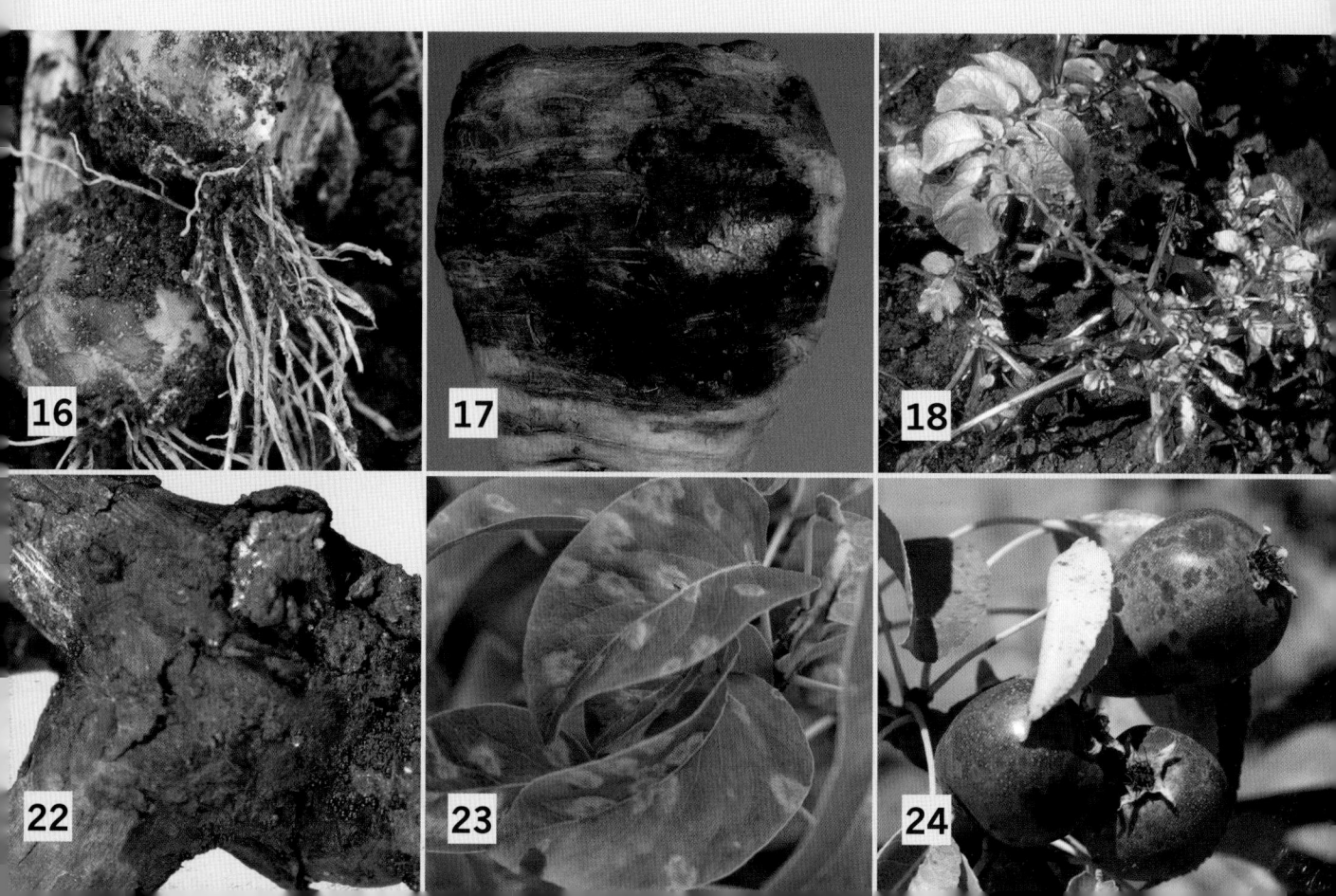

25 SCLEROTINA

This serious and persistent fungal disease affects lettuces, cucumbers, celery, tomatoes, and beans. Plants rapidly yellow and collapse with wet stem rot and fluffy white mould. Quickly remove and destroy diseased plants.

26 SCORCH

Hot sun and cold dry winds can both scorch leaves and flowers, turning them brown and crisp. Sun scorch is especially damaging if there are water droplets on the plants. Avoid watering at the hottest times of day and ensure that greenhouse plants have adequate shading.

27 SILVER LEAF

Plums, cherries, apricots, and peaches are affected by this fungal disease. Leaves develop a silvery sheen, cut wood is darkly stained, and branches die. Infectious spores are produced in autumn and winter, so prune in summer.

28 STRAWBERRY VIRUSES

Strawberries are susceptible to a number of viral infections spread by insects or by pests in the soil, such as eelworms. The symptoms include yellow-blotched or crumpled leaves and poor growth. Dig up and destroy infected plants and rotate your crops.

29 TOMATO BLIGHT

Outdoor tomatoes are more susceptible to this fungal disease than those in the greenhouse. Watch for rapidly spreading wet rots on leaves and brown patches on fruit. Quickly remove and destroy infected material.

30 TOMATO GHOST SPOT

This fungal infection causes pale green or yellow rings to appear on tomatoes. There will be no further deterioration and the discoloration does not make the fruit inedible. Keep the area surrounding your plants tidy to reduce sources of infection.

VIOLET ROOT ROT (not illustrated)

Root vegetables and celery are damaged by this fungus. Usually found on wet, acid soils, it produces a mass of purple threads around roots, which then rot. Lift and burn infected plants.

WHITE BLISTER (not illustrated)

This fungus produces shiny, white pustules on the undersides of brassica leaves, sometimes distorting them. Remove infected leaves or badly affected plants. To avoid further infection, rotate crops and grow resistant varieties.

Common nutrient deficiencies

Plants need a balanced intake of nutrients to remain healthy; mainly nitrogen, potassium (potash), and phosphorus, plus essential trace elements. Nutrients are often present in soil, but "locked up" if the pH is too high or low, or conditions are dry, so it pays to improve your soil.

1 BORON

Typical symptoms include splitting and discoloration of root vegetables and poorly developed ears of sweetcorn. Heavily limed or dry soils are the cause. Apply borax with horticultural sand.

2 CALCIUM

Apple bitter pit (p.240) and blossom end rot of tomatoes (p.240) are the most common signs. Calcium uptake is limited in dry and acidic conditions, so water consistently and add lime to acid soils to raise the pH.

3 IRON

Leaves of affected plants turn yellow between the veins and brown at the edges. Iron is locked up in alkaline soils, so apply acidic mulches and use a chelated iron treatment.

4 MAGNESIUM

This is a common deficiency in acid soils, after heavy rains, or use of high potash fertilizers. Older leaves are the first to yellow, then they turn red, purple, or brown between the veins. Treat with Epsom salts as a foliar spray.

5 NITROGEN

Nitrogen washes out of soil easily and all plants, except peas and beans, can become deficient, showing yellow leaves and spindly growth. Dig in well-rotted compost and add high nitrogen fertilizer.

6 POTASSIUM

Leaves tinged yellow or purple, and poor flowering and fruiting, suggest deficiency, especially in potatoes and tomatoes. This is a common problem on light soils, where potassium washes away. Apply sulphate of potash or tomato food.

1

2

3

4

5

6

Useful websites

Seeds & plants

CHILTERN SEEDS
Bortree Stile,
Ulverston,
Cumbria
LA12 7PB
01229 581137
www.chilternseeds.co.uk
Vegetable, fruit and herbs

D.T. BROWN
Bury Road,
Newmarket,
Cambridge
CB8 7PQ
0845 3710532
dtbrownseeds.co.uk
Vegetable, fruit and herbs

DOBIES
Long Road,
Paignton,
Devon
TQ4 7SX
0844 701 7623
www.dobies.co.uk
Vegetable, fruit and herbs

EDWIN TUCKER
Brewery Meadow,
Stonepark,
Ashburton,
Devon
TQ13 7DG
01364 652403
www.edwintucker.com
Vegetable, fruit and herbs

MARSHALL/UNWINS
Alconbury Hill,
Huntingdon,
Cambridge
PE28 4HY
01480 443390
www.marshalls-seeds.co.uk
Vegetable, fruit and herbs

MR FOTHERGILL'S
Kentford,
Suffolk
CB8 7QB
0845 3710518
www.mr-fothergills.co.uk
Vegetable, fruit and herbs

PLANT WORLD SEEDS
St. Marychurch Road,
Newton Abbot,
Devon
TQ12 4SE
01803 87293
www.plant-world-seeds.com
Unusual vegetable varieties

SEEDS OF ITALY
A1 Phoenix Industrial Estate,
Rrosslyn Cresent,
Harrow,
Middlesex
HA1 2SP
0208 427 5020
www.seedsofitaly.com
Vegetable, fruit and herbs

SIMPSON'S SEEDS
The Walled Garden Nursery
Horningsham,
Warminster,
Wiltshire
BA12 7NQ
01985 845004
www.simpsonsseeds.co.uk
Vegetable and fruit

SUFFOLK HERBS
Monks Farm,
Coggeshall Road,
Kelvedon,
Essex
CO5 9PG
01376 572456
www.suffolkherbs.com
Vegetable, fruit and herbs

SUTTONS
Woodview Road,
Paignton,
Devon
TQ4 7NG
0844 922 2899
www.suttons.co.uk
Vegetable, fruit and herbs

THE ORGANIC GARDENING CATALOGUE
Riverdene Business Park,
Molesey Road
Hersham,
Surrey
KT12 4RG
01932 253666
www.organiccatalogue.com
Vegetable, fruit and sundries

THE REAL SEED CATALOGUE
PO Box 18,
Newport,
Pembrokeshire
SA65 0AA
01239 821107
www.realseeds.co.uk
Vegetable, fruit and herbs

THOMPSON & MORGAN
Poplar Lane,
Ipswich,
Suffolk
IP8 3BU
0844 2485383
www.thompson-morgan.com
Vegetable, fruit and herbs

VICTORIANA NURSERY GARDENS
Challock,
Ashford,
Kent
TN25 4DG
01233 740529
www.victoriananursery.co.uk
Vegetable, fruit and herbs

Plants & sundries

BLACKMOOR NURSERIES
Blackmoor, Liss,
Hampshire
GU33 6BS
01420 477978
www.blackmoor.co.uk
Fruit trees and bushes

CHRIS BOWERS & SONS
Whispering Trees Nurseries,
Wimbotsham,
Norfolk
PE34 3QB
01366 388752
www.chrisbowers.co.uk
Fruit trees, bushes and vines

DEACON'S NURSERY
Moor View,
Godshill,
Isle of Wight
PO38 3HW
01983 840750
www.deaconsnurseryfruits.co.uk
Fruit trees, bushes and vines

J. TWEEDIE FRUIT TREES
Maryfield Road Nursery,
Terregles,
Dumfriesshire
DG2 9TH
01387 720880
Fruit trees and bushes

JEKKA'S HERB FARM
Rose Cottage,
Shellards Lane,
Alveston,
Bristol,
Avon
BS35 3SY
01454 418878
www.jekkasherbfarm.com
Herb seeds and plants

KEEPERS NURSERY
Gallants Court,
East Farleigh,
Maidstone,
Kent
ME15 0LE
01622 726465
www.keepers-nursery.co.uk
Fruit trees, bushes and nuts

KEN MUIR
Honeypot Farm,
Rectory Road,
Weeley Heath,
Clacton-on-Sea,
Essex
CO16 9BJ
01255 830181
www.kenmuir.co.uk
Fruit trees, bushes and vines

READS NURSERY
Hales Hall,
Loddon,
Norfolk
NR14 6QW
01508 548395
www.readsnursery.co.uk
Fruit trees, bushes and nuts

THE CITRUS CENTRE
West Mare Lane,
Pulborough,
West Sussex
RH20 2EA
01798 872786
www.citruscentre.co.uk
Citrus plants and sundries

Garden sundries

DEFENDERS
Occupation Road,
Wye, Ashford,
Kent
TN25 5EN
01233 813121
www.defenders.co.uk
Biological pest control

HARROD HORTICULTURAL
Pinbush Road,
Lowestoft,
Suffolk
NR33 7NL
0845 402 5300
www.harrodhorticultural.com
Garden and greenhouse sundries

LADYBIRD PLANT CARE
The Glasshouses
Fletching Common
Newick
Lewes
East Sussex
BN8 4JJ
www.ladybirdplantcare.co.uk
Biological pest control

TWO WESTS & ELLIOT
Unit 4, Carrwood Road,
Sheepbridge Industrial Estate,
Chesterfield,
Derbyshire
S41 9RH
01246 451077
www.twowests.co.uk
Garden and greenhouse sundries

Index

Acknowledgments

Author's acknowledgments
Thanks to the following: Chauney Dunford, Alison Shackleton, Alison Donovan, Esther Ripley, and the team at Dorling Kindersley for your hard work and much appreciated input; Malcolm Dodds who, as ever, has patiently been my technical support and emergency photographer; and finally Judy and Paul Whittingham for their enthusiastic growing and willingness to compare notes.

Dorling Kindersley would like to thank:
Robin and Brenda Beresford-Evans, Mike Aldridge, and the growers at Cannizaro Allotments, Wimbledon, London.

Dobies/Suttons, Floranova, Marshalls/Unwins, Thompson & Morgan, and Victoriana Nursery Gardens for their kind permission to reproduce their photographs.

Commissioned photography
Peter Anderson

Index Elizabeth Wiggans

Proofreading Emma Callery

Picture credits
The publisher would like to thank the following for their kind permission to reproduce their photographs:

(Key: a-above; b-below/bottom; c-centre; f-far; l-left; r-right; t-top)

6 GAP Photos: Jo Whitworth (r). **7 GAP Photos:** Pat Tuson (c). **Harpur Garden Library:** Jerry Harpur (br). **Photolibrary:** Stephen Hamilton (t). **8 GAP Photos:** Maxine Adcock (cl); Lynn Keddie (bl). **8-9 The Garden Collection:** Nicola Stocken Tomkins, Clinton Lodge. **9 GAP Photos:** Friedrich Strauss (tc). **10 GAP Photos:** Lee Avison (tr); Geoff Kidd (cra). **Photolibrary:** Mark Winwood (tl). **11 GAP Photos:** BIOS/Gilles Le Scanff & Joëlle-Caroline Mayer (b). **Victoriana Nursery Gardens:** (c). **12 GAP Photos:** Elke Borkowski (r); Juliette Wade (l). **13 The Garden Collection:** Nicola Stocken Tomkins, Designer: Karen Maskell HCFS 2002 (br). **Photolibrary:** Mark Bolton (l). **14 GAP Photos:** Charles Hawes (bl). **Photolibrary:** Corbis (br); Jerry Pavia (tl). **16 GAP Photos:** Fiona Lea (br). **Marianne Majerus Garden Images:** Marianne Majerus (t). **18 Alamy Images:** David Chapman (bl). **Chauney Dunford:** (tl). **GAP Photos:** Friedrich Strauss (tr). **20 GAP Photos:** BBC Magazines Ltd (br); Elke Borkowski (cb); Rob Whitworth (bl). **21 Chauney**

Dunford: (tr). **22-23 Garden World Images:** Lee Thomas. **24 Corbis:** Ryman/photocuisine (cb). **Getty Images:** Michael Rosenfeld (bl). **Photolibrary:** Joff Lee (tr). **25 Getty Images:** Spencer Jones (tl). **Photolibrary:** Fleurent (ca). **31 Mike Shackleton:** (tc). **33 GAP Photos:** Michael King/Design: Deborah Bird (bl); Michael King/Design: Greenfield Primary School (br); Clive Nichols/Location: Chelsea 2001 (bc). **34 Photolibrary:** Howard Rice (cl). **35 Alamy Images:** Gary Curtis (bl). **37 Thompson & Morgan:** (tr) (crb). **38 Getty Images:** Michael Rosenfeld (tr). **39 Photolibrary:** Riou (tc). **40 Photolibrary:** Francois De Heel (tl). **41 Thompson & Morgan:** (tr). **44 Dobies of Devon:** (tl) (tc). **iStockphoto.com:** (cl). **Photolibrary:** Michael Howes (bl). **Thompson & Morgan:** (tr). **47 Corbis:** Paul Taylor (cr). **GAP Photos:** Lee Avison (cl). **50 Corbis:** Ocean (bl/tatsoi). **GAP Photos:** Jonathan Buckley, Design: Sarah Raven (c). **51 Corbis:** amanaimages (fcr); photocuisine (br). **GAP Photos:** Juliette Wade (cl). **Photolibrary:** Jo Whitworth (cr). **52 Getty Images:** James Carrier (c). **Photolibrary:** Gerard Lacz (bc). **53 Photolibrary:** Foodfolio (bc). **54 GAP Photos:** Abby Rex (tr). **55 Alamy Images:** Brian Hoffman (tl). **The Garden Collection:** Torie Chugg (tc). **Garden**